View from the Booth

View from the Booth

FOUR DECADES WITH THE PHILLIES

Chris Wheeler

as told to
Hal Gullan

Foreword by
Tim McCarver

CAMINO BOOKS, INC.
PHILADELPHIA

Manufactured in the United States of America

1 2 3 4 5   12 11 10 09

LIBRARY OF CONGRESS CATALOGING IN PUBLICATION DATA

Wheeler, Chris, 1945–
View from the booth: four decades with the Phillies / Chris Wheeler
as told to Hal Gullan; foreword by Tim McCarver.
p. cm.
ISBN 978–1–933822–22–8 (alk. paper)
1. Wheeler, Chris, 1945– 2. Baseball announcers—United States—
Biography. 3. Philadelphia Phillies (Baseball team)—History.
I. Gullan, Harold I., 1931– II. Title.

GV742.42.W53W54 2009
796.357092—dc22
[B]   2009031086

Interior design: Rachel Reiss

Photo section photographs courtesy of Miles Kennedy, Rosemary Rahn,
Ed Mahan, Al Tielemans, Paul Roedig, Rusty Kennedy, William Gordon,
Tom Briglia, Dave Schofield, and the Phillies Photo Library.

This book is available at a special discount on bulk purchases for pro-
motional, business, and educational use.

Publisher
Camino Books, Inc.
P.O. Box 59026
Philadelphia, PA 19102

www.caminobooks.com

I would like to dedicate this book to the memory of my parents, Teresa M. and Christopher H. Wheeler— and to my best friend, Renée Gosik.

Contents

Foreword

by Tim McCarver

If I believed in reincarnation, I might think that in his first lifetime Chris Wheeler was a nineteenth-century ballplayer, learning about baseball from its infancy. Perhaps "Wheels" Wheeler would have been "Wee Willie" Keeler, the five-foot, four-and-a-half-inch outfielder who had 200 hits in nine consecutive seasons, once batted .424, and knew baseball inside and out. If Chris wasn't Willie, and didn't retain his knowledge of the game, then perhaps he has been channeling him and other baseball immortals since he became a Philadelphia Phillies broadcaster in 1977. That might explain how this bright personality has been able, for more than 30 years, to give startling insights into the game without having actually played it, at least on the professional level. Ask the players. They will tell you that quite simply, "He gets it." The fans of Philadelphia have been so fortunate that Chris has been a part of their lives. I have been fortunate, too.

Playing baseball and broadcasting baseball are similar in that they are extremely difficult crafts that, when done well, seem almost effortless. Most fans watching games on television think that the players they see and the broadcasters they hear are doing something so easy that they could do it, too, if someone handed them a glove or microphone. That's one of the game's accessible charms. However, there have been a vast number of players with talent and announcers with potential who never made it because they didn't receive the right training. I can say with experience that I wouldn't have played for 21 years in the majors if I hadn't received terrific instruction, when I was starting out in the St. Louis Cardinals system, from Eddie Stanky on catching (and life), George Kissell on the fundamentals, and George Crowe on hitting. I can also say with certainty that I wouldn't have had an even longer career as a baseball broadcaster if Chris Wheeler hadn't taken time with me at the very beginning.

I officially retired as a player with the Phillies in 1980. At the age of 38, when most men are at the pinnacle of their professions, I was starting anew as a rookie broadcaster for Philadelphia. Like most ex-jocks, I was an individual with single-vocational skills and a lot of self-doubt. I knew that I had accumulated a great deal of knowledge about baseball from the vantage point of the catcher's position and from talking endlessly with some of the craftiest players, managers, and coaches the game has ever known. But was I going to be able to communicate that knowledge of the game to the fans? I wanted to apply the same diligence as an announcer that I did as a player, but I didn't even know how to get started.

Bill Giles (then the Phillies' vice-president, business) informed me that I would be paired with Chris Wheeler for about 30 games in 1980 on PRISM, the team's cable outlet. Poor Chris was handed the job of tutoring me over the winter so that I wouldn't go up in flames. We did our work in a tiny cubicle over at Channel 17. The first time we sat there, Chris put on a video of a game from 1979, minus the sound. Then he waited for me to start describing the action as if I were broadcasting to people in their homes. After a minute of silence, he said, "Go ahead." I stammered, "Go ahead and *what*?" I was experiencing sheer terror. Chris helped me relax, and I started to find my voice, both figuratively and literally. Most of the time, what I said that day was inane gibberish, but Chris was encouraging whenever I came up with anything remotely analytical. More comfortable, I was eager to proceed. It was a tedious three-month process, but by spring training, having absorbed so much from the man on my side, I was confident enough to move into the booth.

During my time with the Phillies, I continued to learn on the job just by being with Wheels. From him I learned that a broadcaster has the responsibility to be informative and stimulating, prescient and provocative. I realized that his biggest gift was that he always went beyond the obvious, finding unique, interesting ways to communicate what was happening in a game. He showed that during its ebbs and flows there is time for humor, serious thought, and real analysis. He also knew exactly how to mix commentary with visuals. Just as he educated me on the inner workings of a broadcast, he taught the fans how to understand baseball without being didactic. He believed that elucidation leads to anticipation, which makes it more enjoyable (by the way, he also taught me what "didactic" means).

All these years later, Wheels keeps on rolling. He is still one of a kind. He has an uncanny ability to blend his exhaustive, game-by-game research and knowledge of the players with the *now* of a telecast. And it's all done seamlessly. He has never allowed his being a lifetime Phillies "phanatic" to interfere with his calling every play in every game with accuracy and professionalism. And, of course, wit.

Those same traits can be found in this book. Its pages are labors of love, and significantly allow Wheels' fans, the fans of the terrific Phillies franchise, a chance to get a close-up view of one of our most underrated broadcasters, who also just happens to be one hell of a guy. So, pay attention and enjoy.

A Word of Thanks

So many generous people have contributed so much of their time and effort to the production and promotion of this book, it's hard to know where to start. And I'm bound to leave people out who will come aboard after this has to be submitted. You know who you are. My thanks to you, as well.

As always, I'm indebted to the person closest to me, who shares in everything I do. Renée Gosik was invaluable in many ways, but most importantly in keeping me focused and productive. Writing is a new adventure for me, and a time-consuming one. In reviewing everything, Renee could say with some authority, "Chris, that just doesn't sound like you," and I don't recall that she was ever wrong. Speaking of writing, I had a talented and tireless collaborator in Hal Gullan. I also appreciate the careful efforts of his associate, Elsa Efran. I owe a lot to our publisher, Edward Jutkowitz, and our editor, Brad Fisher. And my special thanks to Tim McCarver for his wonderful Foreword.

We wouldn't have gotten anywhere without the help of everyone in the Phillies organization, beginning with David Montgomery and including the "retired" Larry Shenk, Tina Urban, Bonnie Clark, Christine Negley, Melissa Maani, Dave Buck, Scott Palmer, John Brazer and all their associates, Dave Smith of Retrosheet.org, and the guy I share the cover with, the Phanatic's best friend, Tom Burgoyne. My thanks also to Bob Bacine for his good counsel. Wonderful photographers like Miles Kennedy made everything come alive, adding visual impact to our words. Rich Westcott, who knows more about Phillies history than anyone, was a reliable source of inspiration and information. How often I consulted *The Phillies Encyclopedia* that he co-authored with Frank Bilovsky. And, of course, my thanks to everyone in and behind the booth.

I'm also indebted to so many friends at Penn State, starting with Doug Anderson, Dean of the College of Communications, and including Steve Sampsell, Mike Poorman, Ryan Jones of the *Penn Stater*, bookstore manager Tom Bauer, his associate, Bill Keister, and a host of dedicated alumni. I guess the theme of this book, and of my life, is how fortunate I've been to have had so much encouragement along the way, from home to State College to Citizens Bank Park, and now extending to a book of my reflections on nearly four decades with the one employer I sought. Most of all, I want to thank each of you for sharing them. I hope you will enjoy reading this as much as I enjoyed writing it.

—*Chris Wheeler*

A Word of Introduction

Since I was a kid, two things have been a big part of my life—the game of baseball and the Philadelphia Phillies. That I have been lucky enough to combine the two into a dream-come-true career of 39 years remains almost incomprehensible to me. Last summer, when my co-author Hal Gullan approached me about writing about nearly four decades with the Phillies, my first reaction was to say no. I've had several writers float the idea, and I'd let it drift away. But it just seemed right this time.

Baseball is a game that lends itself to stories and memories. I have spent countless hours with fascinating personalities like Richie Ashburn, Harry Kalas, Paul Owens, Dallas Green, Bill Giles, Hugh Alexander, Andy Musser, Tim McCarver, Larry Shenk, John Vukovich, Pete Rose, Mike Schmidt, Steve Carlton, Larry Bowa, Greg Luzinski, Eric Gregg, Charlie Manuel, and a host of others. My wish is that sharing that time with you may prove stimulating, often funny, and sometimes even poignant. Anyway, it just seemed the right time to write it all down. As it turned out, winning a World Series was a wonderful bonus. Maybe as you read this, we'll be in the midst of another exciting run with many of the same players you've grown to love. I can only hope so—and, through these pages and pictures, share my storybook journey with you.

CHAPTER 1

What Am I Doing Here?

As I think about it, I can't recall a time when I didn't want to be a broadcaster. There may not have been a microphone in my crib, but what made it all possible was that I had the most supportive parents in the world. Whatever I showed an interest in, they shared. Maybe it was the result of growing up to the comforting tones of By Saam and Bill Campbell, or an early obsession with a ball, bat, and glove, but I always thought in terms of the Phillies and baseball. I did a lot of simulated games for an audience of one, while my amused parents wondered where this would lead. If my childhood wasn't quite like *Leave It to Beaver*, it came pretty close. A lot of kids today might envy it.

You don't have to be born within the city limits to consider yourself a "Philly guy." I arrived at Fitzgerald Mercy Hospital in suburban Delaware County, on April 9, 1945, to Terry and Chris Wheeler. I wasn't a "junior." For the record, I'm Christopher Charles; my dad was Christopher Herbert. Thirteen months later, my brother Fred came along. Living first in Yeadon, my parents were eventually able to purchase a home in 1952 on Tyson Road in what was then the pretty, largely rural town of Newtown Square. It's still pretty, but not all that rural. We kids had a lot more room to roam in those days. I don't recall ever being bored.

I also had the advantage of going to great schools—St. Anastasia's, Devon Prep, and Marple-Newtown High, where I graduated in 1963. Like most kids, I loved sports of all kinds, but baseball was always my favorite, a big part of my life. I played Little League, Babe Ruth, American Legion ball, and one year on my high-school varsity. I not only loved playing, I continued to enjoy watching and listening to the games. I would follow the flow of the Phillies announcers, not only the legendary Saam and Campbell, but also Gene Kelly and Claude Haring. Later it would include my future partner—and former player—Richie Ashburn. I'd mimic the way they talked, their calls, how they described the action. They were as much my heroes as the players.

My parents never considered it a chore to take me to my practices or to amateur games—or those great trips to that memorably green expanse of Connie Mack Stadium to see major-league baseball in person. And it wasn't tough for them because they loved baseball themselves.

When neither of them could make it, I was allowed to go to games on my own, even at a very young age, or with my buddies. Seems like a long time ago. Sometimes I would just take the bus to the 69th Street terminal and then board one of those green PTC Phillies Express buses that went directly to the ballpark. Talk about adventure. Other times I would make the trek to 69th Street, then board the Market-Frankford El to Broad Street, take the Broad Street Subway to Lehigh Avenue, and then walk the seven or eight blocks to Connie Mack Stadium, where I'd buy a ticket and have the time of my life. Even though my parents knew I was a responsible kid and appreciated my passion for the game, can you imagine anyone allowing a preteen to do that today? And back in those days, I loved doubleheaders. Two games for the price of one. Now that I have to work them, they aren't quite as much fun. But these new split, day-night doubleheaders are necessary to generate revenue.

I hoped to go to college, whatever profession I might eventually pursue. I understood that my parents weren't rich, and they had the education of two sons to consider. Fortunately, I had the opportunity to go to Penn State and take advantage of its in-state tuition. My brother went to Shippensburg. I loved everything about State College, including its natural beauty, the exciting environment, and the opportunity to be on my own. Initially, I was a political science major, but I'd switched to journalism by my second semester. Practical or not, the pull of being a broadcaster was just too strong. And Penn State had (and still has) a great communications department.

In my sophomore year, when I was 19, my world suddenly changed with stunning impact. I got the call at six one frigid February morning. My father had died of a massive heart attack. He was only 47, a typical World War II veteran who had been a heavy smoker. He had always been my role model, the solid foundation of our family. The shock must have been even more devastating for my mother. She was typical of the women of that era. Her life revolved around her family—completely devoted to her kids but dependent on her husband. She didn't even have a driver's license. My life became very serious that day. How could I help her, my brother, and myself? It made me an instant adult.

First, I had to graduate and lay a foundation for success. It took some odd jobs to get through, from washing dishes at a fraternity house to doing construction work during the summer. Somehow I also managed to work my way into my first experience on the air, doing some play-by-play for baseball and basketball games on the student radio station at the time, WDFM. Of course, at Penn State, the emphasis was on football. I got to do a weekly radio show in 1966 with a first-year football coach named Joe Paterno. Now that *was* a thrill. I graduated in 1967 with a degree in broadcasting. Still, it's a long way from college to a big-league broadcast booth—like going from "A" ball to the majors.

After graduation, there wasn't much time to celebrate. I don't have to tell you how tenuous and temporary broadcasting jobs can be. Over the next four years, I mixed in a six-month active duty stint in the U.S. Army, in Louisiana and Texas, with short stops at WCAU Radio in Philadelphia, WBBM in Chicago, and CBS Radio in New York, getting my feet wet. Chicago's a great city, but I remember my stay there as especially tough. One month after I'd arrived, in December 1968, my car was stolen. The weekend of that legendary "Ice Bowl" football game up in Green Bay, there was so little heat in my apartment that I used my oven to try to keep warm. But at least I'd accumulated some experience to flesh out my résumés. I submitted them to all four of the major sports teams in Philadelphia, although the Phillies were still my favorite. Amazingly, they actually hired me. On a date I'm never likely to forget—July 5, 1971—I started work as assistant director of publicity and public relations. If I wasn't yet *on* the air, I was pretty much floating on air.

I'm often asked about how I got to be a member of the Phillies' broadcast team. It might be more dramatic to describe a heroic saga of struggling against the odds, spending years in the minors with lots of long bus rides, gradually learning my craft while subsisting on a meager salary. Fortunately, it wasn't like that at all. My big break came on September 26, 1976, five years after the Phillies hired me. On a blustery, cool afternoon in the Montreal Expos' old Parc Jarry, all the elements came together. If it wasn't the perfect storm, it came pretty close.

In my PR job, I had a great advantage. My boss was "The Baron," Larry Shenk, a wonderful guy to learn from, and probably the most professional public relations director in the game. Best of all, as his assistant, I got to travel with the team. It was a great opportunity to hang out in both the radio and television booths, getting to know the broadcasting duo of Harry Kalas and Richie Ashburn, listening and learning how they covered a game, and picking up everything I could. Kalas had come to the Phils from Houston in 1971, arriving at the same time as the opening of spacious, multipurpose Veterans Stadium. Montreal (and former Phillies) manager Gene Mauch wasn't alone in calling it "the best new park in baseball." Harry made an immediate impact, even as he faced controversy by re-placing popular local broadcaster Bill Campbell. "Whitey" Ashburn, a longtime fan favorite as a player, meshed with Harry in a way rarely matched in our sport. But Whitey had his own style, includ-ing a whimsical sense of humor that only endeared him all the more to the listening audience—and he could be less predictable than the weather in Montreal that afternoon. You just never knew where he was going, and if it included his partner.

It was no ordinary day, but the culmination of a long season. The Phillies were playing a makeup doubleheader. If they won either game, they would be crowned champions of the Eastern Division and would qualify to play for their first National League championship since the beloved "Whiz Kids" of 1950. As it turned out, Greg Luzinski hit a three-run homer, Jim Lonborg pitched a complete game, and the Phils won 3-0—setting off a wild celebration in the visiting team's clubhouse. Rivers of champagne flowed, and grown men acted like the children they once were, which is what makes such scenes so spontaneous. Of course, almost everyone got soaked, including me, and didn't care. It's hard to describe how much fun this is the first time.

There was only one problem. A second game was scheduled, and it had to be played. I don't think this exact situation has ever happened again—a team winning and celebrating a championship and then having to go out the same day to play again. That's what makes this unpredictable sport of baseball so fascinating. There is always a possibility you'll see something you've never witnessed before. Understandably, none of the regulars wanted to play in the second game. So manager Danny Ozark had to put together a makeshift lineup and send it out to face the Expos, who also wanted to be anywhere but here. Thankfully, the game was rained out after seven innings, and played in a crisp time of 1:51.

This reluctance to return extended to the broadcast booth, where Harry and Whitey also had to get dried off and go back to work. Ashburn began to consider alternatives. For some time, he had made me part of their on-the-air act. Whitey would say, "There's this guy named Wheeler who works in our public relations department. He's constantly handing me incorrect information that I use on the air, so if I make a mistake, it's not my fault." People must have been wondering just who this clown was who screwed up everything. And so when I wandered back into the booth, Whitey simply said on the air, "Here's this Chris Wheeler I've been talking about" and then said to me, "Wheels, I know you've always wanted to do this, so I'm going to take off and leave you here to work with Harry." Pure Ashburn.

Sure enough, Whitey took off his headset, handed it to me, and I'm on the air doing color with the best play-by-play man in the business, Harry Kalas. It doesn't get any better. There was no time to be scared. How many years had I done this, talked about the game and situations I saw, with everything but an audience? Could the real thing be all that different? And, more important, I knew this was a one-shot deal. So I decided to have some fun. Fortunately, I also knew something about each player on both teams. "You can run on this Expos pitcher," I'd say (I still remember his name—Denis Blair), and wouldn't you know it, the Phillies player on first would break for second and make it. I'd refer to a hitter's strength or weakness, and very soon he'd do something to illustrate it. I'd say where and why a player was positioned in the outfield, just as I do today, and he'd turn a potential hit into an out. It was happening just like I'd imagined. I was having a ball, saying whatever I wanted to, because I knew I'd never have the chance again.

Unbeknownst to me, however, our audio was being piped into the box of Montreal's general manager, John McHale, because the Expos weren't televising the second game. Our vice-president, Bill Giles, happened to be with McHale on that memorable day. Later I learned that he asked Giles, "Bill, just who is this announcer of yours? He's really good. He knows our players better than we do." Initially, Giles was a bit defensive, saying that I was one of his PR guys and admitting, "I don't know what the hell he's doing in there." But eventually Bill told me that he agreed with McHale, adding, "I may have to use him some more." Now, if this were a motivational book, I'd say that it pays to be prepared for opportunity when it comes. But I'd be less than honest if I didn't add that, fortunately, I *was* pretty hot that day, and good things just kept happening.

As luck would have it, By Saam had retired in 1976, and Andy Musser was working radio alone except for home Sundays, when Robin Roberts helped him out. Giles felt Musser should have a partner for 1977. He decided that since I was with the team all the time anyway, he wouldn't have to pay me any more money (as he later told me), and he might just have an analyst on his hands.

The rest, of course, is history. In 1977, I worked radio when the games were televised, and I'm still around and having the time of my life. Yes, I may have a face for radio, but today they even expose that to our television audience. It all began because of one of

Whitey's whims. I could write a book just about them, and about him. Stay with me, if you would, and I'll tell you some of my favorite Richie Ashburn stories.

CHAPTER 2

Whitey, Julie, and Ruly

THERE'S NO BETTER WAY to get free food than to be a Phillies broadcaster. For as long as I can remember, starting with my first assignment on radio, people have been providing us with all kinds of goodies while we're on the air. The procession really picked up through the years as Harry and Whitey became established as our primary broadcast team. Many contributors were just regular fans who would send the stuff up to the booth, but there were also creative folks who somehow managed to avoid security and find their way *into* the booth, bringing with them their favorite dishes for us to enjoy. The only thing in short supply was privacy. We'd have visitors from all over the fourth level at Vet Stadium stop by just to say hello and to see what was on the menu that evening. I'm able to eat almost anything, although I'll have to say that most of what people brought us was really good.

As you know, Harry made a point of mentioning birthdays, anniversaries, and special events over the air. It's certainly a welcome way of bonding with our widespread family of fans. More often than not, our food donors would leave notes with their names and sometimes their business affiliations, hoping that their generosity might be acknowledged with an on-the-air announcement. Of course, some of them were not only fans but actually in the food business. I've no idea what sponsors pay to have their products pitched by baseball broadcasters, but I'm sure it's substantial. So any mention of a product is certainly worth the investment involved in bringing it to our booth. Whitey particularly enjoyed thanking people in that unmistakable Nebraska twang he never lost. "I want to thank the Kratzenmeier family from Lebanon for the wonderful funnel cake," or "Betty from Bucks County for the delicious brownies."

He could get away with saying just about anything because, well, he was Whitey. People sensed the genuine quality in how he added color and conviction to what he saw on the field. ("Hard to believe, Harry," he noted when a player gave up an out by laying down yet another of the sacrifice bunts he hated.) Even though Whitey might go for some time without saying anything, you could hear the tapping of his ever-present pipe. Sometimes it might seem a bit eccentric, but even the familiar sounded spontaneous. Most of it was, including those pregame interviews I'll get to later. Preparation wasn't part of Whitey's DNA, at least not on the air. "This is a simple game, Harry," the plaque still says in Whitey's words on the wall of our broadcast booth. But there was nothing simple about Richie Ashburn. When it was his turn to do play-by-play, all the old competitive fire returned. Our laid-back partner put the food aside, ready to go back on the field and *show* them how to do it. It was easy to understand why he had excelled—not only at baseball, but later at tennis and squash. Only the complexities of golf were challenging for him to master. He was a competitor to his core, however colorful his candor. It may be that so long after his playing days, the fans still loved him so much because he said things they were thinking—an outspoken, authentic "Philly guy" they related to, no matter how Midwestern his roots.

Although this story has been told many times, like many stories about Whitey, I don't suppose it will ever grow old. One of our favorite places was a local pizzeria on Packer Avenue near the ballpark called Celebre's. They made the best pizza imaginable, and would frequently surprise us with a delivery at just the time, late in a game, when the free food from the press box was depleted and our stomachs were beginning to growl. On other occasions, irrepressible Whitey would make an announcement over the air that we'd like some pizza, even naming the toppings. Sure enough, about a half-hour later, an unmistakable smell would come from the back of the booth as a guy walked in carrying at least two large pies from our favorite place. Whitey would tell one of *us* to pay the tip, and he'd be back at the mike, thanking Ronnie and the guys from Celebre's for the delivery.

Then one day Marketing informed us that the Phillies had made a deal with a major pizza sponsor, and the plugs for Celebre's would have to stop. Whitey didn't pay much attention to the edicts of people in authority, but at least he tried to abide by this one. However, one night we were involved in a late, rain-delayed game, there was no food on the counter behind us, and the thought of a Celebre's pie was on our minds. Between innings, Whitey hatched a plot that was vintage Ashburn.

When we came back on the air, my part of the scam was to remind him that he had a special announcement to make. We always noted birthdays, anniversaries, special events, groups of fans at the game, and the like. So between pitches, I said to Whitey, "Well, I know there's a birthday that you almost forgot to bring up because this has been such a long night." "That's right, Wheels," he replied. "We'd like to send our best wishes to the Celebre's twins, celebrating a birthday today. Happy birthday, Plain and Pepperoni!" When he asked me how old they were, I managed to say, "I hope about 20 minutes," and then pretty much lost it. I had to lean back to keep my own laughter contained, while others retained their composure by leaving the booth, but Richie Ashburn simply chuckled as he returned to the mike. He was doing play-by-play that inning, and I was the analyst. And yes, less than half an hour later, two beautiful boxes arrived. This time *we* got the birthday gifts, in the form of plain and pepperoni.

Whitey so enjoyed making special announcements, even when not putting one over on Marketing, that occasionally he'd come up with something right out of left field. One day in Candlestick Park, he made a point of welcoming "a good friend and local Philadelphia jeweler and his lovely wife having a wonderful time enjoying their second honeymoon here in this beautiful city of San Francisco." He went on and on about what a great couple Mr. and Mrs. X were. The next day, Whitey discovered that the lady in question

was *not* Mr. X's wife. I'd love to know how that situation was re-
solved, but Whitey just took it all in stride.

Whitey enjoyed eating even while on the air, not only between
innings. Celebre's pizza was a special favorite, but popcorn from the
press box was his constant fare. Listeners could hear him shaking
the bag and then dumping a crunchy handful into his mouth. Talk
about live broadcasting. One night, while he was eating his popcorn
and calling a play, I had to become an instant pinch-hitter. His call
began something like "ground ball to third . . . so and so to his left,"
but then Whitey started making some utterly unintelligible sounds.
It was scary. Was he having digestive problems or a stroke? I took a
quick look at him and simply jumped in: "He gloves it . . . throws to
first in plenty of time...two outs." Then I turned back, with evident
concern, to Whitey: "What just happened? Are you all right?" "Yep,"
he said, not missing a beat, "bit my tongue, and just wanted to have
you work on your play-by-play."

Our favorite Richie Ashburn stories still resonate. Sometimes
things would linger in his mind for a long time, and then just pop
out. Yet rarely was anyone offended by what he would say. To paral-
lel it with a prominent current ballplayer—that was just Whitey being
Whitey. It was fun being in his world, but it was also unpredictable.

We were doing a televised game one night when Whitey said out
of nowhere, "We'd like to send our best wishes along to former
Phillies owner Ruly Carpenter. Ruly was involved in a car accident
today. We understand that he is OK, and we certainly hope that all is
well." But then, even more abruptly, Whitey went off on a tangent
about Ruly's father, Bob Carpenter, who owned the Phillies prior to
his son's taking over. It seems the elder Carpenter still owed Whitey
something like $500 from a long time ago. "I should be asking for
that money with compound interest, but you know how cheap the
Carpenters are." Could Whitey be serious—or was he just kidding?

So there I was, wondering where all this came from and where it
could be going. As for Ruly being in an auto accident, I didn't know
anything about it, and Whitey wouldn't normally have heard before
the rest of us. Well, I thought, there's a first time for everything. As
soon as the inning ended, we looked up and there was Larry Shenk,

running down the stairs to the TV booth with a serious look on his face. "Whitey, who told you Ruly was in a car accident?" Shenk asked breathlessly. Looking up, Whitey took a drag on his omnipresent pipe and said very calmly, "Well, I had dinner with some guy in the press room tonight, and he told me." To which Shenk replied, "You had dinner with *me* in the press room tonight, and I told you my wife, *Julie*, was in a car accident."

There was dead silence in the booth, except for the sound of the stage manager telling us we had 15 seconds to go back on the air. So I innocently asked, "What are we going to do?" And, of course, Richie replied, "Just leave it to me, pal." The game resumed, as did the normal Whitey banter, with his customary complaints about umpiring calls and other things that were bugging him. Then he smoothly switched gears: "Fans, I'd like to correct something that was said last inning by yours truly. I was given some 'misinformation' by Phillies PR man Larry Shenk and I've learned that it was his wife *Julie* who was involved in the car accident and not former Phillies president *Ruly* Carpenter." After wishing Julie well, Whitey added that Larry Shenk "needs to work on his enunciation." More vintage Ashburn. He screwed up, but with his great sense of humor, he made it seem like somebody else's fault (normally mine).

Now fast forward to spring training the following year. Whitey and the Shenks were living at the same condo complex, where they both owned units. Whitey was riding his bike by the pool when he saw Julie Shenk with her arm in a sling. After they exchanged pleasantries, Whitey inquired, "Hey, Julie, what's with the sling?" "Well," she replied, "I was in an auto accident last September and I'm still having problems with my shoulder." To which Whitey replied, "You were? Nobody told me!" Had Larry Shenk been nearby, he might have worked further on his enunciation.

What about Ruly Carpenter? He remains a huge Phillies fan. To this day, he rarely misses a game, and loves to talk baseball. However, on that particular September evening, with the team headed toward another dismal finish to their season, Ruly, also an avid college football fan, chose instead to watch Notre Dame play Vanderbilt on the Thursday night ESPN game of the week.

So when the phone started ringing with anxious friends inquiring about his "automobile accident" that day, he had no idea what they were talking about. As Carpenter recalled, "All these people kept saying I'd been in a car accident. When I told them I hadn't, they wouldn't take no for an answer. After all, Richie Ashburn was saying it during the Phillies game. So it had to be true. I can appreciate their concern, but I was just trying to watch a football game and getting kind of annoyed. Finally I had to take the phone off the hook."

As for Bob Carpenter and that overdue $500, maybe Richie still felt the residue of all those years when players earned only a fraction of the multi-millions that drove even baseball enthusiasts like the Carpenters out of the game. Perhaps it was Whitey's belated tongue-in-cheek way to take a shot at those frugal owners he had to deal with, even though he liked the Carpenters personally. If so, it was a pretty harmless missile, and nobody enjoyed it more than the Carpenters themselves.

Whitey didn't believe much in preparation. There is a good deal of truth in his assertion, after getting something completely messed up, "Boys, my fans expect that of me." And they did. It was like listening to your favorite comedian do the same routine over and over. That Whitey was genuinely absentminded added to his persona. I remember once, after packing for a road trip, he got to the ballpark before realizing he'd left his suitcase on the curb in front of his Bryn Mawr condo. "Boys," he'd say, "my job begins when the game starts." Here were the rest of us, preparing our notes prior to a game, when Richie Ashburn would just saunter into the booth and ask, "Wheels, who's chucking for us today?"

Whitey's attitude certainly didn't change when he was asked to do pregame radio interviews, hardly his favorite assignment. And he felt undercompensated for taking that extra job. "Boys," he'd say, "if I screw up enough, maybe they'll take that show away from me." Sometimes he'd just come to the ballpark, take the elevator up to the press box, and grab the first person he could find to interview. More often than not, it was a broadcaster for the opposing team. Every guest would be given a watch. Lanny Frattere of the Pirates was on so often, he thanked us for providing him with all the Christmas stocking-stuffers he ever needed. He also threatened once to appear wearing our watches on both arms all the way up to his elbows. Nor did Whitey's conversational style change in these interviews. With the Reds' Marty Brennaman, I recall Whitey holding his stopwatch under his guest's chin, while the mike remained in his other hand, where the stopwatch should have been. Fortunately, Marty brought this to Whitey's attention about 30 seconds into the show, and they started over.

I think the most hilarious interview was with the colorful and garrulous Harry Caray of the Chicago Cubs. Caray didn't need an interviewer. He was really upset, going on and on about the impending free agency of pitcher Greg Maddux, and how the Cubs were going to lose him. He was vehemently opposed. He wanted Maddux re-signed at any cost. "He's the best pitcher in this organization, and they're going to let him walk! Can you believe this?" Finally, Whitey got a word in, asking, "Well, Harry, do you think you have any chance to sign Maddux?" The bemused Caray responded, "Well, no." In interviewing his good friend, "Popeye" Don Zimmer, then a coach for the Cubs, Whitey finally met his match. "Well, Zim," Whitey asked, "Who's pitching for you tonight?" And Zimmer replied, "I don't know. Who you got pitching tonight?" Whitey's response: "I have no idea."

Here we were, doing all that prep work. Sometimes I'd sit up late into the night, typing notes and stats on stencils, which was part of my job back then as publicity man. Whitey wouldn't read them. "Who cares about that stuff?" Another job I had was as a sort of producer of our radio broadcasts. I would update the out-of-town scoreboard, and I'd save each game's highlights. So, when the game ended, I'd have a cue sheet of them. If, say, someone hit a home run, it would be all cued up, ready for our engineer to rebroadcast, when the game ended, on our highlights show. It's possible, though, that Whitey's postgame shows were even more unpredictable than his pregame interviews. With so many highlights to save, there was a good deal of potential for missing one. I remember telling Whitey once, "I'm sorry. We just didn't get Bake McBride's hit in the fifth inning." "That's OK," he replied, "I've got it, pal." Whitey plowed right ahead and then at one point said, "In the fifth inning, Bake McBride comes up…" Silence. Except for my frantic whisper, "I told you, we don't have it." Of course, Whitey went right on, telling the radio audience, "Well, once again my producer, Wheels, has screwed up this broadcast and forgot to inform me that we don't have Bake McBride's hit, but trust me, folks, it was a bullet, and the Phillies took the lead, 6-5." This sort of thing would happen over and over.

The one statistic Whitey did care about was stolen bases, perhaps because of his own speed as a player. He wouldn't read or write down much of anything else, but he always knew a guy's stolen-base total. Yet he retained the goal of managing the Phillies, an ambition we tried to discourage. He'd say, "Boys, if I ever managed this team, you wouldn't have enough fingers for your World Series rings." And the fact is, in 1972, when the club was looking for a new manager, the *Inquirer* took a poll asking fans who would be their choice. Whitey won hands down. He did get an interview. Danny Ozark was hired, but from that day on, Richie Ashburn referred to himself, with some justification, as "the people's choice."

Whitey certainly had a broadcasting style of his own, personally connecting him with his legion of fans. Would his droll, laid-back, irreverent, spontaneous, candid, seemingly effortless approach work so well in today's media mix of prepackaged entertainment and information? Such a hypothesis doesn't seem very relevant to me. Whitey's way earned the unprecedented affection of people throughout our demanding market for decades, and not just baseball fans—this unique man who had two Hall of Fame careers, one on the field and another in the booth. When he died, too soon, at the age of 70, it was Mayor Ed Rendell's idea to have his body placed in Memorial Hall, where thousands of fans filed by to pay their respects, an extraordinary tribute. The entire 1997 team attended in full uniform, saluting one of their own.

A few years before, when Richie Ashburn had been belatedly enshrined in Cooperstown, it seems just as appropriate that he ended his remarks on a light note. Looking back, not to his achievements, but to having been the MVP of the worst team in baseball history, he recalled New York Mets manager Casey Stengel's comment that it had truly been a team effort—no one could be this bad on their own. In fact, Whitey had ended that season by hitting into a double play, for the Mets' 120th loss. Then Whitey deftly turned that memory around, saying, "I couldn't have gotten here on my own. Thank you for making this the greatest day of my life." For my own part, what I shared with Richie Ashburn, and what I owe him, will stay with me always. So will the smiles.

CHAPTER 3

The Happiest Umpire

IF WE JUDGE THE EFFICIENCY of an umpiring crew by how little their work is noticed during a game, then Eric Gregg was hardly the ideal arbiter. He certainly didn't blend in. It wasn't only his weight, with which he always struggled. Eric's personality was also outsized. His evident joy in everything he did couldn't be contained. Even his routine calls were dramatic. He simply loved everything about the game, especially interacting with players and fans. Who can forget his surprisingly agile dancing with the Phillie Phanatic, matching the equally rotund mascot move for move? For a big guy, the man we liked to call "E" was really light on his feet. Unfortunately, Eric's antics could easily overshadow just how conscientious he was about his chosen profession. Day in, day out, at least in my opinion, he was an excellent umpire. In calling a game, your judgment and your eyes are more important than your size.

Not surprisingly, my favorite stories about Eric involve girth and mirth. For a number of years, I was part of the PRISM cable telecasts, working with a variety of partners and doing both play-by-play and color. Founded by Ed Snider, PRISM started with a small number of homes wired in the South Philadelphia area, near the major sports venues. Bill Giles shared Snider's vision for cable's bright future, and the two formed a partnership permitting a number of Phillies games to be aired on this new pay-TV phenomenon. Of course, it eventually expanded beyond anyone's expectations into what is now Comcast SportsNet.

While serving as analyst, one of my duties was to head downstairs in the eighth inning and grab a postgame guest. I normally would place myself at the far right side of the Phillies' first-base dugout at the Vet and hang out with the camera guys. I carried a microphone and had a telex in my ear to hear Andy Musser's play-by-play. In this way, I could also continue contributing to the telecast.

One night between innings, I was looking toward home plate, where Eric had done his usual good job calling balls and strikes. We'd known each other for some time, so I waved over in his direction and expected the same familiar reaction in return. But this time the big guy had a funny look on his face, and he started walking over toward me, making a motion with his hand to his mouth. My first reaction was that he was taking exception to something he thought I'd said about him over the air and was going to give me a hard time about it. I couldn't remember saying anything negative, but he kept on walking until he suddenly loomed over me.

"What's up, E?" I said. "Are you OK?" "Oh, man," he replied, "whatever you do, don't let them take a camera shot of me from behind. You know, the league is all over me about my weight. I split my pants a few innings ago, and I don't want to give them any more ammunition." Naturally, I was relieved that he wasn't mad at me. He just wanted my attention. With that trademark huge smile of his, Eric made his way back to home plate. The game continued. There were no compromising camera shots from the rear during or after that final inning. He must have gingerly backed into the umpires' dressing room for the necessary repair work. But I have a feeling this probably happened more than once.

Another time we were playing a day game in St. Louis. Now, in the old days at Busch Stadium, the playing surface was AstroTurf, which seemed necessary in the new state-of-the-art, multipurpose stadiums that also housed a pro football team. Few places in this hemisphere got hotter than the midsummer turf in St. Louis for a day game. The games used to start at 12:15, and it was absolutely brutal for the players and the umpires.

Leading off for the Phils was the colorful "Dude," Lenny Dykstra. He legged out a hit, as he so often did, and almost immediately stole second. That is, he *appeared* to have safely stolen second—to me, to his teammates, and probably to most of the spectators. But the second-base umpire that day, Eric Gregg—who, after all, was closest to the play—called Lenny out. The Dude jumped up and started screaming at Gregg. Dykstra had a fairly limited on-field vocabulary, as the TV cameras made clear to anyone capable of lip-reading, and he leveled every example he could think of at Gregg. Well, Eric, who had heard a lot worse in his West Philly days, simply stood his ground, just nodding his head. The madder Lenny got, the calmer was the umpire's response. Eventually, Gregg started to laugh— which only infuriated Dykstra more.

It was obvious by now that the Dude was trying to get thrown out of the game. Players understand that there are certain words which, if leveled directly at an umpire, will normally result in an immediate ejection. You can use profanity, but you can't make it personal. A player can use a word like @#$%^&*, but can never tell the umpire that *he* is a @#$%^&*. Clear? Lenny had definitely stepped over the line, but however personal his remarks, it just didn't look like Eric was going to toss him out.

By now, Phillies manager Jim Fregosi had made his way out of the dugout to get into the argument and protect his player. His rich mix of expletives exhausted, all Lenny could do was dust himself off and head back to the dugout. Normally, managers can get even more upset than their players. But Lenny was still in the game. So Fregosi was coming out less to protect his player than to see what was going on. Fregosi and Gregg were talking very calmly, until the umpire began to smile, and this time it was the manager who laughed out loud. Later both confirmed that, yes, Dykstra would normally have been thrown out of the game, but not today—not in that relentless Midwestern heat. Eric had already made it plain to Lenny that he could stand there all day and call him every name in the book, but that if the umpire had to stay out there on that brutal AstroTurf, Dykstra would, too. And so, like it or not, Lenny Dykstra played all nine innings in the sizzling sun of a typical midsummer day in St. Louis. He was probably still cursing on his way back to the hotel.

Change comes slowly to baseball. When I reflect on the new in-stant-replay rule, I'm reminded of another typical Eric Gregg story. It was late in September 1979, at the Vet. The "We Are Family" Pitts-burgh Pirates were headed to a memorable World Series that year, while the injury-riddled Phils simply anticipated the off-season (al-though better days were to come, surprisingly soon). But it was still those two storied Pennsylvania franchises renewing their intense ri-valry, and emotions ran high.

The game began at the peculiar hour of 5:05 p.m. It wasn't long before the late-inning shadows were making it tough for anyone to see very clearly. The lights were on but having little effect by the time Keith Moreland stepped up to the plate for the Phillies. There were two men on base. Moreland hooked a low line drive to left that almost immediately disappeared somewhere in the vicinity of the foul pole. As it happened, in that game, Eric Gregg was umpir-ing at third base.

Eric hesitated for just a few seconds, but then emphatically sig-naled fair ball. Home run! The Pirates went nuts, both third base-man Bill Madlock and left-fielder Lee Lacy rushing over to confront Gregg. What then transpired was one of the best arguments involv-ing both teams ever seen at Veterans Stadium. Eric called in his col-leagues for a conference—something umpires always try to do when they're at all uncertain about a decision. Then he reversed his call: Foul ball. Now it was the Phillies' turn to protest. After manager Dal-las Green, who could get a little agitated himself, heaved a bag of baseballs onto the field, he was ejected by home-plate umpire Doug Harvey, granting "Big D" the pleasure of hearing our account of the rest of the game from his office. There were a good many other can-didates for ejection that evening, from both teams.

Why had Eric seemed so certain in the first place? As he later ex-plained it to me, the story is one for the ages. He said the ball went out so fast he simply lost it in the mix of ballpark lights and twi-light. Of course, he had only two choices—fair or foul—a 50 percent chance of getting it right. He looked down the line and saw the Phillies left-field ball girl, Mary Sue Styles, jumping with excite-ment. If Mary Sue says it's fair, Eric reasoned, that's good enough for me. Home run, and all hell breaks loose from the Bucs' bench and their players on the field.

Meanwhile, in the broadcast booth, we had the advantage of looking at our own video replay—several times. Sad to say, there's no doubt Moreland's blast was a foul ball. Close but foul. About the same time, on the field, Eric was having second thoughts about what had actually happened—just as the Pirates' storm hit him and his umpiring crew. Then he heard a rare voice of reason. The late Bill Robinson, a former Phillie now with the Pirates, walked over to Gregg and volunteered, "We just saw the replay in the clubhouse, and Chris Wheeler keeps saying it's a foul ball." Until the day he died, Eric and I used to laugh about that game, when he was in the middle of one of the best baseball arguments of his life, and as he put it, "The last thing I needed to hear was you telling everyone on TV that I'd screwed up!"

Eric wasn't a favorite only in Philly. I love this story from St. Louis. After the umpires held their customary pregame lineup card exchange and ground-rules meeting, the Cards took the field. Eric had third-base duty that night, where he stood for the National Anthem next to Cardinals third-baseman Tom Lawless.

Frank Coppenbarger, now the Phillies' equipment manager and director of travel (and an author himself), was then the umpires' room attendant at old Busch Stadium. He and Lawless came up with the idea of having some fun with Eric that night. Lawless sniffed the air and said to Gregg, "Man, doesn't it smell good here tonight? Just smell those hot dogs and hamburgers. Wouldn't you like to have one?" Eric, of course, said, "Yeah, that sounds great." Lawless then pointed to the third-base bag, on which a cheeseburger had magically appeared. "How about this one, E?" Since the game was about to start, there was no way Gregg could consume it, but there's a great photo in Frank's office of Eric holding that cheeseburger and flashing his thousand-watt smile. How many umpires find players who like them enough to have that kind of fun on the field?

Growing up on the mean streets of West Philly, and witness to enough tragedy to sink someone of any size, it's almost a miracle that Eric Gregg became a man so esteemed for his sunny disposition. Once he understood that he lacked the skills to make a living playing the game he loved, Eric Eugene Gregg applied himself to learning how to officiate it. He was only 24 when he became the third African-American umpire in major-league history. During the next 23 years, he worked World Series, playoffs, All-Star Games and perfect games, and amassed some vivid memories—from surviving a game-ending California earthquake to working the plate at the first night contest at Wrigley Field.

Always a proud "Philly guy," Gregg was careful to lean over backward not to seem to favor his Phillies (as with that reversed call in 1979). Some people said he had too wide a strike zone, but in baseball, umpires are known for their personal strike zones, and the players are OK with it—as long as they remain consistent. Umpiring gave Eric a good living, a handsome suburban home for his wife, Conchita, and their four children, paid college tuitions, and made possible the pleasures of a comfortable lifestyle replete with fine cigars and steaks. Still, he was an umpire, employed to make close calls. And the very vocal and visible Gregg stood out physically as well. It was never easy staying within the 300-pound weight limit desired by major-league baseball. On Opening Day of 1996, another big man, John McSherry, a dear friend of Gregg's, collapsed and died of a heart attack. The shock of McSherry's death induced Gregg to enter a weight-reduction program at Duke University.

It was not his weight alone that motivated the abrupt end of Gregg's career. It was the result of some unfortunate advice. Since the 1970s, there had been periodic confrontations between those who ran Major League Baseball and the umpires' union, leading to strikes and lockouts. During the 1999 dispute, the prominent lawyer advising the umpires suggested a radical tactic: they should all resign in protest. When, eventually, a settlement was reached, a majority of them were rehired. Gregg was one of those who were not. The commissioner had no legal obligation to take them all back. Ignoring the pleas of Eric Gregg's legion of influential friends, including some in Congress, Major League Baseball remained firm. He would never umpire again. All he received was a modest settlement.

Despite the always-dapper attire he wore in public, topped by his trademark wide-brimmed hat and the good cheer that never waned, something went out of Eric the day he left the field. He remained a familiar figure all around Philly, hosting the patrons at Chickie and Pete's sports bar, officiating at WIP's famed Wing Bowl, appearing often on the air, or just mingling with fans in and around the new Citizens Bank Park. No more colorful or congenial figure ever called balls and strikes.

On June 5, 2006, Eric suffered a massive stroke from which he never recovered. He was only 55. Fittingly, his son, Kevin, works today in media relations with the Phillies—a legacy of this wonderful man who graced our game. It's hard to think of Eric Gregg, even in his involuntary retirement, without smiling. In the end, he may no longer have been the happiest umpire. He simply made everyone around him happier.

CHAPTER 4

Coming to Life

WHAT A LUCKY GUY I AM. Here I was on Comcast Sports-Net's postgame show with Leslie Gudel on October 15, 2008. The Phillies had just finished off the Los Angeles Dodgers in five games to clinch their first National League pennant in 15 years. A tough 5-1 win behind the trio of Hamels, Madson, and Lidge, coming through again in the biggest game of the year—at least to that point. Charlie Manuel couldn't stop smiling. Not far from the visiting manager's office, his players' celebration was raucous but restrained. The big prize still lay ahead: the World Series, starting the following Wednesday in either St. Petersburg or Boston. We had no preference. We only hoped the Phils could sustain the momentum they'd built up with a great late-season run and an impressive two rounds of postseason play. They had failed in 1993, as in 1983, to take that final step—a world championship.

Dodger Stadium remains one of the most attractive and scenic of major-league venues, although it has been extensively renovated. There are now more seats closer to the field of play. The fences have been moved in, helping to make this park, with its magnificent view of the San Gabriel mountains, more hitter-friendly—especially during day games. One area, however, that has remained just about the same is the tiny visitor's clubhouse, with its adjacent cramped manager's office and trainer's room. We were soaking in the triumph of our team's National League championship only about 50 feet from where I'd witnessed a very different scene 30 years ago. Grown men

were crying unashamedly in the same room where they'd prepared
for that game four hours earlier. Tug McGraw, who would become a
hero in Philadelphia only two seasons later, was unable to hold back
his tears. I kept thinking that here, only 30 years ago, I'd been the
same age as many of the players. Now I could be Brad Lidge's dad,
or Cole Hamels' grandfather. But 1978 seemed like yesterday—only
this sure was a lot more fun. It's easier to handle triumph than
tragedy. Baseball may be only a game, but don't try to convince millions of Phillies fans, spread over 3,000 miles and beyond, on that
night in 2008. We were all one in our joy. And from that cramped
clubhouse our team couldn't wait to bring the trophy, and hopefully
a bigger one to come, back to the city of Philadelphia.

I was thinking of calling this chapter "The Great Awakening"—
because that's what the mid to late '70s were for the Phillies, culminating in the great season of 1980. When Veterans Stadium opened
on the unseasonably frigid afternoon of April 10, 1971, I was just a
fan sitting in section 334, the seats provided by my old WCAU 1210
pal, Andy Musser. Frank Lucchesi was the manager. The team finished a dismal 67-95, 30 games out of first place, but drew 1.5 million
fans to the new ballpark. Our leading hitter in 1971 was my future
broadcast partner and great friend, Tim McCarver—who batted .278.
Our most popular player was a homegrown right-hander named
Rick Wise. He'd made his major-league debut in 1964, pitching game
two of the memorable Father's Day doubleheader in New York,
where *all* he had to do was follow that perfect game by Jim Bunning.
Rick was such a great athlete, hitting two home runs in a game twice
in 1971; it's little wonder the fans loved him. So when he was traded
during spring training for a gangling left-hander with a prominent
Adam's apple from the St. Louis Cardinals named Steve Carlton—
to say the deal was not well received is a massive understatement.
Needless to say, "Lefty" Carlton went on to merit a re-evaluation.

After being hired by my first mentor with the Phillies, Larry
Shenk, in May 1971, I had to serve my mandatory two weeks of summer camp as an active member of the U.S. Army Reserve. This
turned out to be in West Point, Georgia, not far from Atlanta. While
I was gone, Wise pitched his no-hitter against the Pete Rose–led

Reds, and hit two homers in that game. I heard about it early the next morning to the sounds of reveille. Great timing. My first official day with the Phillies was July 5th. During that first summer, I started to travel a little with the team, getting a taste of life on the road. I also began moving occasionally from my seat in the press box with the sportswriters to the area that really fascinated me—the broadcast booth of By, Harry, and Richie.

By the following season, there were plenty of changes in the ballclub. A man who would mean a lot to me had taken over as general manager. Paul Owens, nicknamed "The Pope" by Dick Allen because of his striking resemblance to Pope Paul VI, was now the man in charge. His unique way of making his point left no doubt about that, as we'll explore in the next chapter. Although the team's record was even worse in 1972, finishing last again at 59-97, Carlton was on his way to "legend" status. Lefty won 27 games, nearly half the team's total, and the NL Cy Young Award.

Under first-year manager Danny Ozark, the Phillies made some progress in 1973, and in 1974, inspired by Dave Cash's cry of "Yes We Can!" (which has since been used by others), they made a run at respectability. They finished at 80-82, even threatening to win the East, eventually taken by the Mets. Attendance continued to climb, approaching two million. The passionate Phillies fans in this great baseball town embraced an emerging, entertaining team. The Pope and his associates had assembled a group of all-star talent, developed through the farm system and key trades—primed to compete with baseball's best in the Bicentennial year of 1976. At third base was a potential superstar named Mike Schmidt. The powerful "Bull," Greg Luzinski, was in left field, and reliable Bob Boone was behind the plate, plus shortstop Larry Bowa and superb fielder Garry Maddox in center. Carlton continued to lead an improved pitching staff that included Jim Lonborg, Larry Christenson, and Jim Kaat—anchored by a bullpen of McGraw, Gene Garber, and Ron Reed.

The Vet opener merged the centuries, the first ball delivered by a "Paul Revere" on horseback to "Rocketman," who jetted with it above the field. The Phils never lagged in imaginative opening-day stunts, but they lost that day to the Pirates, 5-4. It didn't exactly boost expectations when manager Danny Ozark, who had butted heads with Carlton since taking over the reins in 1973, bypassed Lefty for the opener and opted to start newly acquired left-hander Kaat instead, setting up a little early-season intrigue.

Fortunately, it wasn't a portent of things to come. Instead, this very talented team went on an exciting rollercoaster ride that would unsettle the stomachs of old and new fans alike. By late August, the ballclub had opened up a 15½-game lead on the Pirates, and things were looking really promising. But in Philly, despite our enthusiasm for our teams, we are conditioned from birth to expect the worst. Could it hold up? Everything still looked good on July 13th when President Gerald Ford came to the Vet to throw out the first pitch for the 49th All-Star Game. For the first time ever, the Phils had five players selected for the National League roster, with Luzinski starting in left. Even Ford's appearance seemed a positive omen. His college roommate at Michigan was the father of Stephanie Carpenter, wife of the Phillies' president. And the NL won, 7-1, beating a new phenom—"The Bird," Mark Fidrych. The stars seemed to be aligned. Could this finally be our year?

Then it happened. Shades of 1964, an epic collapse when the Phils were so far ahead they'd been granted permission to print World Series tickets. I still have a pair. From August 24th to September 17th, the Phillies managed to go just 6-17, while the Pirates were getting really hot. Our lead slipped to only three games. The old stories all resurfaced of prior years of promise submerged in a tidal wave of disappointment.

As always happens in the long season of baseball, certain games stand out. I remember two in particular. The first seemed to typify what would turn into the late-season collapse of 1976. The Phillies, still maintaining their substantial lead, were in Cincinnati in late August for a four-game series with the Reds. They won the first game but then dropped two straight, setting up a Sunday afternoon to remember. The date was August 29th. We took a precarious 4-3 lead into the bottom of the ninth. Ron Reed was on the mound. Dan Driessen walked and stole second, followed by a base hit to left by Rose, sending Driessen to third. Runners at the corners, nobody out, and Riverfront was rockin'. Ken Griffey grounded to Schmidt, who threw Driessen out at the plate, with Rose advancing to second. One out, and Joe Morgan the batter.

Two pitches later, things were looking a little better as Morgan lined out to right. George Foster came up, and Reed went to 3-2. I'm not alone in believing that one reason baseball appeals to so wide an audience is that, unique among athletic contests, there is no clock. You can't take a knee. You can't dribble out the time, and you can't ice it. Nope, you have to get those 27 outs, one way or another, and sometimes the last strike is the hardest. What happened next seems unbelievable, but I can still see it unfold. With the count full and two outs, Rose and Griffey took off on the pitch from Reed. Foster swung and missed. Game over. Only the ball got away from Bob Boone, to the backstop. The image of Rose tearing around third and headed for home, his helmet flying off and that mop of his flopping in the wind, is forever ingrained in my psyche. Of course, he scored, the game was tied, and the press box shook with all the energy of those delirious Reds fans. Worst of all, I had to compose myself and write down what had just happened in the official scorebook when all I wanted to do was hurl it across the room. We lost the game in 15 innings, and the wheels were greased for our skid.

The losing ways would continue for five more games, but then came that other significant contest—the one I think really turned things around for the Phillies of 1976. It needn't be the same old story. After a sweep by the Astros in which the club scored only three runs in three games, and two more losses to the Mets in New York, it was getting really grim. In the Sunday game, on September 6th, Larry Christenson took the mound. He was opposed by left-hander Mickey Lolich for the Mets. Lolich had been an All-Star in the American League for the Detroit Tigers, and still had good stuff. But so did L.C., who stepped up big time in that game. He was always a tough competitor, but unfortunately was dogged by serious arm problems for almost his entire career. Whitey loved Christenson because he was a fun guy who could hit. Those were the only pitchers Ashburn liked. When one complained about a lack of run support, Whitey delighted in telling him all he needed to do was to

pitch a shutout and hit a home run. Well, L.C. nearly complied. He
went eight and a third innings, as the Phils stopped the bleeding
with a 3-1 win. And, to Whitey's delight, he also hit *two* home runs
for good measure.

The season was finally secured later in September when the club
started to win more consistently again, although they had never entirely lost their lead. Finally, the Phillies won the East on that magical day in Montreal, September 26th—the champagne flowing in
the visitors' clubhouse at old Jarry Park—that led to the start of my
life in broadcasting. How ironic that I would be paired on radio the
following season with Andy Musser, who had given me those tickets
for Opening Day at the Vet back in 1971.

Now it was on to the postseason to face the "Big Red Machine."
There was only one round of playoffs in those days, East vs. West,
best of five games for the National League pennant. Same in the
American League. It wouldn't take long to determine our World Series opponent. Because of an alternate-year formula, we got to
open the 1976 playoffs at home, but against this formidable opponent. Still, the first game looked promising as we sent Steve Carlton to the mound against the Reds' fireballing young lefty, Don
Gullett. It was windy that night of October 9th when the Phillies
took the field for the first postseason game in Philadelphia since
1950. When the wind was swirling in that huge oval, it could be really treacherous. There is no such thing as a routine out in such
conditions. The Reds had the bases loaded in the top of the first inning, but there were two outs when the always-dangerous Johnny
Bench stepped to the plate. The crowd, more than a little restless,
let out a huge roar when Bench hit one of those mile-high, big-
league pop-ups. Inning over, right?

The collective sigh of relief didn't include reliable Larry Bowa, as
he saw the ball circling directly over his head. Now, Larry Bowa may
be the best shortstop ever to wear a Phillies uniform (although
Jimmy Rollins lately is making a strong case to contest that honor),
but he hated pop-ups. And in the biggest game of his life, with
62,640 fans roaring, he had to fight those dreaded Vet winds and
catch that elusive ball when it finally came down. No one was going

to call him off. "Bo" told me later that his first thought was, "Oh, bleep, those fans think this inning is over. They have no idea how tough a play this is." Lurching around on those "happy feet" he'd often exhibit when going after a sky-high pop-up, he managed to make the catch, and then tried to get his heart rate back to normal as he headed to the dugout. As one respected baseball man told me, "Bowa's the best I've ever seen, but I'd never teach his technique to a kid. Nothing he does is smooth or by the book. It just works." Major-league players, even those as talented as Bowa, are no different from the rest of us. He can laugh about it now, but he was scared to death when that ball, headed up into the pitch-black night, finally came down and nestled safely into his glove. Oh, we lost that game, 6-3, after leading by a run. We also lost the second game, 6-2.

Then it was off to Riverfront Stadium, that "house of horrors" for visiting teams—and game three. Facing elimination, the Phillies led 6-4 heading into the bottom of the ninth, with reliable Ron Reed on the mound. Called "Slinky" by his teammates, the six-foot, six-inch Reed was probably trying to put out of his mind his last experience at Riverfront in August. But before you could blink, George Foster and Bench both went deep, the game was tied, and that queasy feeling returned. Gene Garber and Tom Underwood followed Reed, but the Reds bled out a run on an infield chopper by Griffey that scored Dave Concepcion, and both the game and the series were over. Just like that. The Phillies had won 101 games that season, but were swept by a great team that would go on to sweep the Yankees, as well, in four straight. Those Reds could boast of two consecutive World Series championships, in 1975 and 1976—the last National League team to accomplish this feat.

There was understandable disappointment in the Phillies clubhouse, but also a sense of pride—and resolve. We were getting there. We had simply lost to a better team. I remember flying back to Philadelphia the next day in our Delta charter, thinking there were better days to come—as long as we could keep this potent lineup together and mature as a team. I'm sure such reflections were shared by others. And, as for that Big Red Machine, like all special teams, their days of domination were numbered. Before too long, three of those players—Rose, Morgan, and Tony Perez—would wind up in red-and-white pinstripes and help lead the Phillies to more postseason play—but that's for later.

THE ORIGINAL "GAME of inches," with an off-season that used to be called the "hot stove" league, baseball will always be especially a game of opinions. I continue to believe that the 1977 Phillies were the best team the club ever put on the field. Steve Carlton went 23-10 and won another Cy Young. Christenson, Lonborg, and Kaat made up the rest of a solid rotation. Greg Luzinski, who knocked in 130 runs, finished as runner-up for the league MVP to George Foster. Schmidt, Maddox, Bowa, and Boone were at the top of their games. The signings of Richie Hebner and Ted Sizemore added good players who fit right in. But what solidified the team was a controversial deal at the trading deadline with the St. Louis Cardinals. Yes, it seems like we traded with the Cards a lot.

Bake McBride came to Philadelphia. To this day, I believe McBride to be the most underrated Phillie of this era. In his time here, he made a tremendous contribution both in the outfield and at the plate. To get him, we had to give up three young players, including promising left-hander Tommy Underwood. It is to Ruly Carpenter's credit that he ultimately agreed to the deal. Always a development-oriented owner who believed in putting the team together from a strong minor-league system, Ruly was especially high on Underwood. I remember Larry Shenk telling me, the night we had to make calls to the media to announce the deal, how reluctant Ruly was to go through with it. Eventually, he decided that it was Paul Owens' prerogative to make such decisions, and The Pope must have a pretty good reason for this one. And thus "Shake and Bake" became a Phillie, and right field was now in good hands.

The team sustained its success, winding up with the identical record as in the preceding season (an impressive 101-61), champs again of the NL East. This time our opponent would be Tommy Lasorda's Los Angeles Dodgers. A Norristown native, the colorful Lasorda had been a longtime minor-league manager in the Dodgers organization, now getting his chance to lead the big club. Respected skipper Walter Alston was stepping down after 23 years at the helm. The postseason got off to a better start for the Phils than it had in 1976. We won game one in L.A., 7-5, scoring two in the ninth to overcome a Ron Cey grand-slam home run. The next contest, however, was a loss as Don Sutton pitched a complete game and Dusty Baker hit another slam. So it was back to Philadelphia, tied at 1-1, with the expectation of a raucous crowd awaiting game three.

October 7, 1977 was a late-afternoon start for a game that will be forever remembered as "Black Friday." So much happened during those three hours that it was like a miniseries in itself. Baseball crowds, however loud, are not normally viewed as intimidating, but that day the fans cracked a terrific pitcher named Burt Hooton. In 1972, then a Chicago Cub, Hooton had no-hit the Phils. This game started off promisingly enough for Hooton, with the Dodgers scoring two runs in the top of the second. He got a break when Steve Garvey was called safe by home-plate umpire Harry Wendelstedt. The bottom of the second seemed like it would be uneventful until a two-out single by Bob Boone advanced Richie Hebner to second. Then it started. Hooton walked eight-hole hitter Ted Sizemore to load the bases, and the crowd really started getting on the Dodgers' hurler. Hooton appeared to be throwing pitches, right down the middle of the plate, that Wendelstedt called balls. The exasperated Hooton kept asking the umpire, "Where was *that* pitch?" as he spread his arms in disbelief. With the crowd roaring now on every pitch and waving hankies (the precursor of the rally towel), Hooton managed to walk pitcher Larry Christenson, Larry Bowa, and Bake McBride to force in three runs, giving the Phillies a 3-2 lead. Davey Lopes, now a valued coach with the Phils but then the Dodger second-baseman, reminded me that at one point during the debacle Lasorda came out to try to calm Hooton down. To this day, Lopes claims he has no idea what Lasorda was saying. "I had never heard a ballpark that loud in my life," Lopes recalled. "I just went back to second and hoped we'd get out of the inning." Hooton didn't. His afternoon ended after just one and a third innings of work, hooted off the mound by fans actually affecting a game.

The Dodgers scored a run in the fourth to tie it, but then came unglued in the eighth as errors by Reggie Smith and Ron Cey contributed to two runs. The Phillies took a 5-3 lead into the ninth. The crowd of 63,719, in a frenzy throughout the game, just knew this one had to be over when Gene Garber retired the first two Dodger hitters on harmless ground balls. It was Garber's third inning of work. With the fans on their feet since the start of the inning, no one was overly concerned when pitch-hitter Vic Davalillo beat out a perfect drag bunt. Then another pitch-hitter, Manny Mota, hit a towering fly ball to left that looked like the end of the game. But the ball kept carrying, and Luzinski kept drifting back toward the wall. As he jumped, the ball went off his glove and the Plexiglas fronting the Dodgers' bullpen. Davalillo scored and Mota pulled up at second with a double. However, the Bull's throw back to the infield got away from Sizemore, and Mota went to third. Then came the play that still haunts Phillies fans, turning the atmosphere from potential party into a morgue. Lopes hit a smash directly at Mike Schmidt, who had no time to react. The ball caromed off of Schmidt's glove but went right to Bowa, who planted, grabbed it out of midair, and fired a bullet to Hebner to get Lopes at first on a bang-bang play. Game over? Only Lopes, probably the fastest right-handed hitter in the league, was called safe by first-base umpire Bruce Froemming. The game was tied at 5-5.

What followed was a sequence of events that still gives me nightmares. The crowd started to boo Froemming, but then lapsed into almost a stunned silence. I can still hear Ruly Carpenter and others, in the executive box next to our radio booth, screaming at Froemming and throwing chairs against the wall. Naturally, bad things continued to happen. Garber, trying to pick off Lopes, threw the ball away, sending the speedy Lopes to second. One of the game's great clutch hitters, Bill Russell, singled him home for a 6-5 L.A. lead. After the Phils went quietly in the bottom of the ninth, ending the game, all the second-guessing began. Thankfully, especially for manager Danny Ozark, there was no talk-radio or endless cable TV analysis in those days—because Jerry Martin had almost always been a defensive replacement for Luzinski in left field when the Phillies had a lead. In this instance, Ozark had opted not to do it, with disastrous results. And our great sports town, all set to erupt, went into a collective funk that seemed to envelop the entire tri-state area.

My old friend Jack Downey, a wonderful character who passed away in 2008, had been my first boss at WCAU radio, and then opened the still very popular Downey's Pub at Front and South. A great fan himself, Downey recounted how his place, like just about every other bar and restaurant in the area that October evening, was jammed with screaming fans. Everyone was ready to explode as the Phillies were primed to find themselves only one win away from the World Series. After the final out, his place emptied like someone had reported a bomb scare. People just drifted off into the night. At the Vet, it was like a wake. As for our clubhouse, the scene was one of shock and disbelief. Brave faces and brave words—"We'll get them tomorrow"—but I left that night wondering how in the world any team could come back from a loss like this.

The following day, Saturday, was dreary and rainy, as miserable as the mood in the city. We all wondered if the game would be played that night at all, but after a 17-minute delay, National League president Chub Feeney decided it would start, rain or no rain. The brutal conditions were not quite what the Phils would experience in game five of 2008's World Series. The field was actually playable because of AstroTurf. The grounds crew could focus on the dirt cutouts—the mound, the bases, and home plate—where the water couldn't be absorbed. After Dusty Baker's two-run homer in the second inning gave the Dodgers a 2-0 lead, the playing conditions remained miserable. Tommy John, who later would have the famous ligament-replacing surgery named after him, was brilliant that night, pitching a complete game seven-hitter, with eight strikeouts. He had a disappearing sinker in those days, and some felt he did something else to the ball to make it sink. But he bested Steve Carlton, and it was the Dodgers who went off to play the Yankees in the World Series. Some blamed the rain for our loss that night, but I'll always believe it was Black Friday that doomed us in the deciding game. Baseball is a contest of skill, but it is also played between the ears.

I've always loved following the fall classic, whoever might be in it, but I just couldn't watch it that October. One bad call, leading to a sequence of bad breaks, may have denied us our World Series. It turned out to be an exciting and successful one, with a whopping national 30-share TV rating. These two old rivals from the glory days in New York, but now representing both coasts, going after each other. I remember having dinner in a Manayunk restaurant and hearing people buzzing about the show Reggie Jackson was putting on. First one, then two, how about three home runs? Normally, I would have headed straight for the TV to watch this amazing show. But this night the chicken piccata and Pinot Grigio were a lot more inviting.

I sometimes lapse into saying "we" or "us" or maybe "our team" as if I were a part of it on the field. I try not to do this on the air. That kind of personalization may work in other cities, but never in Philly. However, in the 1970s, I was caught between being a front-of-fice guy, a broadcaster, and a contemporary of the nucleus of the ball club. As noted earlier and expanded on later, we had all kind of grown up together. Bowa came to the major leagues in 1970, Luzinski in 1971, Schmidt and Boone in 1972. After six years with the team and a lot of time hanging out with the players and their families, I could feel their frustration in coming so close to every player's goal—competing in a World Series.

Eventually, you grow out of that mentality, and a transition takes place. And, of course, money changes a lot. Things have come a long way from when I started. The players represented themselves, and had to take part-time jobs in the off-season to support their families. I can still remember when the stars of our team would go and play basketball games in different parts of Pennsylvania and New Jersey against high-school teachers or some other pickup teams. They would get $100 a man for that night's game and the next. It seems like a hundred years ago. Today's players are still just regular people, but they are also multimillionaires, their agents representing them with management. Yet the camaraderie of being one of the elites who can play in the major leagues exists to this day. And while today's fans are probably more demanding (and today's expanded media more intrusive) of high-profile athletes than they were in the simpler times of the 1970s, they still love the grand old national pastime, and the players still love to put on a show for them. As always, anything can happen once the home-plate umpire yells "Play ball!" Hopefully, we won't have to sit and squirm through another Black Friday, but the players, broadcasters, and fans who lived it will never forget that day.

THE 1978 TEAM had a good season, going 90-72: a drop-off from the previous two years, but still good enough to win the East ahead of the hard-charging Pittsburgh Pirates. Dick Ruthven, who had been a Phillies draft choice and pitched for the club from 1973 through 1975, returned to bolster the starting rotation. For the powerhouse Pirates, I always felt that the key to their staff was workhorse Kent Tekulve, my future broadcast partner and still a good friend. "Teke" was from the old school of relief pitching, which basically meant, "Give me the ball and I'll stay out there as long as it takes to finish the game."

As the regular season came to its conclusion, the Phillies and Pirates were locked in a thrilling pennant race. As luck would have it, the season would close with a four-game series between the two. Doesn't that always seem to be the case in baseball? The series would include a make-up twi-night doubleheader on Friday, September 29th, with day games set for Saturday and Sunday. The Phillies came to Three Rivers Stadium that weekend with a three-and-a-half-game lead and had to win just *one* game to claim their third straight NL East crown. It may have sounded easy, but the proud Pirates, only a year away from a world championship, still boasted such powerful hitters as Willie Stargell and Dave Parker.

Friday night was a disaster. We lost both games of the doubleheader in the ninth inning, a crushing setback. Game one ended in shocking fashion when slow-footed catcher Ed Ott, who had started the inning with a rare triple to center, came all the way around to score when Garry Maddox's throw went into the Phillies' third-base dugout. The dugouts in Three Rivers in those days had neither steps nor screens in front of them. There was nothing to stop a ball from rolling or to prevent an extra base. Game two featured a great pitching matchup between Steve Carlton and Bruce Kison. The Pirates' right-hander was one of the most disliked players in the league, a sentiment the Phillies shared. Kison was a tall side-armer whose specialty was pitching inside. He wasn't hesitant about drilling any hitter who leaned over the plate. I've gotten to know Bruce now that he is a major-league advance scout, and have found him to be a really nice guy. Today Kison laughs about those confrontations: "I wouldn't have liked me either, but I had a job to do. I had to intimidate those great right-handed hitters on the Phillies, and get them out. But those days sure were fun."

In that game, however, Luzinski homered early for the Phillies. Then, can you believe it, Kison countered with *his* first home run of the year. It was tied, 1-1, in the bottom of the ninth. Parker, who normally had trouble hitting Carlton, led off with a double, advancing to third on another error by the normally dependable Maddox. Here we go again. After Carlton intentionally walked Bill Robinson and Willie Stargell, Warren Brusstar was brought in from the pen to replace Lefty. With "Scrap Iron" Phil Garner batting, Brusstar was called for some ticky-tack balk, and Parker trotted home with the winning run. Two losses, both by one run, and the Bucs had some serious momentum. It was a frustrating night, but not a long one. Games were a little different back then. Game one was played in 2:11, and game two in 2:07. And the winner in both games? You guessed it, our old pal Tekulve. I can't believe how much I used to dislike him.

Still, we only needed to win one more game to pop the corks. Saturday afternoon was a new day, and a new opportunity, wasn't it? Well, the great Stargell, Mr. "We Are Family," wasn't ready for the season to end. He blasted a grand-slam home run in the first inning off young lefty Randy Lerch, a talented pitcher the Atlanta Braves thought they'd acquired a few years earlier (a great Pope story we'll share in the next chapter). But then Randy settled down, and, like Christenson in 1976, *he* hit two home runs himself and gave the team a solid five innings. Meanwhile, the Phillies' bats finally came alive. When we put up a four-spot in the eighth and took a 10-4 lead into the ninth, things were looking good. But the Pirates, with their potent offense, had already won two games in their final at-bat the preceding night. And sure enough, they came right after reliever Tug McGraw, and promptly loaded the bases. By the time Ron Reed replaced McGraw, the score was 10-7, with only one out. Bill Robinson greeted Reed with a base hit, and it was 10-8. How tough could it be to win just *one* game from these guys? Naturally, up stepped Stargell, representing the tying run. Reed struck him out. One more to go. The next hitter was Garner. What a relief seeing that ground ball off his bat headed to the almost-automatic Bowa. The game was over. For the relieved Phillies the celebration was on. We were NL East champs again. It hadn't been easy. I've never seen a more wild and crazy clubhouse celebration.

The Dodgers were the opposition again, as the playoff series opened in Philadelphia. L.A. took both games, 9-5 and 4-0, our nemesis Tommy John shutting us out in game two. Another long flight to the West Coast, facing long odds. But the Phils came out smoking in that third game on Friday night. Lefty put on a one-man show against Don Sutton. The Phillies won the game 9-4, highlighted by Carlton's home run—the last homer hit by a Phillies pitcher in postseason play until Joe Blanton's blast against the Rays in 2008. The team was still alive, with game four slated for Saturday afternoon.

It got off to a promising start as leadoff man Mike Schmidt (yep, he was hitting first that day) doubled. Then Bowa walked, and Maddox singled to right to load the bases off lefty Doug Rau. Nobody out. But Luzinski, who loved to hit in Dodger Stadium, struck out. José Cardenal hit a bullet to short for out number two, and Jerry Martin popped up foul to end the inning. But it was far from over. Bake McBride blasted a pinch-hit home run in the seventh to tie the score at 3, and this tense, potential elimination game for our guys eventually went to extra innings.

In the 10th, as it had before against the Dodgers, some strange stuff seemed to seize our normally most sure-handed fielders. Tug retired the first two batters he faced, before walking Ron Cey. Dusty Baker then ripped a line drive to center that handcuffed Maddox.

Garry dropped it for an error. And up came that ever-reliable, clutch-hitting shortstop, Bill Russell. He lined a single to center, Cey scored, and Dodger Stadium went nuts as their team headed to another World Series. For the Phils, it would be a grim, 3,000-mile flight home after another bitter disappointment. And that's where we started this chapter, with the raw emotions permeating that snug visitors' clubhouse in 1978—only to be cleansed by the World Championship team of 2008.

At the time, I thought our prospects were bright for 1979, especially with the welcome arrival of one Peter Edward Rose, and his winning attitude, to supplement the strength already on our roster. But, as it turned out, our pitching staff was decimated by injuries, and this would not yet be the year. The Phillies and the rest of the league were steamrolled by those Bucs, led by their inspirational captain, Willie Stargell. They still had the same stable of mashers the Phils had put away on next to the last day of 1978, and went on to win it all in 1979. Our commitment was to get healthy and make another run, only with a different ending. Shouldn't so talented a group find a way to finally get over the hump?

CHAPTER 5

The Pope of Pattison Avenue

WHEN I ARRIVED TO WORK for the Phillies, my first general manager was the legendary John Quinn. "J.Q.," a career baseball man hired by Bob Carpenter in 1959, had already been a major influence on the development of other teams, particularly the powerful Milwaukee Braves of Hank Aaron, Joe Adcock, and Eddie Mathews. Carpenter wanted the best front-office man in the business, and there was no one more established or "old school" than Quinn. It extended to his daily attire. He dressed like your grandfather might have. He always wore a suit, a stiffly starched white shirt, cuff links, and a tie. Add a high collar and hat and you'd have had Connie Mack. And the man always had the distinct smell of his favorite after-shave. Whether it was Old Spice or something else, you always knew when John Quinn entered the room or if he had been there. Quinn believed that to be a serious professional, you had to look the part. More than once, there had been some situation with the club that required his attention at an unseemly early-morning hour, when the team was staying in a hotel on the road, or during spring training or at those infamous "winter meetings." And sure enough, the man would show up fully dressed, like he was the headline speaker at a banquet.

Quinn expected the organization to look the part, even down to Larry Shenk's brand-new, without-a-clue PR assistant. After I'd started my employment and set out for my first spring training in February 1972, replete with my wire-rimmed glasses, sideburns,

open shirt and sandals—a poster boy for the rebellious 1960s—
Quinn let me know immediately through The Baron that such an
appearance was simply not acceptable at any time or place. The
message was clearly conveyed. I was now in the major leagues, not
about to participate in a protest march in front of the White House.

Quinn liked to think of himself as fair-minded, but he was very
careful in dispensing the Carpenter family fortune. When Richie
Ashburn, nearing the end of another typically productive year, felt
he merited a nice raise, Quinn disagreed. Stressing Ashburn's lack of
power numbers, Quinn insisted, "You hit too many singles." To
which Whitey replied, "If I hit my singles any further, they'd be
outs." Even the somber Quinn had to be amused at that line, but in
those reserve-clause days, the teams had the hammer, and it was
take it or leave it.

Yet it was Quinn, ironically such a standard bearer for the status
quo, who would wind up in the middle of a series of events that
changed the whole system of professional baseball as we know it
today. In 1970, he initiated the trade that would have brought All-
Star and Gold Glove center-fielder Curt Flood to Philadelphia. The
only problem was that Flood was very comfortable with the star-
studded Cardinals and didn't want to leave. He refused to report.
Why exchange a storied team like the Cardinals, where he was used
to playing in World Series games, for a team that didn't win consistently? Why play in front of fans that seemed to be so mean-spirited,
in a dilapidated old ballpark like Connie Mack Stadium? It may be
that Flood also recognized the racial overtones that helped drive
Dick Allen out of Philadelphia, and wanted no part of that soap
opera. Ironically, Allen was part of the package the Phillies sent to
the Cardinals in the Flood deal, which also would make Tim Mc-
Carver a Phillie for the first time. Flood took his fight all the way to
the Supreme Court, but he lost.

He returned to the major leagues in 1971 to play for Ted Williams'
Washington Senators, but was only a shell of the star he had been.
He hit just .200 with only 35 at-bats before retiring to a life of paint-
ing and writing. However, Flood did see the reserve clause over-
turned in 1975 by an arbitrator. He died of lung cancer in 1997 in Los

Angeles at the age of 59. What he started would change the game forever and bring the unbridled wealth that so many players possess today. Jackie Robinson may have broken the color barrier, but it was Curt Flood who players should thank for the opulent lifestyles so many of them enjoy.

The Phillies were awarded two players because of Flood's failure to report. One of them, Willie Montañez, became a fan favorite who hit 30 home runs in 1971, a flashy center-fielder who would later exhibit such skill at first base. And it was John Quinn who also would engineer that key deal with the Cardinals, trading Rick Wise for Steve Carlton. This venerable baseball lifer left an indelible mark during his tenure with the Phillies.

Bob Carpenter never lost respect for Quinn's ability or professionalism, but the team had fallen on hard times, with a dismal sixth-place finish in 1971 and a poor start in 1972. With so many empty seats in its huge new ballpark, it seemed time for a change in the front office. On June 3rd, the media was summoned to Carpenter's office during the ninth inning of a game at the Vet. Carpenter and Quinn greeted them with the news that J.Q. was "retiring." Paul Owens, the team's director of the minor leagues at the time, was to replace Quinn. I remember that as one of the more confusing days I would experience in the PR department. There were some questions left unanswered during that strange Sunday afternoon. Quinn's departure was handled with the kind of amicable dignity that reflected the nature of both men. After responding to reporters' questions as best he could, J.Q. retired quietly with his wife, a pleasant lady whom everyone called "Mom," to their apartment near the art museum. He had made it easy, but this was the kind of succession Larry Shenk and I hoped we'd never have to try to explain again.

Paul Owens now was the man in charge of baseball operations, and he wasted little time in putting his imprint on the organization. Little more than a month later, he fired manager Frank Lucchesi and decided to put on the uniform himself, heading downstairs to become field manager. It was quite a drastic step. Owens felt the Phillies had some good core talent, but he had to shake things up— get down there, see who was part of the future, and start removing the dead wood. Pope felt that the only way to get to know the players was "to live with them every day." So we now had a combined general manager and manager for the rest of that brutal 1972 season. We still finished last, 59-79, but one way or the other, Owens was determined to turn things around. As for my own role, in a year that had started in spring training with a reprimand from John Quinn, the acquisition of Steve Carlton, and a huge upheaval in the front office, I was learning that this was going to be an unpredictable, fast-moving business. It required the ability to improvise, and it sure wasn't going to be dull.

It's fitting that Paul Owens would always be known as "The Pope." A character right out of a Damon Runyon novel, Owens was a man who deserved a name that distinctive. He was more than a mentor who taught many people like me how to be a baseball man. And it wasn't always a pleasant experience. I know I'm not alone in feeling that my chest still may be bruised from one of his long, bony fingers jabbing at me while he made his point. Tall and thin, slightly hunched over, Owens had huge hands. He might not be venting at you personally, but he was very emotional when making his point. You just stood there and let him poke away, hoping this wasn't going to be a long exchange. Pope favored contact in making his points, but he didn't hold grudges. He could be livid at that moment, but by the next day he was your best friend. What never changed was his passion for the game.

That "fire in your belly" was one of the favorite expressions of an Owens protégé he elevated to run the ballclub late in 1979. Dallas Green was Owens' farm director. After years of Danny Ozark, it seemed like time for another change. Owens and Green were on the same page, believing in "tough love" as the method of imparting life's lessons. To a young guy like me, without a father since college, it isn't a reach to say they were like father figures. You knew that the more Pope and Dallas got on you, the more they cared about you. Maybe I didn't realize it at the time, but it sure struck home as I got older and understood their methods. One thing that always fascinated us about Owens was what he could do with his omnipresent cigarette. While jabbing away at his subject with his right hand, he would hold a fully lit Camel in his left hand. The ash would continue to grow—two inches, three inches—but somehow would never fall off. Finally, he'd just flick it off and keep talking. It was mesmerizing.

Owens had been a good minor-league player, hitting .407 one year in a league in his native New York State. However, he never made it to the major leagues, something he shared with other successful baseball executives. His contrast with Quinn was striking. J.Q. never was a physical person, given to close contact or confrontations. On the other hand, Owens was intensely physical. He had his share of fist fights, and it was never a good idea to provoke him. He was a man's man, deceptively strong in that long, lanky frame, but he never was afraid to show his emotions. Probably two of the most enduring memories of the 1980 season were of Owens and Green holding the World Series trophy and Pope tearfully kissing a champagne-soaked Tug McGraw.

Still, in his own way, even as he got close enough to evaluate each player, Owens always knew where to draw the line between being a guy's friend and his boss. He wondered if perhaps, being around the same age, I was getting too friendly and close to the players. Even before the age of free agency, front-office negotiations could be sensitive. I tried to walk that line carefully, and Owens seemed to understand that I had a difficult role. Since some of the current players and I had kind of grown up together—Boone, Carlton, Luzinski, Schmidt, Bowa—it's natural to think they might have wanted to know if I had any inside information on trades and front-office happenings. This was especially true of a guy like Bowa, who had antennae for everything. I think I did a pretty good job of separating the two roles, but Pope made sure that I didn't cross the line. It was no fun having him in my face (or chest).

The fact is that one of our jobs in publicity was to try to protect the players and avoid potential conflicts. It was much easier back then than it is today, with so much more media. That we did get to know the players personally was another reason we'd want to look out for them, especially in terms of their media dealings. It's so much tougher for today's Phillies publicity staff to do that, however hard they try. Nowadays, it's almost impossible to contain a story or withhold personal information when an athlete is involved. During my time with Larry Shenk, we tried to do things on our terms. Although we had our share of leaks back then, it got to the point where we never would announce anything. One day I said to Larry, "You know, we ought to call ourselves the 'Department of Confirmation and/or Denials' because that's all we do."

Once I got into trouble with famed Associated Press reporter Ralph Bernstein. I didn't witness the incident, but evidently Larry Bowa had a beef with Ray Kelly Jr. of the Camden *Courier-Post* about a story he had written. Bowa got Kelly to come into the clubhouse and "jumped" him, both literally and figuratively. Not a good thing. During the game, word spread about what had happened. Media members wanted to talk with Bowa in the clubhouse after the game. Obviously, this was a sensitive subject, and we tried to make it as short an interview as possible and then get the writers away from Larry. Well, when Ralph got his teeth into a story, nobody was more tenacious. He just wouldn't quit. So finally I stepped in and said, "OK guys, that's enough." That threw Ralph into one of his legendary rages, directed at me, which was fine because it gave Bowa time to move away into the sanctity of the trainer's room. The short shelf life of what happened wouldn't be the case today, with cameras and sound equipment everywhere. The story would have led the local sports shows and would have featured on Comcast and ESPN. Bernstein complained to Ruly Carpenter, Paul Owens, and Larry Shenk, but they all agreed I'd done the right thing, and that was the end of it. And Ralph and I had a lot more pleasant than nasty experiences throughout the rest of his storied career.

Paul Owens did more than back his players up. He was the best judge of baseball talent and people in general that I've ever seen. As farm director, he had signed Schmidt, Bowa, Luzinski, and Boone. After he went down into the dugout, he carefully developed a plan for the inevitable housecleaning. Pope then acquired Garry Maddox, Manny Trillo, Bake McBride, Tug McGraw, Ron Reed, Gene Garber, Pete Rose, and many others who helped make 1980 so memorable. From farm director to his 12 years as general manager, twice serving as field manager and then as a senior advisor to later GMs, Pope was the face of the success of the Phillies organization.

Firm in some ways, he was also innovative and adaptable. He would use the term "bounceability" as a trait that he admired, and he sure lived his life that way. He created the concept of a spring-training complex with the clubhouse in the center and four fields emanating out—he called it "spokes on a wheel." His creation was copied by other organizations and remains in place at the Paul Owens Complex in Clearwater. It has been modernized but still retains The Pope's design. He would stand on the roof and go back and forth from field to field, watching the four diamonds, missing little. Believe me, the players and instructors always knew when Pope had moved over to check them out, and they didn't want to disappoint him.

On the major-league level, Owens felt he should travel with the team as much as possible. Although he believed that a lot of people can tell you who could play and who couldn't, he wanted to know what made the guy tick. What were his hobbies, his interests? You didn't need to be a saint to become a great player, or dead serious to become a student of the game. Owens acquired a character like Jay Johnstone, who had worn out his welcome with other teams, but Pope loved his bat. Tug McGraw had a reputation as a talented flake who would never live up to his potential, but he became a star with the Phillies. The list goes on and on.

Not everything worked, but Pope's track record was amazing. Owens didn't miss many trips. He loved life on the road and the camaraderie that came with the whole vagabond existence of a player away from his home ballpark. He could be seen everywhere—on the team bus, in hotel lobbies and bars—constantly interacting with club personnel and the public. The man was in his element wherever the team found itself, like no one I've seen before or since.

At the ballpark, he liked to move around to different locations and watch batting and fielding practice for both teams. You rarely saw him hanging out behind the batting cage or in the clubhouse or dugout. He felt these were the places for the players, coaches, and managers. So when he showed up in one of these locales, look out—he was there for a reason. He liked to watch individual work habits to see which players were taking their ground balls and fly balls seriously, and which were loafing and simply going through the motions. He wanted to know who was preparing properly for the game. Are our players doing the things they need to do to get better? How about the opposition? He might be involved in a deal for one of these guys later on. It was valuable to gain some up-close feel for the players' habits. Some people might consider this insignificant. But Pope was the most thorough of baseball men, leaving nothing to chance. He might have trouble remembering names, constantly calling people "Slugger" or "Big Guy" or something similar. But he would know what was more important—if the guy could hit, pitch, or field his position. He had this invaluable ability to see the whole picture. I think people sometimes underestimated Pope's intelligence. If they did, they would pay for it.

Alcohol was very much a part of the baseball culture back then. There were hard drinkers and hard livers on every level of the game. But in those relatively simpler times, the beat writers could often be found drinking with the players and front-office personnel. Occasionally there might be a flare-up, like the one I'd had with Ralph Bernstein, but they were few and far between. We all relied on each other; we were in it together. The writers were inclined to look the other way and not report something unpleasant that they had witnessed. There just wasn't that insatiable desire for dirt that now permeates our culture. It was in everyone's best interest to accentuate the positive and try to get along. Back then it worked. That couldn't happen today.

However competitive, the GMs had their own little private club. Growing up in the game, they had a lot of shared experiences. They weren't at all like the present-day breed of younger, more detail-oriented, highly educated executives. They didn't have to worry about free agency, salary arbitration, long-term guaranteed contracts, egomaniacal agents, and many other things that have changed the game—not necessarily for the better. Two men could make a trade and not sweat over a lot of minutiae involving contracts.

And that sets the stage for a Pope story that we still laugh about to this day. At the baseball winter meetings, where a lot of transactions used to happen, every GM would have his own suite at the hotel headquarters. And every suite would have a well-stocked bar for entertainment purposes. That was where the wheeling and dealing took place. Eddie Robinson, a good baseball man and GM of the Atlanta Braves at the time, met with Pope one night in the Phillies' suite to talk about their compatibility for a deal. The conversation started with a few cocktails, went on from there, and eventually an agreement was reached between the two clubs. The next day, the Phillies announced that we had acquired versatile right-handed pitcher Ron Schueler in exchange for shortstop Craig Robinson (a native of Abington, Pennsylvania) and right-handed pitcher Barry Lersch. It sounded like a good deal for the Phils, but almost immediately a problem arose. Apparently, Robinson was under the impression that he had traded for promising young left-handed pitcher Randy Lerch, not the veteran Lersch. Now, there may have been only a difference of one letter in the spelling, but it was not making the Braves very happy. They'd traded for the wrong guy. So what happened? Well, to this day we believe Pope got the better of Robinson that night and early morning because he'd stayed a little more coherent. The fact is, Pope could not only hold his Jack Daniels, he'd rebound with that bounceability that he so admired in others. The trade went through, and the participants maintained a good relationship, although I'm not sure if they made any more deals.

With no agents to concern them, Owens and other GMs could deal directly with the players. One day, Larry Bowa walked into our publicity office with that anxious, worried look of his etched all over his face. "Wheels, what's going on? Pope called me and said to be down here in an hour and to see him in his office." This time I didn't have to fib to Bo, because I had no idea what was going on. For a player (or one of us), being told that Pope wanted to see you one-on-one was like going to the principal's office or waiting for your father to come home while you were holding that bad report card. But off he went into Owens' office, expecting the worst. When Bowa came back out about an hour later, he had an ear-to-ear smile and a rare (in that era) guaranteed two-year contract. He also had a story to tell about Pope.

He'd walked quietly into the office, and there was Owens behind his desk, playing with a yo-yo. I'd seen him do this before—for no apparent reason, he would just take it out of his desk and start bouncing it around, doing tricks like "rock the cradle" and "walking the dog" and then asking for a critique of his ability. After Larry got over that distraction, Pope made some small talk and then said, matter-of-factly, "Well, what would you think if I offered you a two-year contract?"

Owens had been always been a Bowa fan, from the time he was in a hotel room when West Coast scout Eddie Bockman asked to see him. Bockman put a bed sheet on the wall and rolled film from an old projector, showing this young kid from Sacramento playing shortstop and running the bases. He didn't look much like a skilled ballplayer at first, but the veteran scout really liked him and wanted to show Owens. Pope told Bockman to slow the damn thing down so he could get a better feel for the kid's ability. Bockman replied, "That's regular speed—he's that fast." From that day on, Pope was sold on Bowa. He also came to love Bowa's work ethic and what he had done to make himself a major-league player. He genuinely wanted to reward Bowa, but I'll always believe Owens also wanted to see the look on Bowa's face when he told him what was up with his contract. He just lived for those moments.

Because Owens had the ability to adapt and change with the times, he was able to adjust to the new system of players' agents and negotiating contracts. But he never liked it. It's still kind of nostalgic to remember those early days, however unfair to players, when it was just man-to-man. Before the onslaught of talk shows, cable, cell-phone cameras, and YouTube, players weren't so reticent to go out at night. And the media was more into reporting what actually happened during the game instead of all the personal stuff. I guess Jim Bouton's *Ball Four* was the first shot across baseball's bow, starting the run-up to today's 24/7 coverage. Excesses that had always been a part of the game used to be contained within the clubhouse.

It wasn't just the PR guys who promoted our team. Every winter we'd have a "Phillies Caravan," including players and management, that made an exhausting tour of towns within our marketing area to drum up interest for the coming season. This was a true endurance test that would take us as far north as Scranton and west to Harrisburg. Two stops a day—one for lunch, another for dinner—complete with pre-dinner media sessions and post-meal autographs and the viewing of our highlight film from the previous season. It was my job to make our miserable projector perform while the players and rest of the traveling party hit the exits for the bus or a nice, cozy place in the hotel to unwind.

I remember one enjoyable but really grueling day when we'd had a luncheon somewhere in Pennsylvania and then headed to Lancaster for the nighttime affair. After dinner and the highlight film, we were unwinding in the lounge of the hotel where the banquet had taken place. I was sitting at a table with Bowa and Luzinski, while Pope was across the way at another table, maybe 30 feet from us. It happened to be Pope's birthday. A small cake had been ordered from the hotel for him, and it was brought to his table. Unfortunately, Owens was being harangued by someone who apparently had attended the banquet. Now, people generally understood that this was our time to relax after a long day of socializing, and they were generally courteous, but this guy was buzzing around Pope like a green fly. He just wouldn't leave. Pope started to look agitated. The three of us glanced at each other with an "uh-oh" expression because we had seen that look before. Suddenly the man was holding the small cake in his hand, and Pope had put his hand under the guy's wrist. Then, out of nowhere, Owens flipped the man's wrist and the cake hit him smack dab in the face. Splat! Pope then took a little of the icing with his finger and put it in the guy's ear. In an instant, Bull was out of his seat, while Bowa and I just sat there with our mouths agape, wondering what had just happened.

Afterward, Pope filled in the blanks for us. The guy had continued to bug him, even after having been asked to leave. By the time the cake arrived, Pope just decided he had had enough. "So I told him to pick up the cake so I could get a better look at it," recounted

Pope. "Then I said, 'move it a little to the left…now a little to the right' until I could tell it was lined up perfectly—and POW, it was a direct hit." We kidded him later that the directions he gave the guy sounded like he was trying to set the sights on a rifle. Anyway, the guy started yelling at Pope that he was with the FBI and would never give him a day's rest. Pope responded in his distinctive, high-pitched voice, telling the guy just where to go. Bull separated the two, and eventually our visitor was led away, never to be seen again. To this day, we have no idea if the man in that Lancaster lounge was actually a federal agent, but Pope said he never heard from him. We were all left with yet another Paul Owens story to tell—and a birthday to remember.

Owens had married a Belgian woman, Marcelle Le Clerc, while overseas with the Army during World War II, and it was a love affair that never dimmed. They were a great pair who really cared deeply about each other. She passed away a short time after he did. Marcelle could bring out the kind, warm side of this occasionally gruff man. It's funny sometimes how your view of people changes over the years. Owens certainly was demanding of all of us. And it was well-publicized that the players' intense dislike of Dallas Green helped unify and motivate many of them in our 1980 championship club. Green sometimes benched the Bull, playing rookie Lonnie Smith in his place. He had little time for the sensitivity of Garry Maddox, giving Del Unser playing time in center field. He butted heads with Bowa constantly. But they all respect him now. Like Pope, whatever his means of motivation, Green only wanted you to be your best. Neither man had time for excuses.

Just as I remember when Owens became GM and later manager after firing Frank Lucchesi in 1972, I'll never forget late in that lost season of 1979 when Pope decided we needed to make another managerial change. It wasn't a hasty decision, because he always erred on the side of caution. As usual he had done his "reconnaissance." After the '72 season, Owens had hired longtime Dodgers minor-league manager and big-league coach Danny Ozark to take over as skipper. And the team had really improved under Ozark, winning the division in 1976, '77, and '78. But it failed to reach the

World Series. Then, too, our talented, once-young team was aging, and that window of opportunity was closing. To Owens, the time had come to make a change. It was going to be tough for him because he really liked Ozark, but he felt that the players needed to hear a different voice.

I was in my room in Atlanta on the afternoon of September 1, 1979. The season had been lost to injuries and the runaway Pirates, but we still had a month to go. I was working on the daily stats and notes, still doing double duty as the traveling PR representative and a part-time broadcaster. A lot of the pregame material now is computerized, but in those days we had to type everything on mimeograph stencils—and it was a lot of time-consuming work. We typed the pages line by line after updating all the stats and notes. Make a mistake and it was time to get out the toxic-smelling correction fluid, fix the error, and then hope you didn't type the same dumb thing again.

The phone rang in my room, and it was Pope. He sounded a little agitated and said, "I need you in my room right away to talk about something." I got up there really fast, because you never wanted to keep him waiting. His suite door was half open, so I knocked and walked in. There sitting on the couch was "Big D" himself. "Bet you're surprised to see me," said Green, "but I know you know why I'm here." We spent some time talking about a press conference to announce Ozark's firing and how we were going to word the news release that was being prepared back in Philadelphia by Larry Shenk. It was a tough day because we all really liked Danny Ozark. But we accepted this as a part of the business—an unpleasant part but still something that just happens, and then you have to move on.

A leadership role demands decisive action. Paul Owens felt that was needed again in 1983. Our team that season had been dubbed the "Wheeze Kids" because of the number of veterans, including former "Big Red Machine" stars like Pete Rose, Tony Perez, and Joe Morgan. Owens didn't like the way the club was performing, even though they were in first place. And so he fired another man he really liked, manager Pat Corrales, and went back down to the field again. The team responded, staging a September rally to win the National League East before losing the World Series in five to the Orioles. As for Corrales, a tough, quiet man to this day, he accepted his firing and left Philadelphia without a whimper. Two weeks later, he wound up managing the Cleveland Indians, becoming only the fourth manager in history to manage teams in both major leagues during the same season.

Looking back, I think one reason I went from being a wet-behind-the-ears kid without a clue to being a respected friend of The Pope was that he could see, mistakes and all, how seriously I took my job—or, you might say, my jobs. He appreciated people who worked hard at what they did, who "knew how to act, how to be a professional." In that way he was much like John Vukovich, another tough, good man I still think about and miss every day. They were most critical of the people they cared for the most. They could chew you out, but never hold a grudge. They always looked you in the eye, no matter who you were, and told you how they felt. Vuk may not have said quite as much as Pope, but he always made his point.

Paul Owens loved to tell stories. He'd start a lot of them with the disclaimer "to make a long story short...," but they never were short. The last time I got to spend some time with him was late in 2003. The Vet was in its final days, and Paul had come to the ballpark that night to visit. Larry Shenk came to our broadcasters' office to tell us that Pope was in the minor-league office, holding court. When I walked in, he gave me a big hug—the man was an interminable hugger—and I had to fight back tears when I saw how frail he'd become over the summer. But he had us in stitches, telling some of the same stories we'd heard over and over. We never got tired of his versions. Finally, it was time to leave, which precipitated another hug from this wonderful man, and then it was back to work. We had a game to broadcast that night, and nobody understood that better than The Pope.

He managed to attend the closing ceremonies at the Vet, although everyone knew his days were numbered. He received a nice reception from the crowd, who understood what this man had done for the Phillies in his long and illustrious career. Paul Owens died on

December 26, 2003. Although reared in Salamanca, New York, he was buried in the part of the country he had come to call home—South Jersey. Standing by his gravesite that dark, cold morning with Schmidt, Luzinski, Bowa, and Vuk, we knew an era had passed with the death of our Pope of Pattison Avenue. This is a man who did not get cheated. He lived every day like it was his last. I'll carry a part of him in my heart forever and thank him for being such a huge influence on the wonderful life I have today.

Leadership comes in many forms. Larry Shenk, another mentor, friend, and role model, is so consistently calm—truly the eye of the storm. When I started in the organization, pretty sure I knew a lot and ready to do battle with anyone, he'd reason things out for me. "Calm down, Wheels. We have to deal with these guys every day." The Baron still is a big part of the Phillies, although he's now technically retired. And it was Larry who gave me the nickname "Wheels," a moniker I wear proudly.

After the Carpenter family sold the ballclub and Bill Giles became operating partner and president, the overall management went through a transition. We had no general manager for several years, because a "gang of six," as they were called, ran the baseball operation until Woody Woodward was hired as GM in 1987. An experienced baseball man, Woody seemed like the perfect choice for the job, but it wasn't to be. Woodward saw a lot of things he didn't like and wanted to clean house. I think his plans were a little too radical for some in management, and he seemed to be moving too fast. So Giles fired Woodward in June after just eight months on the job, admitting it just hadn't worked out. I personally liked Woody and had some fine baseball talks with him. Since he'd had some experience in broadcasting, we had things in common.

In June 1988, Giles named Lee Thomas to replace Woodward, and he would be with the Phillies through 1997. His crowning achievement was constructing the 1993 National League champions, for which he was named "Major League Executive of the Year." With his close friend and former teammate Jim Fregosi, Thomas assembled an unforgettable team of "throwbacks," as Harry Kalas called them: Kruk, Dykstra, Daulton, Incaviglia, Greene, Mulholland, Williams, Hollins, Thompson, Schilling, Eisenreich, Duncan, Andersen—what a cast of characters and bizarre personalities! I can still get a laugh out of a lunch or dinner audience when I use the line, "The 1993 Phillies were a memorable team, but you sure didn't want your daughter bringing some of them home." Lee Thomas was a warm guy, a former major-league player himself, who had worked his way up to a GM job. I remembered him from his days as the Cardinals' traveling secretary, when he would hand in those dreaded, aforementioned stencils that he'd labored over. I could feel his pain. Lee was a guy who used to like to fly by the seat of his pants a lot, making some moves from his gut. Fregosi, his close friend and former California Angels teammate, was more cautious and inclined to think things out. They made a great team, and many of their moves bear that out.

That fun group of '93 never could repeat the glory of their magic season. Injuries and age took their toll and finally led to Thomas firing his friend following the 1996 season. Fregosi was the third manager fired by Thomas, who also had both hired and dismissed Lee Elia and Nick Leyva. John Vukovich even got a chance to manage briefly in 1988. It appeared that we were having trouble retaining a manager. In their defense, however, the Phillies just weren't very good in those years. Their lapses can't all be laid at the feet of their managers. Since that time, Terry Francona, Larry Bowa, and Charlie Manuel have had longer tenures, with Bowa and Manuel having success with better players, and Francona becoming a lot smarter once he landed in Boston. Surrounded by their talent, he won two World Series with the Red Sox.

One thing I always admired about Lee Thomas was his candor and self-deprecating humor. He never took himself too seriously, and although he possessed an explosive temper, he also had a ready smile. He liked to call people "dear boy." The one thing that would cause him to explode like a summer thunderstorm was golf. Lee really wanted to play the game, but it drove him nuts. He had a powerful left-handed swing, but the ball rarely went where he desired, a common problem for many of us who love the game but are exasperated by it. He would occasionally throw a club, and we had to

turn away so he wouldn't see us laughing. One time we were playing at Bellaire Country Club in Clearwater when Lee's iron off the
tee to a par 3 was mishit into a creek, well short of the green. Guess
what happened next? Suffice to say that that club was never used
again. The last time we saw it, the 6-iron was hanging from a tree
branch, ready to initiate some interesting conversations for the future golfers who happened to look up there.

Lee used to agonize over decisions to fire employees. One day, I
was on my way out to lunch in Atlanta when I ran into him in the
hotel lobby. He invited me to join him, and we started to walk down
Peachtree Street to Underground Atlanta for lunch. Lee was a good
conversationalist, but was very quiet that afternoon. After ordering,
he finally looked at me and said, "I've got to fire my farm director. I
screwed up, and it's not working." Then he let out that infectious
laugh of his and waited for a reply from me. Not able to come up
with anything brilliant, I looked at him and simply said, "Why?" It
turned out that Lance Nichols, Lee's minor-league director, was running everything like a boot camp, and there was an open revolt from
the troops. Sure enough, a few weeks later, Nichols was gone.
Thomas had made his tough decision.

Ed Wade, who succeeded Thomas as GM in 1998, was just out of
Temple University when he spent a summer working as an intern in
the PR department with Larry Shenk and me. He came from Car-
bondale, upstate, where his father was a funeral director. Ed would
experience that crushing season of 1978 up close and then move on
to work for the Pirates and Astros before coming back to his home
area to serve as Thomas' assistant. Perhaps because he didn't seem
tough, hadn't played professionally, and before Lasik surgery looked
like conservative columnist George Will, he wasn't afforded the
same respect a true "baseball man" would have been given. He became a target of the fans and some loud local media. His treatment
was unfair in many ways. Ed was a good judge of talent and did a
commendable job. I thought it was classy when Pat Gillick acknowledged Wade for developing and bringing in a lot of the talent
that enabled us to win the World Series in 2008. Wade had to fire a
man he really liked and admired, Terry Francona, and then hired

and fired the immensely popular Larry Bowa, which only brought him more wrath from the fans. It was another example of the necessity to make tough decisions by the man who occupies that seat, a pattern that can't be avoided.

Gillick, who is sure to be a Hall of Fame executive someday, had a strong three years in Philadelphia, winning a world championship before retiring and turning the job over to his assistant, Ruben Amaro Jr. Ruben, Philadelphia-born and Stanford-educated, may seem a poster boy for the present-day GM, except that he actually was a major-league ballplayer. Ruben certainly possesses all the qualities to be a great general manager. He looks to be off to a great start.

When I think about all the changes since I came aboard in 1971, I reflect on the career of someone like David Montgomery, who also started with the Phillies in '71. Now general partner, president, and chief executive officer of the ballclub, David had recently graduated from the University of Pennsylvania. He was a part-time football offensive line coach, working for his friend Jack Turner at Germantown Academy, when another guy who was doing a little coaching there took notice of him. Robin Roberts was very impressed with Montgomery and recommended him to Bill Giles, who interviewed David and hired him on the spot. But Giles didn't have a position in mind. Montgomery wound up in the team's ticket office at a starting salary of $8,000. I was hired a few months after David and started at $10,000. He has gone a little farther in the organization than I have. I once asked him how come I made more than he did that first year. He said I had a career path, but he had no idea what he was going to do. I think it has worked out pretty well for both of us, and David's the best person anyone could ever call "Boss."

This chapter has been mainly about Paul Owens. I'd like to end it with a story I know he really liked. The Vet had a room down the first-base line we called the "scoreboard control room." It was not a pleasant place to watch a game. There was tinted glass to protect the sensitive electronic equipment, and there was a lot of noise from the machines used to operate the massive left and right center- field scoreboards. When I worked my first game at the Vet, I was given a seat behind home plate, where the PR man kept the official team scorebook and helped look up information required by the media. Larry Shenk, my boss, was working in that tightly confined space down the first-base line. One night, he told me he took a look at me sitting there in the fresh air and said to himself, "What the hell am I doing in here while my assistant is sitting out there?" So we swapped jobs the next night. Thus began a fun time for me, from 1971 to 1976, as part of the crew that ran that amazing operation.

The staff included public-address announcer Art Wolff, who did the job for one season before Dan Baker took over and still is the voice fans hear at every game. Also on hand were Cal Adams and Joanne Levy, who were in charge of gathering information and processing it onto paper tape that would be fed into a computer and then shown on the scoreboards. In the next room was the organist Paul Richardson—"Maestro," as we liked to call him—who did such a great job entertaining crowds at the Vet for so many years. The final two people were Dennis Lehman, the heart and soul of the room, and myself. Denny, who now is a vice-president with the Cleveland Indians, had worked at Connie Mack Stadium as a press runner and came to the Vet to work with Larry Shenk in the PR department. He was a bright young guy, out of La Salle University, with a wicked sense of humor. You never knew what he was going to put on one of the boards. We used to come up with quizzes and try to amuse (or annoy) people. For example, we would have a multiple-choice quiz and ask the fans to guess a famous person's last name. Harry wasn't all that pleased when the crowd found out that his middle name was Norbert. One time we put up, "Guess the player who holds the record for fewest RBIs in a season with 600 plus at-bats." Answer: "Richie Ashburn." It didn't take long before Whitey was at the door, wanting to know what was going on with that. We just had a lot of fun. We were young and slightly immature.

One night the Phillies were scoring a ton of runs and the place was going nuts. Now, I've mentioned that Denny Lehman had a wicked sense of humor. Out of nowhere he came up with one of his famous one-liners. The colorful mayor of Philadelphia, Frank Rizzo, had recently experienced a little problem and told the *Philadelphia Daily News* that to prove he was telling the truth, he would take a lie-detector test. As it turned out, he failed. That news, featured in the press with big headlines, certainly didn't please Rizzo. So this night, with the crowd roaring, Lehman put up on the board, "This town hasn't had this much fun since the lie-detector test." I thought it was pretty funny, but we didn't consider the consequences.

The next morning, I was sitting in my office when Ruly Carpenter suddenly appeared and asked me if I had a minute to come down to his office. Ruly and I had developed a good relationship and spent a lot of time talking, but this time his tone was a little different. He owned the club but was the least ostentatious man of wealth I've ever known. His office was tiny. He got right to it: "What the hell did you and Lehman do last night?" I'd already seen the back page of the *Daily News* that morning with a huge picture of the lie-detector line from the previous night, so I had a suspicion about where this might be headed, but I played dumb. I knew Ruly never read the sports sections because they used to infuriate him, so I hoped that this was about something else. Anyway, Ruly went on, "I just got a call from 'the Bambino'"—everyone's nickname for Rizzo—"and he's not happy." I was trying not to laugh when Ruly said, "Rizzo roared into the phone, 'RUDY'"—he called him Rudy—"what the *&%^&&*^% are you doing in my stadium?" Ruly had no idea what Rizzo was talking about and asked the mayor to tell him what had made him so upset. So Ruly had to sit there and listen to Frank Rizzo chew him out about a back-page feature in the *Daily News* concerning something flashed on the scoreboard of a city-owned stadium. Still, when I told Ruly what Denny and I had done, he couldn't contain a big laugh. He just told us to please use a little better judgment next time. Then he suggested I get back to work, while he headed over to The Pope's office to share the story with him. I'm sure that Pope enjoyed it as much as we did, but that was the last time we ever did anything in that room to tick off the mayor.

CHAPTER 6

Learning from the Best

WE SHOULD NEVER STOP LEARNING in life. Sometimes we are learning and teaching at the same time and not aware of it. That's why conversations and the lost art of listening are so important. Baseball can seem deceptively simple. There is the old "see the ball, hit the ball theory" and other expressions that simplify the game. But one thing I've learned after almost 40 years around a major-league baseball team is that I'm still learning. The people who have been a huge influence on me come from many places—from the front office like Paul Owens and Dallas Green, from the playing field, and from the broadcast booth. Each personifies a different quality, but what they've all had in common is the healthy curiosity to keep listening and learning themselves. And their willingness to impart this knowledge to eager disciples like me.

I've already said a lot about Larry Bowa, but the fact is I could start off every chapter with a new story about him. Bo's three months younger than I am, which he will bring up occasionally. When I played the game at the amateur level, I was a shortstop, and I pitched. I loved the shortstop position more than any other, and was drawn to it when I joined the Phillies organization in 1971, one year after Bowa's debut in the big leagues. That could be one of the reasons we clicked early on. I've never been able to put my finger on any one special reason why he and I developed the relationship that exists to this day, but I can cite the experience that helped launch it.

We were on a long road trip in 1972 that would include five cities, plus an exhibition game in Spartanburg, South Carolina, home of one of our minor-league franchises. Part of the trip was the journey through Atlanta, Cincinnati, and Houston, three of the hottest cities imaginable for a summer visit. In those days, the clubs used to play their minor-league teams to give each a taste of major-league baseball—and also help the team with a big gate. We had a luncheon that afternoon and then headed to the ballpark for a night game. We got there early since we weren't going to check into a hotel until later that night in Atlanta. So there was a lot of time to kill. Bowa had been ragging me to work out with the team. I always had an excuse at home, but here on this day in South Carolina, I didn't. So I put on a uniform and went out on the field with quite of bit of trepidation. I made my way to the shortstop area where Bowa was taking some ground balls, and he invited me to join in. I was 26 at the time, could still move around a little, and didn't embarrass myself picking the grounders and throwing to first. I was starting to get a little winded, as he and I alternated on ground balls, when he came over to me and said, "You played, didn't you?" I just answered "Yeah," and we kept working.

That was the highest level of respect you could get from a big-league player, and I'll always feel it was the beginning of the enduring friendship that exists between us today. We started out as kids and now are approaching that unearned senior citizens' status that simply comes with the years. We would talk about the game for hours, and 38 years later we still do. I always enjoy my time with him because it's funny as well as educational. He may have one of the quickest minds of any man I've ever met. It's a mismatch to get into a one-liner contest with Bo, because you will lose. But I love hearing people try it, even though I suspect their inevitable fate will be stunned silence.

Bowa still makes his home in the Philadelphia area. Before game two of the League Championship Series in 2008, I drove him to the ballpark and, of course, we talked more baseball. He really liked our team and thought it had the potential to go all the way. He certainly wanted to see that happen if we knocked off his Dodgers. Of course, all that "Kumbaya" stuff ended a few hours later when Brett Myers threw a pitch behind Manny Ramirez. Bowa erupted like old times, and kept that anger on simmer for the rest of the LCS. But not surprisingly, one of the first calls I got after we won the World Series was from a really happy Bowa. The Phillies will always be his team no matter where he works.

Things haven't always been perfect between us, but we've made it work. When I first went to the booth, it wasn't easy to suddenly have to criticize not only players on your team but many who had been your friends. And Bo could be tough on me. Still, following one season, he thought it would be fun for me to have a little vacation and drive with him to his Seminole, Florida, home near Clearwater. So we got into his little Mercedes sports car and the two-day journey began. He wouldn't let me drive, and he wouldn't let me sleep. As always, he wanted to talk. When I would nod off, he'd just push me and I'd be awake, trying to respond to whatever new subject was on his mind. Now that was a long trip. I was never happier than when we finally arrived in Seminole to be greeted by his wife, Sheena.

I remember hearing on the radio the first day that an arbitrator had ruled in favor of Andy Messersmith and Dave McNally. This opened up the world of free agency, completing the journey Curt Flood had unsuccessfully started with his challenge to the reserve clause. Even after Bowa moved on to the Cubs and Padres, we'd get together in those cities, or whenever he came back to Philadelphia, and catch up. In those days there was no ESPN or Comcast SportsNet to give Bo his fill of breaking news—so he would make it up. On more than one occasion, he would start a trade rumor in the clubhouse and watch the writers pick up on it until it developed a life of its own. It was just another outlet for his nervous energy.

Was he a great manager? To this day, I don't think I've ever been around a man with more knowledge, or a better feel for the game. He was way ahead of anyone in the other dugout, and his anticipation for situations was remarkable. After his first season guiding the Phillies, he was named Manager of the Year. But if Bo had a weakness, it was his inability to relate to many of today's players. Many simply lack the same intensity and love of the game that his generation possessed, and that remains with him. And it's not always the players' fault, because they came up in a different era. Many of them can't understand the way Larry approaches every day in the big leagues as a tremendous challenge and honor. Bo also had problems with certain media members whom he perceived to be lazy and intrusive. He won't hesitate to butt heads, so it will always be tough for him to be the manager of a team. Still, it could happen again, because he is so eminently qualified. In the last few years, he's worked for one of the game's great leaders, Joe Torre. He loves what he's seen of Bowa on and off the field, and understands how to get the best from him. Whenever I ask Joe how "my boy" is doing, he'll just roll his eyes and laugh. But then Torre always makes a point to say that Bowa's as good a third-base coach as he's ever had working for him. All you have to know is that when Torre went to L.A. from the Yankees, Bowa and Don Mattingly were the two men he took with him, giving them both two-year, big-money contracts.

It's not hard to see where Bo's chip-on-the-shoulder attitude comes from. Mocked as a "Little Leaguer" by members of the media when he first came to the majors in 1970, Bowa weighed about 150 pounds back then and looked almost too frail to compete. But there was no way to know what was in his heart. He was hitting around his weight at the All-Star Break that first year, and if he had been sent to the minors, who knows what would have happened? But, as luck would have it, Frank Lucchesi was the Phillies manager. He had managed Bowa in the minor leagues and knew what other people couldn't see: the incredible fire and intensity that drove him. So Lucchesi told him, "I don't care what happens the rest of this season, you are my shortstop. Go show everyone I'm right." Of all the players I've been around, probably only Pete Rose was more of a self-made ballplayer than Bowa. Cut twice from his high school team in Sacramento, California, Bowa willed and worked his way to become a major-league all-star. In my opinion, he's also a guy who should have had his full 15 years of eligibility on the Hall of Fame ballot to see what might have happened.

Bowa was a right-handed hitter in those days. It would take a couple of years in the minor leagues before he would make the tran-

sition to switch hitting, a change that made his career possible. Bo
likes to tell the story of how, during one of his first professional
games, he had an experience that almost made him pack his bags
and go home. They were playing a night game in Spartanburg on
the same field where he and I would, years later, field those ground
balls. The night was steamy and the lights were really bad. Bo said
he thinks he struck out four times, and was lucky even to foul off a
pitch. He was distraught and told his manager that he wasn't sure
he could keep going. The manager—I think it was Bob Wellman—
told Bowa to hang in there, that the guy he faced that night was
pretty good and was probably going to get to the major leagues.
That pitcher was the great Hall of Famer, Nolan Ryan. It got a little
easier after hitting off guys like Ryan.

One of Larry's biggest thrills was a night in 1977 when he hit his
first and only grand-slam home run. As fate would have it, it was off
the Cincinnati Reds and a former teammate, Joe Hoerner. Bowa hit
the homer off the tarp covering the temporary seats in left center
field, and he literally flew around the bases until he got near third.
The man standing there trying not to laugh was his buddy, Pete
Rose. Pete told me Bowa went by, yelling at him, "Take a ride on
that!" which completely broke up Pete. The sight of Bowa skipping
and jumping toward the dugout like a little kid and high-fiving
everyone who would extend their hands was a joy to behold. He
wasn't showing anyone up—he just couldn't contain himself. It was
sheer, unmitigated joy, and we all got caught up in the moment.

The man who threw the pitch, Joe Hoerner, was a wonderful
guy—funny, with a tremendous, self-deprecating sense of humor.
He only had one pitch, a kind of cut fastball-slider, but he was a big
part of some of those great Cardinal teams of the '60s. Joe had
pitched for us in the '70s and knew the excitable Bowa well enough
not to get mad at him for going nuts. Years later, when both Bowa
and Hoerner attended our Dream Week fantasy camps, it was fun to
hear them talk about that moment. And it still ticked Joe off because, in his long major-league career, he threw only one slam, and
it was to, of all people, Larry Bowa. I used to see Hoerner at Busch
Stadium during the season when he was a partner with former

teammate Dal Maxvil in a travel agency. He had a quick smile, always ready with a story or joke, and we would laugh over and over again about the night that Bowa took him deep at the Vet. Joe died tragically a number of years ago when he was attempting to remove a tree stump on his Missouri property and was run over by his own tractor. That's another guy I still miss.

Pete Rose would come to the Phillies in the fall of 1978 as a free agent. Bowa was as nervous as I've ever seen him during those Rose sweepstakes. Several teams were wooing Rose, including the Pittsburgh Pirates, who offered a thoroughbred racehorse and time around the sport of kings that Rose loved. One late morning my phone rang, and it was that unmistakable voice on the other end. "We got him!" exclaimed Bowa. "What are you talking about?" I asked. "We got Pete. He just said he decided to sign with another National League team where he has some real good friends. That's *got* to be us." Bill Giles did a great job in pulling off that move, because Ruly was reticent to spend the unprecedented money that was necessary to sign Rose. But Bill went to our TV partner at the time, Taft Broadcasting, and convinced them that Rose would help them sell advertising, and the deal was made. Rose was coming to Philadelphia for what Pete described as an amount of money "a show dog couldn't jump over."

It's not surprising that Rose and Bowa got along so well, considering their physical tools and what it took for them to get to "The Show." Pete loved to shell out nicknames. For example, Bowa became "Pee Wee," and Mike Schmidt was "Herbie Lee" because, according to Rose, "He looks like a Herbie Lee." One of the best monikers he imposed was on a new outfielder from Atlanta named Gary Matthews, whom Rose started calling "Sarge." Gary wanted to know why, and Rose told him, "Man, you just look like one of those mean, nasty drill sergeants." It stuck, and my colleague still answers to that name and loves it, especially since it was given to him by Rose. I was lucky enough to spend many hours talking baseball with Pete, and that was like getting a Ph.D. in your field. He would plop himself down next to you on the team bus after a game and say, "What do you think about this pitch to so-and-so in the seventh?"

What do I think? I would give my opinion, and then he'd come up with something that would really open my eyes. My nickname? He would call me "Wheeeeel," dragging out the e's and eliminating the s. Hard to write, but he still comes out with it every time I see this exceptional baseball player, who should be in the Hall of Fame.

If there is one word that describes Larry Bowa, it's intensity. He just wants to win, but especially at baseball. How can you not try to do *your* best around a guy who's always given everything he has to make himself and those around him aspire to be the best that *they* can be?

WITH JOHN VUKOVICH, it was toughness. No less than Pope, he was a consummate professional—mentally and physically, the toughest man I've ever known. The second quality John possessed was loyalty. Certainly, he had his own goals, but they would never be realized at the expense of another. If he was your coach, the manager knew he could count on a guy who had his back and who would be a real asset in the clubhouse. And Vuk worked with a lot of different managers, treating them all with respect. As a player, he was marginal, which nobody appreciated more than he did. He was an exceptional defensive third-baseman, but not much of a hitter. One season with the Cincinnati Reds, he won the third-base job in spring training, and manager Sparky Anderson told him to just catch the ball and not worry about his offense. That team had plenty of it. But the Reds got off to a slow offensive start, were having trouble scoring runs, and had this great young hitting prospect, George Foster, sitting on the bench. So they moved Rose into a new position at third base. Foster took over left field, and the "Big Red Machine" was born. And naturally, the guy Rose replaced was Vuk. He would have his moments in the big leagues with the Brewers and Phillies. He was so respected in the clubhouse and by his teammates that Dallas Green kept him active as a player for the entire 1980 season, even though he got only one at-bat. Vuk had grown up with a lot of the stars on that team, and Green knew he wouldn't hesitate to get into anyone's face.

Despite his intimidating demeanor, those of us who really knew the man I always called "Johnny" saw a gentler side and his own brand of self-deprecating humor, especially about his offensive skills. He would roar with laughter when he was teased about it by people he liked. One of them was the respected Orange County columnist Mark Whicker, who had been in Philadelphia with the *Bulletin* and had a great relationship with Vuk. One day Whicker, making sure he had an audience, sauntered up to Vuk with a lopsided grin. Vuk was in his normal repose, leaning on a fungo bat, squinting through a late-day sun with that weather-beaten baseball-lifer face of his. "Whick" said to him, "Hey, did you hear they named a convenience store chain after you?" Knowing some wise-guy comment was coming, John replied, "All right, let me have it." So Whicker said, "Yeah, it's called Circle K, after your career." Everyone, including Vuk, just cracked up. Just in case you're not sure of the meaning, when a player strikes out and you put it in your scorebook, it's recorded as "K," and circled as an out. We could never see a Circle K store again without thinking about that day.

Vukovich appeared to have gotten a huge break in 1987 when Dallas Green was going to name him manager of the Cubs. Dallas had given Vuk the news and brought him to Chicago. There would be a press conference later that afternoon, after he'd had a meeting with the Tribune Company, owners of the ballclub. Well, Big D and ownership had a little falling out that day, and Dallas resigned. Then he had to tell Vuk to go to the airport and head back to New Jersey. Neither of them would be with the Cubs. Eventually, Vuk was able to laugh that one off, but I think he would have been a great manager. And though he had managerial aspirations, he would never get that close to a top job again. Vuk hated everything about the interview process, and he wasn't about to go from club to club and try to sell himself. He always felt that if you had done your homework and decided you wanted him, then hire him and he would do the job. Could he be stubborn to a fault? Nobody embodied that trait more than John Vukovich, but he was always true to himself.

He and Bowa had a tremendous relationship, from their amateur days in Northern California to their early days in the Phillies minor-league system. Vuk was a reliable regular, and Bowa was the thorn-under-the-fingernails guy who annoyed the opposition. Vuk certainly didn't like him when they competed against each other. That would change, and they became good friends, so very much alike in their mutual desire to win and to play the game the right way. Over time Vuk and I became great friends as well, and we would sit together on our charter flights. He was old-school. If you lost a game, there was a period of time when you kept your mouth shut. That was the way he had been taught. He could never understand the modern player who would be smiling and laughing after a loss. He would always sit on the aisle because of his balky knees, leaving me with the window. Guys would come up to me before we got on the plane, pat me on the back and say, "This is going to be a fun trip for you." After Vuk would growl at me, "Shut up, and don't say a word," I'd respond, "What makes you think I want to talk to you anyway?" and it would be like that for a while. He would stare straight ahead and I would read, until he broke the ice and I could see he wanted to talk. It was nothing personal. He just had to cool off. He knew the game inside and out, and I'd always have strategy and personnel questions for him. But we'd get to them on his terms. I always learned something, which was one reason I wanted to sit next to him. Vuk would conclude many of our talks with "I hope you appreciate how I am continuing your baseball education."

I have so many memories and stories about him. One of his habits was to eat his meals in record time. It was comical to watch him wolf down a meal with his cheeks looking like a chipmunk, swallowing at a rate that would be envied by any canine. That would be followed by a nap with his mouth wide open, and guys walking by and just shaking their heads as they looked at him. No one loved his family more than Vuk—his wife Bonnie, son Vincent, and daughter Nikki. One summer, he was preparing for his daughter's wedding, which he referred to as "the wedding of the century." I made sure to have an audience one day and told him I had an idea for the wedding. I said that since he was going to be up at the head table, why not try to cut his food into small pieces and chew each piece a certain number of times, then put his fork down and take a breath before repeating the process? He actually said he would try. There is a priceless picture in this book of the two of us laughing on that great day when Nikki and Brian were married and Johnny made a point of taking a page out of Miss Manners. There he was, eating like an honored guest at a White House state dinner, while at the same time making certain that we all observed his newly found etiquette. It just didn't look right.

Vuk was a great practical joker and loved to laugh. One time, he and Ruly came up with an idea to scam me into thinking I was being audited by the IRS. Ruly had some official IRS stationery and sent me a letter saying that I had to appear for a hearing when I returned from spring training. I called my tax guy, Joe Brindisi, who was sympathetic, agreed that I had a problem, and said he would accompany me to the government office on Roosevelt Boulevard in April. Of course, I had no idea that Vuk had called Joe and told him to go along with the deal or he would burn down his house or something equally threatening. Joe later apologized, telling me he didn't want to scare me, but Vuk was pretty intimidating and made him go along with the whole thing. One day, I was on the phone with Joe in my Jack Russell Stadium office when David Montgomery, who also knew what was going on, heard me frantically discussing the problem. David went down to the coaches' room and told Vuk that maybe the joke had gone on long enough. I got a call from John to get downstairs to see him as soon as possible about something that had occurred a few days before. When I got into the room, everyone had their heads down, knowing that I was in real trouble with the IRS. Then Vukovich finally came clean that it was just a joke. I was greatly relieved, but I still wanted to choke him.

People were always telling me to do something to get him back, but I always felt it was best to leave him alone. I mean, why poke a sleeping bear with a stick and get it riled up? But one year I had an idea. I had a big old shoulder bag that I used to take on the road—hardly a Gucci. It was blue and tan and had a "Wheels" nametag sewn on it. Vuk hated it. He kept telling me it was embarrassing and he was going to throw it away when I wasn't looking. I knew he was right, but I wouldn't give in. That winter, he had set up a time for me to meet him at a warehouse, where he had worked during past winters, to pick up some wine that he was getting at a great price. Vuk's intention was always to pay as little as possible for everything, assuming he couldn't get it for free. His goal was to "make the guy give it to you for nothing and then make him think he still hasn't done enough for you." So I wrapped up the bag in some nice holiday paper and presented it to him as a Christmas present. I told Vuk, "Man, you do so much for me, I just wanted to give you this present. So thanks again. Please don't open it until Christmas with your other gifts, and make sure your family is around the tree with you." He apologized for not having anything for me, and I got out of there as fast as I could with the wine, laughing all the way over the Walt Whitman Bridge. I waited all that Christmas morning for the call from Johnny, which finally came around 11 a.m. He was belly-laughing, telling me how I'd gotten him good, and how much his whole family enjoyed the payback. And he especially enjoyed the note I'd left inside that simply said, "Merry Christmas, you jerk."

I think most people would agree that our 1980 LCS with the Houston Astros was the best postseason series ever played. We split the first two games in Philadelphia and then lost an extra-inning game at the Astrodome. I had those "here we go again" visions. Now I'd have to spend another off-season, for the fourth time, as one of the club's point men, trying to explain just what went wrong this time. How many seasons would end in this bitter disappointment of failing to get to the World Series? So there I was, sitting on the team bus outside the Dome, sulking and pouting, all alone in my self-imposed misery. And here comes Johnny, walking with his head up and chest out as always, sensing my pitiful mood. Vuk was immensely strong, and before I knew what happened, one of those huge hands whacked me on the shoulder. "Get your head up," he said, "we're going to win this series!" I foolishly replied, "Are you nuts?" His eyes narrowed. So I just shut up and looked out the window. And, of course, we did win the final two games, also in extra innings, and we were headed to the World Series. During that delirious postgame celebration in Houston, Vuk came up to me and hugged me so hard I can still feel it. "I told you so, you little % ^ ^ *&," he roared. And I had to admit he was right again.

Vuk married the love of his life, Bonnie Loughran, shortly after coming to the majors in 1971. Bonnie was, and still is, a beautiful lady who was a member of the initial Hot Pants Patrol at the Vet. The big hangout after the games in those days was the Philadium on Packer Avenue, and that's where he met this woman we always told him was way out of his league. Bonnie didn't know a whole lot about baseball. As mentioned, Vuk wasn't much of a hitter. He tended to pull off a right-handed pitcher's breaking ball, hitting some towering pop-ups. Bonnie always thought that was great, and would brag about how *high* her man could hit the ball.

The battle of Vuk's life started with some headaches in 2001. One Sunday, he called me into an empty room in the clubhouse and said he wouldn't be going to Houston with us that day. They had found something in his brain during a checkup, and he was to undergo surgery the next day. We shared one of those rare, vulnerable moments that men who deeply care about each other try to avoid. There were tears and a hug, and then he got down to business. A man of few words, he said, "I don't want people to know anything today. I'm going to go out and coach third and try to get through it even though I'm having some vision problems. But I wanted you to know why I wouldn't be on the plane later. Please tell anyone who asks that I had some personal business and will be joining the team on Monday in Texas." When Vuk ran out to third base that beautiful May afternoon, he looked up at me in the radio booth, raised a clinched fist, and pumped his right arm. I laughed and returned the gesture, but then had to turn away and fight back my emotions. He made it through the game and had surgery the next day for a benign brain tumor. The news, however, was not all that good. There was a mass remaining that was not malignant but that could not be removed. He would have to be monitored for a long time. And to his credit, this warrior was back coaching third in a couple of weeks— just an amazing feat.

Over the next few years, he would have some more vision problems and had to leave a few games. His final year on the field was

2004. After Bo was fired, Vuk became a special assistant to general manager Ed Wade. That first spring training, when he showed up in street clothes, he looked like a duck out of water and seemed very uncomfortable in that role. But he started to adjust to the new life and was really enjoying more time at home. As much as possible, life off the road became a positive. He could spend a lot more time with his beloved Bonnie. And when daughter Nikki gave birth to triplets (all girls), he had a new calling as both a baseball man and doting grandfather. Life was good.

But no one ever said life was fair, and the headaches continued. We would sit in the booth before games at Citizens Bank Park and talk about his "treatments." Vuk never wanted to go into detail, but he alternated between describing the discomfort and occasionally expressing concern about what was going on. In the fall of 2006, my buddy started to change. The first indication that things weren't right was when he didn't attend the winter meetings. That wasn't like him. He wasn't returning my calls, and when he did, he was struggling with his speech and concentration. He would tell me that the doctors were telling him what to do, but he wasn't getting any better and just didn't feel right. He was steadily regressing to the point where we would be talking and he would completely lose his train of thought and say we'd talk later. It was disconcerting to hear this thoroughly together man struggle to carry on a conversation, and to sense the frustration he must be feeling. I told him I wanted to come over and see him, but he didn't want company. So I honored his preference, something I'll always question. We talked around the holidays, and then I heard he really wasn't doing well. So I decided to drive over to Voorhees, New Jersey, to see him, and not worry if he got angry. It wouldn't be the first time he'd yelled at me. There had been a little snow overnight, and when I pulled up to his house, the paper was in the driveway and there were no tire tracks in the snow. Obviously, no one was home. I had a sinking feeling. Sure enough, Vuk's condition had worsened. He had fallen over the weekend and had been admitted to Jefferson with some breathing problems. He would never leave the hospital. Nor would we ever speak again.

Vuk's final battle was under way—one he could not win. While he was being treated for a series of complications, the doctors weren't able to treat the malignant, inoperable tumor that had appeared in the front of his brain, different from the first mass. I was in Bradenton, Florida, watching the Phillies and the Pirates in an exhibition game when my cell phone rang. Fittingly, Ruly Carpenter was on the line. "I've got some bad news about our buddy," he said, his voice cracking. "He's in really bad shape and the family has decided to disconnect his life support." I was stunned. I had been preparing for the worst, but it was still hard to believe this incredibly tough man wouldn't win this one, too. I drove back to Clearwater and just thought about all the good times we'd had and how much Vuk would be missed.

He died peacefully the next morning, March 8, 2007. The Phillies chartered an airplane and invited many of his friends in baseball from all over the state of Florida to fly up with us. Some of the current Phillies who knew him well were permitted to skip a game that day. Others like Scott Rolen, Terry Francona, Curt Schilling, and Lenny Dykstra took their own means of transportation. His funeral was absolutely jammed, a great tribute to this man who'd had such an influence on so many lives. Larry Bowa, Jim Fregosi, and I sat together in that New Jersey church and alternately laughed and cried. Like many others, we gawked at the never-ending line of people who had come to say goodbye. For someone who had tried to portray himself as such a tough guy, John Vukovich was a man loved by many. His ashes were in an urn on a table in front of us, and there was a picture of Vuk with a big smile. Bo leaned over to me one time and said, "Is it just me or is he looking right at us?" It did appear that way. We both agreed that he would have said something like, "Let's go and get these guys back to spring training. We've got a season coming up, and they need to get back to work."

My last conversation with my friend was in December when he was really struggling and didn't want to be on the phone very long. But he appreciated having certain people calling to check in, and I knew I was one of them. He was more and more incoherent, and it frustrated him. I could tell he knew that he was in trouble. I told

him I loved him and he said, "You know I love you too, buddy."
There was a little silence, and then he hung up. I sat there in my
home office in Blue Bell and cried like a baby, just like I'm doing as
I write this.

Now I alternate between periods of difficulty talking about
Johnny without choking up, and laughing with people who cared
about him as we share stories. He would have been so proud of the
2008 team, the way they fought through a lot of adversity and became World Champions. I'm a lucky man to have had Vuk in my life,
a model of hard work and respect for the game. There was no other
way for him to live his life. He was the consummate professional
who always did it the right way.

When I was still married to Joanne, we used to spend a lot of time
with Greg and Jean Luzinski. Bull lived in Willingboro, New Jersey,
when he began playing with the Phillies. Quite a few members of
the team in the early 1970s lived in Jersey. It was a pretty easy commute to the Vet over the Walt Whitman Bridge, and the guys liked it
out there. We were living in an apartment complex near the Pennsylvania Turnpike in Valley Forge. I'd been a Pennsylvania guy since
birth, but Greg kept bugging me to move to South Jersey and make
life easier on myself with the trip to the Vet. I finally decided it was
a good idea, and we found an apartment in Lindenwold. The problem was that it wasn't yet ready to move into, spring training was
right around the corner, and my lease was up. This was no problem
for Greg and Jean; they insisted we move in with them until our
apartment was ready.

The move to Jersey was something else. I sure didn't have a lot of
money in 1973, so Bull came up with a plan. He said we would rent
a truck and he, his brother-in-law Mike, and I would turn into Allied
Van Lines. So one winter day in January, Greg showed up with the
truck, and we loaded up our belongings and moved into his home
in Jersey. Bull stored my stuff in an empty room and his garage. At
some point during spring training, he came to me and said that
there had been a break-in at his house and some things were stolen.

Joanne had been staying with a friend in Roxborough at the time, so the house was empty. I know I lost a stereo and some other items that were never recovered. Bull always tells people that the burglars didn't take anything of *his*. I guess I had better taste. So he and I had a good story that he still loves to tell. My Jersey experiment lasted just one year. Like a homing pigeon, I was back in Pennsylvania in a condo in Andorra by 1974, but it was quite an experience on the other side of the Delaware.

My introduction to Greg Luzinski was in September 1971. He was a September recall, and the first time I saw him take batting practice at the Vet was an eye-opener. He had a real short, quick stroke and amazing power. He was firing balls into the upper deck that after-noon, and they took off like golf balls. It was pretty easy to see why the Phillies were so high on this guy and his potential.

Bull may seem the strong, silent type, but he has a great sense of humor and loves people. He is a fixture around Citizens Bank Park at Bull's Barbeque, where he can be found before and during games, chatting up fans and signing autographs—and, of course, getting people to partake of the great food they serve out there in right field. Boy, does that place smell good, and do we love it when we get an occasional delivery to the broadcaster's room before a game.

Greg is a solid baseball man, too. He has a great feel for hitting and loves to talk about it. He eventually became a hitting coach for teammate Bob Boone when Boone was managing the Kansas City Royals. This was after Greg had played with the White Sox, follow-ing his career with the Phillies. Bull was a fun guy as a player and loved to go out and have a good time. When you got him going on a baseball conversation, you always learned something new be-cause Bull was also a great observer of the game. He still has a good feel for it, as you'll discover whenever you get a chance to visit with him. This is a guy who could hit .300 despite not running well, es-pecially after he suffered a serious knee injury. One of the more feared hitters in the National League, Greg came within a whisker of winning an MVP award, only to be nosed out by George Foster. His prodigious homers at the Vet were aptly called "Bull Blasts" by that scoreboard cut-up, Dennis Lehman. Before the Vet was demolished, there were a number of seats in the upper deck that had bull's eyes on them, marking the landing spots of some of his more awe-inspiring moon shots. (When Greg would hit a bloop single, Lehman would label them "Bull Burps" on the right-field scoreboard.)

Greg told me a story once that pretty much summed up what our playoff series with Houston was like in 1980. We were into the fifth and final game of that amazing series that featured four straight extra-inning games. This one would decide which team would represent the National League in the World Series. The game was extremely tense and nerve-wracking, even for the players. The dugouts at the Dome were pretty open, and you could easily see the players as they leaned on the railing to get a better view. They could turn to their right and look up and see our location, which was very good and close to the field. So Bull was getting a little uptight himself when he looked up at the radio booth where Andy Musser and I were doing the game and he saw me with my head on the microphone, evidently not able to look at the field. Greg laughed out loud as it dawned on him how tough it was for us up there. At least he could do something about what was happening to determine the outcome. All we could do was watch and suffer. And that was the end of his tension. I wish it had been that easy for us.

Greg is another guy I owe a lot to for helping me to develop an understanding of the intricacies of the game and what the players are thinking and trying to do. I've told him that many times. He's the kind of person who is genuinely happy when things work out for others. That rare generosity is a quality he personifies. But he vows that his moving services will never be offered again.

LIKE RICHIE ASHBURN, Tim McCarver has enjoyed a stellar dual career as a player and broadcaster. After playing for the Phillies from 1970 to 1972, Timmy came back to the club in 1975 and spent a lot of time as Steve Carlton's catcher. In 1980, he joined us in the booth. However, he was activated by the Phillies during the month of September that year so that he could be one of those rare players to have performed in four decades. His last at-bat in the major leagues came on the Sunday after the Phillies had beaten the Expos in a thrilling, rain-delayed, extra-inning game the day before to advance to the National League Championship Series. Timmy ripped a double off right-hander Steve Ratzer, and when he pulled into second, made a point to tip his batting helmet to his colleagues in the booth.

Making the transition from the field to his new career upstairs in 1980 would be one of the best decisions of his life. McCarver spent his first season as a rookie broadcaster, working on network television with Harry and Whitey and with me on the cable TV PRISM telecasts. Timmy was a hard-nosed player who took nothing for granted, and he would be that way as a broadcaster. He wanted to know everything he could about the business and not just show up one day, put on a headset, and start talking. So to get prepared during the off-season in 1979, he and I would meet in a small room at the Channel 17 studios in Wynnefield. It wasn't a very glamorous setting. In fact, all we had was a small TV and videotape recorder. We would simulate broadcasting with the game tape on the monitor, but with the sound turned down. I would do play-by-play, and McCarver would be the analyst. He was a natural right from the start. The job requires someone who not only knows the game, but also understands the mechanics of TV.

You only had to say something once to Timmy, and he had it. I've come to feel that many pitchers and catchers make good analysts because that part of baseball is so vital. Think about it for a minute—nothing happens until the guy on the mound throws the ball. So the complexities of what the pitcher and catcher are trying to do to confuse the hitter in those 60 feet, six inches of real estate are the essence of the game. And since that's what these guys did for a living, those who are able to impart that knowledge can really stand out in describing what's happening.

Tim was immediately comfortable in the ebb and flow of a telecast and commenting on the plays. Replays were starting to become a big part of telecasts, so the analyst needed to try to add something to what the viewer had just seen. Now it's not always possible to come up with something new and brilliant, but we try, and he was saying things I'd never heard before. Typical of his work ethic and desire to succeed, Timmy not only wanted to be an analyst, he also wanted to try play-by-play. It would serve him well when he later went on to join the Mets broadcast team. So we decided to reverse roles one day. I told him the first thing he'd have to do is keep score, so that when he was describing the game, he'd have a record of what had happened earlier. "Keep score?" he said in that distinctive Memphis twang. "What's that?" I couldn't believe what I was hearing, but then it dawned on me that guys like Timmy, who had played the game their whole lives, didn't sit in the stands like us and keep score.

We started with the basics—that every position has a number—and went from there. When a ball is hit to short and an out is recorded at first base, it is scored 6-3. Keeping score sounds pretty simple to those of us who've sat watching a lot of games. But he had to learn it from scratch. Not surprisingly, for this bright man who also was a great bridge player, it turned out to be no problem. Eventually, Timmy did what many broadcasters do—he designed his own scorecard. Through a lot of trial and error, he also adapted some of the features that other broadcasters had created.

I learned so much from Tim back then. I'm still amazed about how much he sees during a game with his ex-catcher's perspective. It bears out my original premise about how important it is to listen to others and then be able to impart that information to your audience. He taught me so many little yet important things. For example, why do the first and third basemen guard the lines in late-inning situations? There are so many variables involved, and just as many opinions. But he always had a reason for why he thought this strategy should or should not be employed. I'd never thought about that stuff before, and I'd watched hundreds of games. I didn't know that when a catcher calls for a breaking ball, he always anticipates it in the dirt, and that it will bounce in the opposite direction from where it first hits. He was saying all these things while we were sitting there doing those mock games, while I was thinking how to retain this new information. I still use many of the things he taught me. One of the criticisms made of Timmy is that he talks too much and over-analyzes. I get the same negatives sent my way. But that's what our job *is*—to talk and analyze. That's why we're in the booth, to provide a different voice from the play-by-play man. We also have a constantly changing audience, and to some extent we're entertainers. While some fans might insist they already know all this stuff, others are sitting there learning something. When I watch another sporting event, I like it when a broadcaster tells me something I didn't know. It helps me to enjoy the game more and to look for that situation the next time. Then, too, when you have the enthusiasm that a guy like McCarver has for his job, you can't wait to go to work. Every game has the potential for something new and wonderful to happen. My feeling has always been that to be compared to Tim McCarver in our business is the highest form of flattery.

We had so much fun when we spent those three years together. Timmy is an interesting, proud man who works hard at everything he does. He is a voracious reader with a love of the English language. I could get away with a lot when we were together, because we were so close. One night, after he had dropped a few of those multisyllabic words of his during the telecast, I looked at him and said, "Timmy, I went to journalism school and you ate dirt for a living for 20 years, so why don't you leave the big words to me?" He couldn't believe I'd said that. We still get a big laugh out of that night when I actually sent him into a state of silence followed by his incredulous reply, "You can't say that to me on the air, can you?"

Not only do his interests go far beyond baseball, but working with Tim McCarver was like having a concierge at your beck and call. All we had to know was what time to meet in the hotel lobby, and Timmy would do the rest. He'd have it all arranged—restaurant reservations, wines, transportation, after-dinner plans. Everything was so much fun. Harry Kalas and I always were a part of the group, and others joined us, like Andy Musser and our director, Ray Tipton. But one thing was understood before departure. The tab would be split equally, and it didn't matter how much fine wine was ordered or how elegant the restaurant. There was never any thought of fast food for Timmy—nothing but the best for "The Catcher," as former teammate Deron Johnson liked to call him. He always goes first class, and if you join him, you do the same, whatever the cost.

Whitey used to go once in a while, but many nights he just stayed in his room and avoided us. Ashburn would say, "Boys, I will be in my suite [he always called his room a suite], reading a good book and dining with the most interesting person I know—*me*."

Timmy had a great relationship with Richie. One day they were playing golf. Both were left-handed players. Timmy was admiring Whitey's clubs. He made the mistake of telling Ashburn that he was thinking about getting new clubs and that those PINGs were real nice. Always generous, Whitey replied, "Tell you what I'll do, pal. These babies are yours for $300." Timmy took the deal right away and only later found out that the Phillies had given Richie the clubs as a gift. To this day, Timmy still has one of the "Whitey" head-covers on his driver. It's yet another way that just the thought of Richie Ashburn makes us smile.

McCarver hates small talk. Get to the point and he'll go from there and have a great discussion, if it's a subject that interests him. One of the worst things you can say to him is the overused expression, "Have a good one!" To which he'll reply, "A good what?" Nametags on people in hotels are another pet peeve. The first day of spring training is the prime example of meaningless small talk. The odds are that you haven't seen some of these people for a few months. Inevitably, the same questions are repeated over and over, whether one cares about the reply or not. So one spring, Timmy came to Clearwater with what resembled a business card, and when people would walk up to him, shake hands, and start to ask the obvious questions, he simply handed them the card in response. There were only answers on Timmy's card. For example, one of the first questions people normally asked was, "How'd you get here?" McCarver's answer simply said, "I drove." Answer number 2 said, "I'm staying on the beach" (for the inevitable "Where are you living this year?"). Answer number 3: "My weight is fine." Number 4: "Ann and the kids are fine." Number 5: "I had a great winter." Finally, number 6: "I don't know where I'm going to eat tonight." I think I still have one of those cards somewhere. Every spring, when the same questions are asked over and over, I always think about Timmy's response.

My first Phillies boss: The Baron

Early days in the booth: with Maddox,
Ashburn, Musser, and Kalas

Friends from the
start—with Timmy

Bill Giles presents...

everything from "The Great Wallenda" to

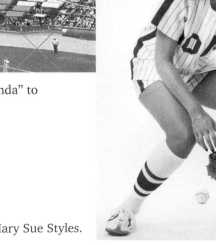

the unforgettable Mary Sue Styles.

It took a mighty Schmidt swing to
hit one out at the vast Vet...

or a Bull blast.

Some of us are still trying.

From Lefty...   to the Tugger...

finally in 1980! The Pope, Big D, Ruly, and soaked friends

Pride of Philadelphia

Memories are forever...

and the men who made them: Ozark, Lucchesi, Owens, Green, and Fregosi in 1999

With Vuk at "The Wedding of the Century"

With Johnny Kruk...

and Dutch: Which of these guys made it on TV?

Hail to the Chief

With Senator
Jim Bunning

Meeting of the minds:
Bowa and Boone

Of course, my own
fan base is growing.

GMs present and past: Ruben Amaro Jr.
and Pat Gillick

President David Montgomery

In 1983, McCarver left the Phillies, expanding his broadcasting career with the Mets and then the Yankees. His superb work and visibility in the New York market started landing him some national broadcast exposure on various networks. He now is paired with Joe Buck as the leading team on Fox, where they do a Saturday game-of-the-week telecast and also work the All-Star Game, the playoffs, and the World Series. He and I have both marveled at his longevity on a network aimed at the youth market and current pop culture. But he has become the best baseball analyst in the business, as the people at Fox have recognized by extending his contract throughout the years. I hope to be there when Timmy wins the Ford C. Frick Award and is enshrined in the broadcasters' wing of the Baseball Hall of Fame in Cooperstown.

Along with Vuk, Timmy is as good a friend as I've known. We still try to stay in touch as much as possible. We have many similar interests. One of our passions is U.S. history, especially the Civil War. One year, Renée and I took a five-day trip with Timmy to tour some battlefields down south. It was a great vacation. We had our photo taken at the spot where Stonewall Jackson was mortally wounded at the Battle of Chancellorsville. We spent a Sunday touring the once blood-soaked fields of Western Maryland, where Union and Confederate troops met at the brutal battle of Antietam. The South called it Sharpsburg after the town where it took place. But the stop that brought it all together was at Fredericksburg, Virginia, when we stood atop Marye's Heights. There the Confederate troops mowed down the Union Army as they marched relentlessly, wave after wave, across an open field between the town and the high ground occupied by Robert E. Lee and his Army of Northern Virginia. It's awe inspiring to think about all the sacrifice and carnage that occurred just below us in 1862. At one point, Timmy turned to me and said in his best Southern drawl, "You know, Wheels, I would have been up here and you would have been down there." Talk about a reality check. That pretty much put what had happened there, and throughout the conflict, in perspective.

Timmy still has the same enthusiasm for the game we love as he did as a hard-nosed player with no back-down in him. Every day is a new adventure and an opportunity for learning, and his zest for life is infectious. He has written several entertaining and informative books that are "must reading" for baseball fans. It means a lot to me that Timmy would take the time to write the Foreword for this book.

While we're talking about some of the people I've learned from, how about the unforgettable Jim Fregosi? But let's save him for the next chapter, along with all those other varied personalities who have guided the Phillies on the field during the past four decades.

CHAPTER 7

I'm the Manager, Not a Coach!

SINCE I STARTED WORKING for the Phillies, we've had 12 different men hired to manage the team. Now, in our constant concern for accuracy, rather than adhering to Whitey's motto, "Boys, don't let the facts get in the way of a good story"—15 men have actually been in that role. That's if we count The Pope's two trips to the dugout and short stints by John Vukovich and Gary Varsho. The won-loss record of these managers seemed to follow a pattern of available talent. "The better the players, the better the manager" is an old axiom that almost always rings true. Check the records for these guys and who they could put into the lineup, and it's not hard to predict the good and bad years.

All the other major sports call their leader coach. Not in baseball. Our guy is the *manager*, and many of them spent a lot of years riding buses to minor-league games and enduring the trials and tribulations of working their way up to the major leagues. So when they get hired as only one of 30 managers, don't call them *coach*.

Nobody fit that path to "The Show" more than the first guy I worked for, Frank Lucchesi. Known as "Skipper Lucchesi" or "Luke," Frank was the epitome of the baseball lifer. He spent 19 years in a myriad of minor-league towns before the Phillies hired him as their leader in September 1969. He had been managing their Triple-A team at Eugene, Oregon. Bob Skinner had begun the 1969 season as the Phillies' manager, but ran into problems with Dick Allen and resigned that August. Coach George Myatt took over as interim manager before Lucchesi was hired to start the 1970 season. That year would mark the end of storied but outmoded Connie Mack Stadium. Lucchesi was a gregarious guy, warm and friendly, with a huge personality that contrasted with his short stature. But there was something about him that always would be a little too "rah-rah" for the hard-edged professional players of that era. The fans loved his energy and his spectacular arguments with umpires. However, those shows would leave many players shaking their heads and, frankly, a little embarrassed about what they had witnessed. Frank had a hilarious pregame radio show, *The Skipper Lucchesi Show*, which he did solo. He would spend a lot of time talking about the priests and nuns he'd met and the hospitals and sick kids he had visited. There wasn't a lot of baseball, which probably was a good thing because he had some really bad teams. In fact, his record from 1970 to 1972 was 166-233. But it's more than a little unfair to judge his managerial ability in view of the talent he was given—the lack of quality players.

Frank's best move was staying with Larry Bowa and believing in his ability. His biggest shortcoming, I think, was his inability to connect with veteran players. That's never a good thing, because the older players can—and will—poison a clubhouse atmosphere if they don't like and respect the manager. That's what happened with Frank.

My first encounter with Lucchesi was memorable because he was the first big-league manager I'd ever met. Now, here I was sitting in his Veterans Stadium office, just the two of us, and boy was I nervous. But he made me feel great. He told me to have fun, to appreciate that I was in the major leagues, and to make the most of it. That conversation lasted only about 15 minutes, but he made a favorable impression on me, and we had established a good, albeit short, relationship.

With the Phillies struggling in 1972 and Frank's act starting to wear a little thin, Paul Owens pulled the plug on the man who had managed so many minor-league teams for him, and went down on the field himself for the first time. Lucchesi would go on to manage the Texas Rangers. He got punched out in an unfortunate confrontation with one of his players, Lenny Randle. I don't think Lucchesi ever recovered from that incident. He bounced around baseball before one last time on the field. Frank was named interim manager by his old friend Dallas Green in 1987, taking over the Cubs for 25 games after Gene Michael was fired. Dallas would depart Chicago shortly after that, which affected Vuk as well.

The Pope's first trip to the field would result in a 33-47 record. But he was more a man on a recon mission to find out what he had and what the team needed to compete. The coaches pretty much ran the games, and pitching coach Ray Ripplemeyer was invaluable handling the pitchers. I do think Owens enjoyed his time in the dugout. He certainly had some good arguments with umpires. One smoking hot night in Atlanta, home-plate umpire Frank Pulli called a balk on a Phillies pitcher. Paul stormed out of the dugout and put on a great dirt-kicking show that seemed to entertain Pulli, one of baseball's good guys. The Pope tossed his hat, then quickly picked it up after getting a warning from Pulli not to do that again or he'd be watching the rest of the game on TV. By the end of 1972, Owens had a pretty good idea of what he wanted to do, and he was now ready to head back upstairs and bring a new man to town to run his ballclub.

That man would be Danny Ozark, a longtime member of the Brooklyn and Los Angeles Dodgers organization. A quiet man with a hangdog appearance, he was the epitome of the way Larry Shenk used to describe himself. "You know," The Baron would say, "God gave me a great personality and a tired face." But Danny loved to laugh and have a good time. He just looked serious. He was a big, powerful man with huge hands. His tremendous physical presence in the clubhouse made him a guy any player would think twice before challenging. Because of Ozark's background with a great organization, and bolstered by the total backing of Ruly Carpenter and Paul Owens, he was a formidable leader in the dugout. The team knew it was time to pay attention to detail.

At the outset, as would happen later with Charlie Manuel, many underestimated both Ozark and his baseball knowledge. Danny never was overly comfortable with the English language. Like Lucchesi, he had the propensity for coming out with malaprops that could leave people scratching their heads. Some were genuinely funny, such as when Ozark observed that "Even Napoleon had his Watergate." But the man could make his point where it mattered.

He knew how to run a clubhouse, this one populated by a few veterans surrounded by a cast of young, rising all-stars. In the 1970s, although every game was broadcast on the radio, not every game was televised. Thus, every move by the manager wasn't dissected over and over by the media. People would actually get up the next day, having not seen the game on TV. So they eagerly awaited the morning newspaper to read about what had actually happened in the game, rather than the analysis that newspaper guys must do today. Now, by the time the newspaper hits the driveway, many fans have seen the game and the postgame show, and may also have seen highlights and commentary on ESPN or Comcast SportsNet. Guys like Ozark didn't have to worry about constant second-guessing of their every move and comment. They could concentrate on their players, and on how to win the game.

One of the low points of Danny's career came late in September 1975. The Phillies were hanging around the Pirates, who were headed for the NL East title with a magic number of one. It doesn't get much better for a team than to reach for that goal—win one more game, which the Bucs achieved that night. Fireworks went off in Three Rivers Stadium, players rolled around on the ground in celebration, and it was over for the Phillies. However, when Danny met with the media, he inexplicably told them his team was still in it, raising more than a few eyebrows. Picture the media frenzy if that were to happen today. Yet Danny was able to survive this major gaffe, and the Phillies did finish second, 86-76. No doubt about it, they were starting to improve under Ozark. Certainly, he had his problems with some players. He was slow to relate to Mike Schmidt at the start of his career and was tough on him. Carlton and Ozark constantly butted heads because Lefty never wanted to come out of a game. But overall it worked out, as the Phillies embarked on one of the most successful three-year runs in the organization's history, with playoff appearances all three years. Yet the team just couldn't get past the first round. As much as anything, that brought about the fateful day in Atlanta when "Big D" came to town and the baseball world changed dramatically for the guys in red-and-white pinstripes.

. . .

IF THE EVEN-TEMPERED Ozark was the right man to oversee a transition, blunt Dallas Green was the perfect choice to bring it to fruition. On September 1, 1979, he strode into the clubhouse, filling the room with his enormous presence and personality. More than once he reminded the players that *they* were the ones who had gotten a good man fired. Now it was time to deal with Green and turn things around. Danny Ozark left Atlanta for his Vero Beach home that day without holding a press conference—a class act to the end.

Danny never lost interest in baseball or the Phillies. He had intended to come to Clearwater in late March 2009 to see a game and visit with his many friends in the Phillies organization. But he called Larry Shenk to say he had a touch of bronchitis and couldn't make it. Ozark added that overall he was in good health. At 85, he was still playing golf four times a week, and generally was enjoying life. We missed seeing him. He passed away in Vero Beach on May 7, 2009.

When Dallas took over, he wielded the hammer immediately, starting to set the tone for 1980. Could he do it today with all the guaranteed contracts, the lure of free agency, and greener pastures for players who disapprove of their manager? It's unlikely, but back then he was the ideal man for the situation. The players, especially those who had known him in the minors, realized from day one that the sea had parted. They might not like Dallas personally, but he didn't care. He had a job to do, and he would do it his way. He would not only scream and holler, he *called* himself "a screamer and a hollerer." You normally heard Dallas before you saw him, because the man reached some octaves that could shatter glass. He spared no one's feelings and would accept neither baloney nor excuses. Between games of a doubleheader in Pittsburgh in 1980, he staged an all-time chew-out that was heard through the clubhouse doors by the media. Green simply stayed on that bunch of players for six straight months, willing them to win, unfazed by any bruised egos. And the players used their intense dislike of Green as their motivation to show him they could get the job done.

Why had The Pope, generally so deliberative, decided on this managerial change before the end of 1979? He was convinced that Ozark probably had taken the team as far as he could, and a new approach was needed. When the Phillies beat the Kansas City Royals in six games in the 1980 World Series, one of my lasting memories will always be the moments shared by Green and Owens. These two very emotional men could not bear-hug each other enough as their tears flowed and the celebration erupted around them. They had come a long way together through their shared minor-league experience. After Owens' controversial move to fire Ozark and replace him with his volatile farm director, the ride had been anything but smooth. But now here they were, world champions. The players grudgingly gave Green his due. It wasn't until years later, when they had left the game, that many realized there had been a method to his madness. All they had to do was check out that finger bearing the red-and-gold championship ring. Having come up agonizingly short for three straight years, now they were part of something that never could be taken away from them, and they knew they had Dallas Green to thank for it.

I think the 1981 team was every bit as good as the one in 1980. Still pretty much intact, they were a confident group, fully prepared to parade down Broad Street again. But, in first place, they fell victim to the devastating strike called by the Major League Baseball Players Association in June, which lasted two long months. When play resumed, it was determined that there would be a split season to be decided by the only "divisional series" in history. With the Expos in first at the end of the season, the Phillies and Expos met in a best-of-five format. The Expos won the first two games in frigid Montreal. Then the Phillies won the next two at the Vet, with George Vukovich (no relation to John) winning game four with a pinch-hit home run. Game five in Philadelphia featured the marquee matchup of Steve Rogers and Steve Carlton. However, that day, Rogers blanked the Phillies 3-0, and it would be the Expos who moved on to meet the Dodgers for the National League pennant. Los Angeles won the deciding game on a Rick Monday home run off Rogers at Olympic Stadium, and the Dodgers went to the World Series to play the Yankees.

When the *Chicago Tribune* purchased the Cubs that year, they asked respected baseball writer Jerome Holtzman to help them pick the man to run their baseball operation. Jerry later recalled how he went through the American League *Red Book* and the National League *Green Book* in search of the man to recommend to the Tribune Corporation. Holtzman told them it was his opinion that Dallas Green was the best baseball man in the game. When Green accepted the Cubs' offer to be their new GM and president, the news leaked out prematurely. Hal Bodley, then with the *Wilmington News Journal* and an old Delaware friend of Green's, broke the story. Bodley, now a broadcaster with MLB.com, was a tenacious reporter. Even though he knew that it was going to make things awkward for Green, it was his job to report this very big story. Dallas had to sit down with Ruly Carpenter and confirm it, and another sea change was about to occur for the Phillies.

One day, while this was going on, Green walked through the PR department office occupied by Larry and me. At the time, the rumors of his departure were swirling, and we wanted him to confirm or deny them to us. I remember flippantly asking, "Why would you want to go to a bad team like that, Big D?" I'll never forget the look I got from Dallas. He stopped dead in his tracks and said, "Why? Because I'm going to have a chance to *run* that place, and we are going to win!"

PAT CORRALES HAD also come through the Phillies organization and was close to both Paul Owens and Dallas Green. He'd had a tough childhood, growing up among Chicano migrant workers in Northern California. Pat was one firm guy, and stories of his confrontations were legendary. A hard-nosed catcher, he took that mentality to managing when he got a chance with the Texas Rangers and the Cleveland Indians in the American League. In the other dugout some nights was another competitive guy, Jim Fregosi. As both men gracefully aged, they started to resemble each other, with their dark complexions and shocks of white hair. Back in those younger days, Corrales and Fregosi remember times when their ballclubs would get into fights over pitchers throwing at hitters. Both deny ever telling their guys to throw at the opposition, but there were some memorable, bench-clearing brawls. The two managers would laugh about it later, but Fregosi made it a point never to wind up in a fight with Corrales. He was a man to avoid.

Corrales was another guy with a good personality who loved to laugh, but who rarely showed that side of himself. He was a stern taskmaster, whose few rules insisted that his players be on time and always hustle. He wasn't with the Phillies very long, managing the 1982 season and a portion of 1983, so I didn't get to know him very well. Since then, we've become good friends, because he's spent so much time in the National League East with the Atlanta Braves and the Washington Nationals. I especially recall one night during our press caravan in 1982, when we were in a hotel bar after a dinner. He suggested we stay and talk for a while, which we did, well into the early-morning hours. I later asked him why he had issued that invitation. He said that was his way of getting to know someone better whom he hoped he was going to trust.

Pat had been mainly a backup catcher during his career with the Phillies, Cardinals, and Reds, but I told him I had been at Connie Mack Stadium the night of one of the most violent collisions I'd ever seen. Corrales was behind the plate and Willie Mays was on first when a Giant doubled into the gap in right center field and Mays took off. In those days, there was nothing more exciting than watching Mays run the bases. The ball and the "Say Hey Kid" arrived at home plate at the same time, and he and Corrales had nowhere to go. Boom! Mays went flying behind the plate, and Corrales went in another direction. Both men lay motionless on the ground as the home-plate umpire went over to Corrales. He saw the baseball still in the unconscious catcher's glove and called Willie out. Both men later staggered to their feet and stayed in the game, giving many of us a memory we'll never forget. I asked Pat about the collision during that conversation, and he said he still ached from the impact. But then he smiled and said, "But he was out, wasn't he?"

The Phillies of 1983 were known as the "Wheeze Kids," in part because older players like Pete Rose, Tony Perez, and Joe Morgan were on the roster. They were not reacting well to Corrales' style of leadership, and some veterans made an end run to the front office, complaining about the manager. On July 18th, Corrales was summoned to Bill Giles' office and dismissed by Giles and Paul Owens. It was an almost unprecedented move—firing a manager in first place. Dallas Green could lean on players and get his way, but his was a unique situation. Long-term, Giles and Owens felt it couldn't work for Corrales. He had a right to be upset, having put together an impressive record with the Phillies of 132-115. But when told of the decision, the always-stoic Corrales simply got up, said "Thank you," and walked out the door. When I asked him later about the way he had handled his dismissal, he replied, "What more was there to say? They had made up their minds, and I was too proud and stubborn to try and talk them out of it."

So he left the Vet, went back to Jersey, and started thinking about what was next. Two weeks later, he resurfaced as manager of the Indians. Pat subsequently went on to a long run as a trusted aide to Bobby Cox with the perennially successful Braves. (In those days, there was a third "given" in Atlanta. In addition to death and taxes, you could be certain your team would participate in post-season baseball.)

So back to the field went Paul Owens again, and the Phillies rode a blistering September by Joe Morgan to an improbable NL Eastern Division Championship, only to lose in five games in the World Series to the Orioles. Owens was never again to be general manager. He became, as would Green later, a "senior advisor." And with Owens relinquishing his GM role, a new manager was needed, and the front office was about to change the way it did business.

ONCE AGAIN THE Phillies would reach into the minor-league system, this time bringing John Felske up to the big-league club. He had been successful in managing the Phils' Triple-A club at Portland, Oregon, taking it to the Pacific Coast League championship. Felske was a career minor-league catcher who'd had the proverbial cup of coffee with the Cubs and Brewers. He was quiet and cerebral, with a laid-back Midwestern personality, polite almost to a fault. However, Felske was coming to manage the Philadelphia Phillies in an "in-your-face" town whose fans took their sports more than seriously. And they expected the guys leading their teams to feel and express things just as fervently. Felske was close to the "Gang of Six" who now ran the Phillies, a connection that came from his days with Milwaukee. The front office had some former Milwaukee guys on board, like Tony Siegle, a whiz with contracts and rules, and farm director Jim Baumer. (Today, Siegle works for GM Brian Sabean with the Giants; Baumer, unfortunately, is deceased.) The Gang of Six moniker came from *Philadelphia Daily News* columnist Bill Conlin, who was looking to describe the way the club was being run without a GM. They were all experienced baseball men, with distinctive personalities.

The most colorful of the bunch had to be Hugh Alexander, known to everyone as "Uncle Hughie." Alexander was born in Buffalo, Missouri, but grew up in Oklahoma and always considered himself a Sooner. He was an excellent athlete in high school, qualifying in 1935 for the Olympic trials as a sprinter. But baseball was his first love. He was a sturdy six-footer, weighing 190, when the Cleveland Indians signed him in 1935. Alexander made it to the major leagues in 1937 at the age of 20. He played in seven games for the Tribe and went 1-11, .071, but was still considered a top prospect.

Alexander's life changed dramatically that off-season when, like a lot of men in those days, he took a job working in the oil fields. One day, his clothing became entangled in a drilling mechanism, and before he could free himself, his left hand had been badly mangled and had to be amputated. Nobody that I've ever met, in or out of baseball, could tell stories like Alexander. When he would get rolling on losing his hand, the tale was mesmerizing. He talked about being given some whisky as a makeshift anesthetic while a Native American doctor completed the surgery. It was painful to hear, but somehow he made it sound almost funny. Possessing a deep voice from years of smoking and drinking, Alexander was someone everyone in the game wanted to be around. Following his injury, he embarked on a career of professional scouting that would be his life for 62 years. We were lucky enough to have him with the Phillies for 16 of them. He also worked for the Indians, White Sox, and Cubs. Not only was he a great storyteller, but with all his experience, Hughie was like a professor of baseball.

Alexander and Paul Owens should have charged admission when they would get together. If Pope was deliberate about player moves, Alexander was just as impulsive. He could pursue a player like a cheetah chasing an antelope. But in many ways they were so much alike. When the two would hold court at Heilman's Beachcomber in Clearwater, we always hoped a nearby couple hadn't come out that night for a nice, quiet romantic dinner. The table seating these baseball lifers was going to be loud—and, as the cocktails increased, it would get louder. And that's when the stories would start.

Alexander had an Oklahoma accent that was right out of *The Grapes of Wrath*. The man could take you back to the days of the Great Depression, and you could almost feel the wind as it came "sweepin' down the plain." He had spent countless hours looking through backstops, trying to find talent for the major leagues. Hughie was a grassroots guy who would think nothing about doing whatever was necessary to sign a player. There were no rules when he started, and no draft. Go find a kid, camp out in his town, find out what it would take, and then go sign him.

By this time, Pope and Hughie had been around each other for so long that they could finish each other's stories. When Alexander started a story, Pope would call out, "Ah, that's number 76." Another story would be "number 101." And on it would go, as Alexander simply ignored Owens and launched into another entertaining tale for a new audience. One of his favorites was a story about lions and the circus, which Uncle Hughie would feel compelled to act out. We always prodded him to make sure he would tell it. Then the show would start. He would leave the table, go to another part of the restaurant, and start crawling back, looking like a Marine going under barbed wire. Good hand out, then stump. Other patrons would stare in disbelief, while we roared with laughter. Part of the act was for him to say, in his best Oklahoma drawl, "Now here come those #$^&*% lions!" We loved it, and Pope always called it "story number 1." Of course, with Hughie, you never knew whether he was embellishing or how seriously to take anything he said, but it really didn't matter.

Alexander's personal life was a big part of his storytelling. We thought he had been married six or seven times, but we knew he had married at least one woman twice. When a newcomer would ask if he'd ever been married, Uncle Hughie would gesture with that strong right hand and say, "Son, I've been married so many times, I can't count them on my hand." To which Pope would add, "Ah, that's number 45."

Pope and Hughie would argue about many things, but thankfully, they never got into a fight. It would come close to that point sometimes, but it never happened. I'll always believe they respected each other too much to let it go that far, but it would have been something to see.

After he left the Phillies and joined the Cubs, Alexander still made his home in the Clearwater area. One of the highlights of spring training would be the sight of him showing up with his wide-brimmed straw hat and taking a seat behind home plate, ready to talk. I always enjoyed my time with this fascinating man. Baseball has changed so much, as has scouting itself. There will never be another generation like the one that produced Hugh Alexander and others like him. I was lucky enough to come along at a time when these men still were a vital part of the game, and could tell spellbinding stories about Ruth, Gehrig, Foxx, and Cobb. What an education, and what a legacy.

Uncle Hughie died on November 25, 2000, in Oklahoma City, at age 83. When a person passes, you'll hear or read that no one got more out of his life than he. Well, I can't believe this ever applied more than to Hugh Alexander. He saw his life's dream end at age 20, but he was still tough enough to spend 63 more years in the game that he loved. Several of those years, in the mid-1980s, were as part of the Gang of Six.

Bill Giles' management team was convinced that their youthful manager, John Felske, would be able to handle the Philadelphia sports scene, despite his laid-back demeanor. To Felske, though, baseball—although a most exciting, challenging game—was not a matter of life and death that one lived 24/7. I'm convinced that he was a good man in the wrong place, simply miscast for our passionate market. The Phillies finished second in 1986, Felske's second season, 21½ games behind the Mets. The highlight of that season was watching the Mets come to Philadelphia, needing only one win to clinch the NL East. The champagne was on ice for three days. Following a three-game Phillies sweep, it was wheeled out of the visitors' clubhouse and taken to another stop, where they finally clinched. We did enjoy those three days. After going 190-194, Felske was fired in mid-June 1987. Although for different reasons than Corrales, he was the victim of another end-run by some players to management. This time they objected to their manager's too-placid personality. A solid man who was never meant to manage in a town like Philadelphia, Felske returned to the Midwest and opened a chain of successful oil-and-lube businesses. He never returned to baseball.

IF FELSKE WAS the poster boy for the anti-Philadelphian, the man who replaced him seemed to personify Philadelphia. Lee Elia was a legend at Olney High, starring in football, basketball, and baseball. His fiery personality may have helped influence Dallas Green to name Elia his first manager in Chicago. He and Dallas were already close friends, and "D" felt comfortable with Lee as his manager. Unfortunately, he was saddled with some really bad Cubs teams. Today, it's hard to imagine what Wrigley Field was like in the early '80s. Now it's a sold-out, raucous venue inhabited by thousands of young people intent on making the hallowed ground at Sheffield and Addison the site of the biggest sustained party in the U.S.A. Back in Lee and Dallas' early days with the Cubs, however, Wrigley Field was just a beautiful old ballpark only half-filled with spectators accustomed to seeing their team struggle.

One especially cold afternoon in 1983, following another thumping, Lee Elia was holding his postgame meeting with the media. Asked about the manner in which the Cubs had been booed that afternoon by the Wrigley faithful, Elia exploded and went into a now-famous rant. His classic line was, "Eighty-five percent of the people in this city work, and the other $@&*%&* 15 percent come out here and boo my players." Now this was hardly an ideal theme, particularly because the Cubs only played day games back then. They were still several years away from Dallas persuading the city and neighborhood that night games wouldn't signal the end of civilization as they knew it. Unfortunately for Lee, cameras and tape recorders in his tiny office preserved his explosion for posterity. Both men can laugh about it now, but it wasn't so funny at the time, when Green was intent on convincing Chicago that the Cubs didn't have to be lovable losers. After everyone left, Lee called Dallas. "Big guy," he said, "I had a little trouble with the media down here today. I got a little hot under the collar and maybe said some things I shouldn't have." Green replied, "Ah, come on, I have your back. Don't worry about it. By the way, what did you say?" When he heard what Lee had said, Dallas roared into the phone for him to get his butt upstairs immediately. It was not a pleasant meeting, and Elia would never really recover from that incident. He was fired in late 1983.

Lee surfaced as the Phils' Triple-A manager at Portland after Felske was hired to manage in Philadelphia. Then Elia was named a coach at the big-league level, and finally took over his dream job as manager of his hometown team in 1987 after Felske was given the boot. It should have worked out, but like many of the Phillies managers of that era, Lee's teams weren't very good—and the manager eventually paid the price. With the club slogging through a poor 1988 season, and Elia feeling the heat from both the front office and the fans, one Sunday afternoon summed it all up. There was a big crowd at the Vet. The Phillies were batting when someone hit a hard ground-ball down the third-base line that was clearly foul. But all of a sudden, to our surprise, there went Elia, bouncing out of the dugout and headed for our old friend, Frank Pulli, who was umpiring at third. And we were even more surprised when what started as a little conversation between two old pals began to get more heated. Suddenly, Elia tossed his bubble gum, and he and Pulli were going nose-to-nose in one of those classic baseball moments. The crowd, which had been pretty quiet during another less-than-thrilling game, quickly came to life in support of their beleaguered manager. Their roar escalated as the argument continued. Then it became deafening as Pulli, with an exaggerated arm thrust into the air, threw Elia out of the game. Lee got in a few more words, kicked some dirt, and headed slowly to the Phillies dugout as the fans showered their local hero with adulation. They loved the emotion he had showed in trying to jump-start his dead-in-the-water team.

Later we learned the real story. As I mentioned, Elia and Pulli were old friends, and Frank loved to have a good time out on the field. So as Elia came up to Pulli, Frank said, "Lee, what the hell are you doing out here? The ball's foul." Elia responded, "I know, Frank, but I'm getting killed around here. The media is on my tail. The fans are mad at me, thinking I'm not the emotional guy they knew. The front office is all over me. I need to get kicked out of a game so they know I still have it." To which Pulli replied, "My pleasure, but let's give them a good show." It was one of the best I've ever seen. Following the game, the umpires are supposed to file a report to the league office about ejections and any possible fines involved. Frank Pulli never filed a report that day. And the fans were back on Elia's side, at least for a little while.

By that time, Lee Thomas was the Phillies GM. One unforgettably emotional outburst wasn't enough to save his manager. With nine games left in the season, he fired Elia and replaced him with John Vukovich. Vuk and Lee were like brothers. In fact, Vuk always referred to Elia affectionately as "The Nut." Those nine games were hard for Vuk, who refused to sit in the manager's office out of respect for his friend, but as a loyal coach he took the responsibility.

It had been a strange time around the ballclub, with managers coming and going. There was a long period without a general manager and a short period with Woody Woodward in charge. I think the club missed the steady influence of Paul Owens. Giles had surrounded himself with solid baseball men. But where Owens was always deliberative, the philosophy now was a little more impulsive.

· · ·

THE NEXT MANAGER, Nick Leyva, a young man with great potential, ran into some of the same problems as his predecessors. We just didn't have the talent to compete with the teams that were winning consistently. Philadelphia is certainly a major media market, but in those days that didn't equate to revenues. Economically, the Phillies remained a "small market team" in an age when free agency and salaries were beginning to explode. Back in 1969, the ballclub was so anxious to get out of antiquated Connie Mack Stadium that they'd agree to almost any deal with the city of Philadelphia. The club's lease for its beautiful new ballpark in South Philadelphia had to be one of the worst ever negotiated in sports history. The Vet had been built for the then-staggering cost of $54 million, a state-of-the-art, multipurpose home for both the Phillies and Eagles. But the city took advantage of the desperation of both pro teams to have a new home. The parking revenues all went into municipal coffers, and the concession revenues were minimal. The Phillies constantly tried to update the Vet as it aged, hoping to be reimbursed. The upkeep was brutal, and eventually the whole stadium began to deteriorate.

When Eagles owner Leonard Tose secretly negotiated a deal to move his team to Phoenix, the Phils did receive a huge break. That potential agreement was scuttled by a newspaper report that started a firestorm in Philadelphia. It kept the Eagles in town and forced the city to look at the teams' leases. Both teams and the city understood that new revenue sources had to be developed, so installing "skyboxes" was planned to help keep the Eagles in town. Meanwhile, Bill Giles was sitting back and thinking that the NFL plays about 10 home games a year and we are here for 81, plus the postseason and the potential for a World Series. Both teams renegotiated more favorable leases with the city, and the Phillies, too, were able to use the skyboxes, but conditions at the Vet continued to decline.

A Cardinals minor-league manager and big-league coach, Leyva came to the Phillies with the highest recommendations of one of the most respected managers in the game, Whitey Herzog. Nick was a positive guy with a lot of energy, but not much experience. It was a real eye-opener for me to realize that I was older than the manager

I'd be working for. How could that have happened? Wasn't I always supposed to be "the kid"? Not anymore.

In 1990, I started doing a pregame show on radio with the manager, Nick being the first. We did about 150 shows a year, pretaped to run 15 to 20 minutes before each game. Baseball's escalating salaries didn't extend to our young, rookie manager or his new pregame show collaborator. I got $25 per show and Nick got $100—and we were both happy for the extra cash. After we finished each show, Leyva would say, "Ka-ching, that's another Ben Franklin." I'm still doing that show nearly 20 years later, although for a little more money. And it's been a real plus in other ways. I've gotten to know each manager a lot better, helping with my daily game preparation. We spend a lot of time together before recording a show, and much of it is off the record. But the manager provides a lot of insight that can be used later. When we're on the same page as the man in the dugout, that's helpful to us as well as to our audience.

Leyva relied a lot on his experienced coaches like Darold Knowles, Hal Lanier, Larry Bowa, and Vuk. One night, we were headed back to Philadelphia on our charter flight after almost completing the first official night game in Wrigley Field. Unfortunately, the game had been rained out after a few innings, so the Mets would have that distinction, playing the Cubs on the following night. That rainout featured one of the most turbulent thunder-and-lightning displays I've ever seen. It was magnificent and frightening at the same time. The storms still weren't out of the area when we departed Midway Airport and our plane was hit by lightning. It's pretty unforgettable. There is a bright flash and boom at the same time, and the plane reacts. Thankfully for us, it was relatively little that night.

I can remember sitting there, trying to be as calm as possible, when Lee Thomas came down the aisle and sat next to me. I feared it might be one of those "Uh oh, what did I say on the air that ticked off the GM?" moments. But Lee quickly got to the point: "I've been told by a lot of people that you know Larry Bowa better than almost anyone, and I'm thinking about bringing him back as a coach. What do you think?" I told him that it would probably be one of the best things he could do to help the ballclub, and Nick. Then I threw in a qualifier: "Lee, just remember this man is extremely popular in Philadelphia and if things don't work out, you'll get crucified if you fire him." To his credit, Lee made the move and Bowa and Leyva became great friends.

There are few better third-base coaches than Bowa. By that time, he already had managed in San Diego, and his strong personality had not gone down well with some of his players. (Although, to this day, one of those who praises Bowa's job as manager is Hall of Famer Tony Gwynn.) Bowa had a pitcher with the Padres named Storm Davis, and the manager thought he was less than a "team guy." One time during a meeting, Bowa singled out Davis and said, "Storm, let's get something straight. That $%^ ^&* SD on your uniform doesn't stand for Storm Davis!" But helpful as he would be to Leyva, Bowa couldn't save his job.

On April 3, 1991, only 11 days after the start of the season, Jim Fregosi replaced Nick Leyva as manager. Leyva had posted a 148-189 record. He was the sixth Phillies manager to be replaced in mid-season since I began working for the club. Fregosi certainly came to the job with the best credentials, lacking confidence neither in himself nor in his ability to run a baseball team. My first meeting with him was in spring training of 1990. He had been hired as a special assistant to Lee Thomas and already was beginning to exert his big personality around the ballclub. I had heard a lot about Fregosi and knew him as an All-Star player (six times) with the Angels and manager of both the Angels and White Sox. Reports were that Jimmy never just slid into a room. No, this big man tended to dominate any room he entered, as I was about to learn first-hand.

Lee Thomas had invited a group of us to dinner at Heilman's Beachcomber on Clearwater Beach, scene of those storytelling sessions with Hughie and Pope. This had been a Phillies hangout since the '50s, and was a comfortable spot for a night out. I sat a few seats from Fregosi, who was holding court. Several times during dinner I was asked for my opinion. I could see that was getting his attention, because Fregosi is a man very much aware of his surroundings, who misses nothing and observes everything. I didn't know it at the time, but I was being sized up. Later on, after we became friends, we talked about that night. Jimmy told me he knew I was one of the broadcasters who had been around the team for a long time. Then he noticed how I was being asked for my point of view by some very important people at the table. According to Fregosi, "I could see you were regarded as a lot more than some guy who broadcasts the games, and I'd better get to know you a little better." And that was Jim Fregosi right from the start. He was polite and accommodating, but he sensed who could help him and who would get in the way. He was very skilled at surrounding himself with people who could contribute to making his situation, and the team itself, stronger.

During spring training in 1991, Fregosi had been asked to do the games on Sports Channel with Andy Musser. He probably would have been good in the booth, but we'll never know. With Fregosi now at the helm, surrounded by some of the characters on his teams, we were off on a wild ride. Lee Thomas had made a lot of good moves during the off-season leading up to 1993, and had assembled a club that looked like it could compete. It was a group of players with a lot of experience, very few of whom were home-grown. The Phillies were going through a period of slim pickings from the minor leagues, so Thomas was forced to trade and sign free agents. The 1993 team was a collection of diverse personalities who needed direction. That's where Fregosi made his best move. Darren Daulton started his Phillies career as a shy, skinny kid from Kansas. He matured into a sturdy veteran catcher who had an impact in the clubhouse, playing the perfect position to become a team leader. Fregosi sensed in Daulton, even when he still had his laid-back personality, what every manager craves: a guy with the potential to police the clubhouse without needing to have his manager and coaches involved. Fregosi would later say that he had probably asked more of Daulton than of any other player. "Dutch" embraced the role, and rarely did Fregosi have to confront a player. Daulton, with his physical presence and respect from his teammates, took care of business. And that group of players, who could have spun into an uncontrollable mess, instead went to the World Series.

Fregosi was also one of the best I've seen at walking the line between being an authority figure, respected by all his players, and being their best friend. Before games, he was a familiar sight in the clubhouse, in his trademark sleeveless undershirt and shorts, with his reading glasses low on his nose. He might be involved in a rollicking card game, laughs and insults abounding on both sides. Other players would be lounging around—some watching TV, some napping. But everyone knew when to switch gears. On the road, things were the same. It was the manager's rule that when the team bus arrived at the ballpark, it was time to go to work. Fregosi's mindset became everyone's. All card-playing ceased. The manager would saunter back to his office, put on his uniform, and take charge. There might be a meeting with the media or his staff before heading for the dugout, but we were all now dealing with Jim Fregosi the manager. It was fascinating to watch this daily transformation and how the players understood that when Fregosi's game face came on, so did theirs.

Fregosi also had a good feel for the city of Philadelphia and the demands put on his time by the media. Understanding and respecting the passion of the fans, he loved being the manager of the Phillies. Even though he was from Northern California, he realized that baseball in our city was not just a game, not merely entertainment, but a way of life. He grasped that newspaper columnists were guys he should know because what they wrote could influence fans. He might also get his point across to a player through them without having a potentially destructive, ego-shattering confrontation. The media, print and broadcast, appreciated his cooperation, even if at times he could be a little condescending.

Jimmy was a man who did not suffer fools easily, although he tried his best to contain that attitude. He had a brash, flippant way about him, and almost anyone could be the target of his barbs. Some were meant to hit a target, but most were only a harmless part of the daily back-and-forth that exists between teams and those assigned to cover them. One night, however, Jimmy misread his audience, getting into a situation not easily overcome. Fregosi liked to do his pregame session with the media in his office. It was a lively exchange, filled with baseball talk, humor, one-liners, plus an occasional rebuke of a reporter who might have asked a question that Fregosi didn't like. It was a Saturday night, when many beat writers used to take some vacation time, and substitutes were sent in their place. For some reason, the subject of WIP radio came up. Sports talk was starting to become a big part of the scene, and some of the veteran baseball guys like Fregosi were still trying to comprehend its importance. So when WIP was mentioned, in terms of something critical that someone had said about him, Fregosi launched into his best chest-out, defiant reply about the insignificance of that station. Then came the line that would haunt him. He said that only "guys from South Philadelphia who [bleeped] their sisters listened to it anyway."

Normally, that would have gotten a chuckle from the assembled audience, and it would be on to another topic. No big deal, just outrageous Jimmy being Jimmy in another pregame session during a long season. The regular guys knew what was on and off the record, and left the latter in the manager's office. But, for some reason, a backup reporter decided to call one of the radio station's hosts and inform him of what Fregosi had said. This particular host didn't have a warm and fuzzy relationship with Fregosi, so he waited until Monday morning to have the drive-time show air the remark, on the premise that it was a story as many fans as possible should hear. Apparently, his definition of maximum exposure beat the importance of immediacy. It produced a firestorm, embarrassing to both Fregosi and the Phillies organization. Jimmy apologized and even led the Columbus Day parade in South Philadelphia that October, but the damage had been done. I don't think Fregosi ever was the same again, especially around the local media. That combination, and some bad teams, eventually led to his firing by Thomas after the 1996 season.

I could tell so many stories about this fascinating man, but I want to make sure I share this one with you. It's the genesis for the title of this chapter. As we've made clear, Fregosi was generally accommodating and friendly, but could also be one of the most intimidating men imaginable. When he would peer over those reading glasses and get serious, look out. He'd make his unmistakable point. One night, we were sitting in the dugout in Atlanta, shooting the breeze, as we did many nights before recording his pregame show. He and I spent hours talking about a lot of topics with the machine off before he would finally say, "Let's go with this stupid show. I don't have all day to sit and talk with you." So he was sitting there with those glasses on, reading something, when a young guy came walking up with a tape recorder. He shyly approached Fregosi and then summoned up the courage to say, "Coach, could I have a few minutes with you?" I just sat there and winced because I sensed what was coming next. Jimmy slowly looked up at the kid over those glasses with the most menacing of stares. "Son," he said, "I worked a hell of a lot of years not to be called coach. I am the MANAGER!" And just as the reporter was about to slink away, Fregosi broke into a big grin and added, "Now, what can I do for you?"

Jimmy taught me so much about the game and what his job entailed. I'll be forever grateful for our enduring friendship and the give-and-take we've had over the years. He even taught me something about broadcasting. It still is a common practice in our business to hear an interviewer go through a long-winded statement, then pause and wait for the subject to reply to his brilliance. Whenever I'd fall into that trap, Fregosi would stare at me and say, "Mr. Wheeler, I thoroughly enjoyed your great analysis, but now would you like to ask *me* a question?" And he was right. So we would start over. I still think about that whenever I'm inclined to make pronouncements instead of doing what an interviewer is supposed to do—ask a question. We also had a signal during the interview to warn me if I had gotten into an area he didn't like, or if perhaps something was going on with an injury or an impending move that I wasn't aware of. If he didn't want to go there with a follow-up question, he would hold his nose as if some foul odor suddenly had permeated the room, and I would know to move on to another subject.

I still love to see Jimmy during spring training or the season itself. Hired originally by John Schuerholz, he is presently a special assistant with the Atlanta Braves. First we trade insults, and then it's down to talking about whatever comes up. I can't think of a time that

I walked away from a discussion with Fregosi without learning some-thing. He left Philadelphia the same way he came aboard: head held high, chest out, and a confidence in his ability unmatched by anyone I've known in this business. This man is the ultimate professional, and the amazing run he put together with that colorful bunch of players in 1993 remains an irreplaceable memory for us all.

TERRY FRANCONA WAS next in line. If Felske was a good man in the wrong place, Francona turned out to be the right man at the wrong time. Lee Thomas had taken a liking to Francona, viewing this bright young baseball mind as part of the wave of the future. And even though youth and inexperience hadn't worked out with Leyva, Thomas was ready to cast his lot with another first-time major-league manager. After all, Francona had enjoyed success at the minor-league level. In guiding the Double-A Birmingham Barons, a farm club of the Chicago White Sox, from 1993 to 1995, he'd posted a 223-203 record and in 1993 was named Southern League Manager of the Year as well as *Baseball America*'s Minor League Manager of the Year. In 1994, *Baseball America* named him their top managerial candidate. He had another distinction that year, managing some guy who was taking a leave from his prior profession and trying to play baseball. As Michael Jordan's manager, Francona did every-thing he could to help him successfully change careers. However, it didn't take long for Jordan to decide to head back to the NBA, win-ning his championships on the hardwood.

Terry is the ideal modern manager. He thoroughly understands computers and how statistics and the information revolution have changed the game. And he was a great face for the Phillies organi-zation during a particularly lean time. Always calm and cheerful, the man we all called "Tito" was able to show up every day with a positive attitude, doing the best he could to make bad teams com-petitive. He was tested immediately with a *really* bad team, during his first season in 1997. In fact, that squad was so bad that it was being compared with the worst in the history of the game—Whitey Ashburn's 1962 Mets. At one point, from June 6th to July 10th, the

Phillies went 3-25! Yes, we actually were that inept not so long ago. By the end of June 1997, the Phillies were 23-56, and 100 losses seemed incvitable. Comparative stories about the Mets' 120-loss season were coming up constantly in the media. Nevertheless, Francona and his staff remained calm, providing our first real insight into his personality and leadership ability. The team would go 45-38 during the final three months of the season, finishing over .500 for August and September. Although their final record was 68-94, dead last in the NL East, it could have been a whole lot worse.

Everyone starts out calling Francona by his given name, Terry. However, he soon becomes Tito because he wants to be called that, and is proud of the nickname. His father, Tito Francona, was an excellent major-league ballplayer who played briefly with the Phillies in 1967. Terry grew up around the game, getting to know his father's teammates and becoming familiar with life in the clubhouse at an early age. Terry himself became a tremendous prospect, projected as a potential major-league star. He was the number-one pick of the Montreal Expos in 1980, and the 22nd overall selection in that draft. In Terry's final season at Arizona, he won the Golden Spikes Award, emblematic of the best college player in the country. His Wildcats team won the College World Series that year, and he was named the tournament's most outstanding player. Francona made his major-league debut in 1981, and during that infamous division series against the Phillies, he went 4-12 (.333). However, injuries to both knees sidetracked his career, and he never realized his potential as a player, bouncing from team to team—the Cubs, Reds, Indians, and Brewers—before retiring in 1990. He might have felt sorry for himself, but that just wasn't in his makeup. Former teammates invariably described Tito as a fun-loving guy with a great sense of humor, but also as a serious student of the game. Forced to ride the bench for the latter part of his career, he spent a lot of time watching and learning from his managers and coaches.

Tito still enjoys making fun of himself and his exploits on the diamond. For example, he likes to tell the story of a pinch-hitting appearance one afternoon at Wrigley Field. The shadows already had passed the mound, and it was not an ideal time of the day to hit. He was sent up to face Nolan Ryan, a Ryan in his prime who liked to pitch late into games. His fastball was intimidating and his curveball just about unhittable. So Francona devised a game plan to go up there and look for a fastball on the first pitch. Ryan went into that big, high leg kick of his that was followed by a loud grunt as he released the ball. Wanting to make sure to get his bat started early enough to hit that fastball hard, Tito did just that.

The only problem was that Ryan had thrown a curveball that had a 12-to-six rotation. Francona took a mighty, belt-high swing at a pitch that wound up in the dirt, missing it by a foot or more. Now Ryan was the ultimate competitor. He never changed facial expressions and was all business. Tito said he could hear the crowd erupt in laughter at his swing and never will forget the sight of the stoic Ryan turning his back to home plate, his broad shoulders shaking in what actually appeared to be laughter. He couldn't contain himself, and his usual stone face split into an ear-to-ear grin that stunned his teammates. Ryan then turned around and finished off Francona with two more pitches. Terry dragged his bat back to the dugout, replacing it in the bat rack along with his helmet. Then he dejectedly took his customary seat on the bench, glimpsing out of the corner of his eye his own teammates' amusement at what they had just witnessed. It's typical of Francona that he can still tell this story, bragging that he has to be the only player ever to make the great Lynn Nolan Ryan laugh on a baseball diamond. And that strikeout is preserved on a video that Francona proudly shows to friends.

Francona was fired by GM Ed Wade on the final day of the 2000 season. Seeing a manager fired is always a difficult experience because all of them invest so much time and effort in their jobs. But the bottom line is that they are generally only as good as their players. Tito got the news on a steamy Sunday morning in Miami before the Phillies were to play the Marlins in the final game of a season in which they would finish a dismal 65-97. Every manager has his own way of leaving the stage, and Francona and his staff decided they would stay and manage the final game. As the team bus arrived at what was then Joe Robbie Stadium, we all knew what had happened and wondered what it would be like in the clubhouse. I had

a manager's show to record and wondered what we might do to fill
the time, assuming that there was no way Francona would want to
do it. Walking into his office, I found Tito seated behind his desk as
usual, no longer exhibiting the upbeat personality I'd come to know.
His normally playful eyes were red from the tears shed that tough
morning. We just looked at each other, and then he said, "Guess we
have a show to do."

I remember suggesting that I'd find a way to fill the time, but he
insisted, "No, let's do it." So I sat down and started recording. About
halfway through the first segment, he started to talk about all the
people who had been so special to him and how much he'd appreciated their help. Then Tito lost it, and that was the end of the show.
I still have the disk of what we were to able to air that day. And to
the credit of this remarkable man, a half hour later he was out on
the field, seated beside me on a couple of high stools, doing a
pregame show for TV. We'd now had some practice containing our
emotions, so this one went off without a hitch, and he provided
some great stuff for the telecast.

Following the game, Francona and two of his coaches, Brad Mills
and Chuck Cottier, got into a rental car and headed to Florida's west
coast to play golf and get away from the media attention. I was a little upset that they left behind the final member of our normal on-
the-road golf foursome—*me*. But unlike a lot of managers who get
fired and fade into oblivion, this was only the start for Francona. He
worked for the Indians in 2001, then was bench coach for the
Rangers in 2002 and the Athletics in 2003. After Grady Little was
fired by the Red Sox after their 2003 loss to the Yankees in the American League Championship Series, Theo Epstein, the young general
manager of the Sox, took a chance on Francona. It's turned into one
of baseball's great stories. In his first season in Boston, the Red Sox
were down to the Yankees 0-3 in the ALCS. That's when all that positive energy and patience that Francona had built up over the years
came into play. (Plus, of course, the bats of "Big Papi" and Manny
Ramirez. He now had a lot of good players.) The Sox were down to
their final strike, then rallied and won. They went on to win three
more. That, followed by a World Series win over the Cardinals, put

an end to the 86-year championship drought in Boston and made Francona a hero throughout New England. They since have added a second World Series trophy, further boosting his popularity.

I'm not going to say that any of us foresaw this much success for Terry Francona, but there is not a person knowing him who didn't have that wish. Always gracious and giving, he's a guy who paid his dues through a series of professional and physical tribulations and managed to come out on the bright side.

Probably surprising to those who don't know him well, he remains a terminal needler and practical joker. Any time spent with him can be fun—and unpredictable. In case you ever play golf with him, make sure you check your bag on every tee. There is nothing he enjoys more than taking the moment when all eyes are looking down the fairway to employ his favorite stealth tactic. While his opponents are hitting their tee shots, he's loosening the strap holding their golf bags. He then loves to roar off first, listening to the sounds of the bags crashing to the course behind him, and the accompanying comments. He will always play the innocent, but there is no doubt about who caused the stoppage of play. It's a side of Francona I wish more Phillies fans had seen.

ED WADE AND the Phillies organization had come to the point where something had to be done to win back the enthusiasm of Philadelphia's fans. Throughout this traditionally great baseball city, the club had become a distant second in fan support behind the Eagles, with the Flyers and 76ers also cutting into their base. Attendance was down as the losses piled up. The team remained a few years away from the dream of a new revenue-producing ballpark, with seasons remaining in unpopular Veterans Stadium. It wasn't that the Vet was so terrible. Actually, it was a good place to watch a game. But the incessant drumbeat of negativity about the ballpark by the media and the Phillies' co-tenant, the Eagles, had made a new park a necessity. The game had evolved into a business that necessitated increased revenues to deal with free agency and out-of-control long-term guaranteed contracts. Ticket prices could only go up so much. Clearly, the answer was to own your own ballpark and find a way to keep as much of the resulting revenue as possible.

An idea that had begun to take shape late in 2000 was that one way to get excitement back into Philadelphia baseball was to bring back to town a man who defined intensity and dedication, and put him back in a Phillies uniform. Who better than Larry Bowa to change the culture of this laid-back, settle-for-mediocrity team? Ed Wade made the decision, understanding that it might eventually turn out to be a problem. As I'd discussed with Lee Thomas years before, Bo is an institution in Philadelphia and has earned that distinction. If things worked out, everything would be fine. If they didn't, and a change had to be made, look out. And no one knew this better than Wade.

So Bowa was hired to replace Francona and be the new Phillies manager for 2001. His first season produced a record of 86-76 as the Phillies finished second behind the Braves, and Bo was named National League Manager of the Year. Attendance went up a little, but the enthusiasm level for baseball was starting to move unmistakably upward. A new ballpark and all the potential that came with it were on the horizon. Vuk and I used to kid Bowa all the time. "Hey, don't mess this up," we'd tell him. "We want to go to that new ballpark together." On flights, Vuk and I used to occupy the first two seats on the left in first class, and Bowa would sit on the aisle in row two on the right. We could hear everything he said, and Vuk used to tell me not to answer him when he would start talking about the negative vibrations he felt around the club. "Don't fire him up," Johnny would remind me. "It will only make things worse."

The great relationship between them—manager and trusted coach—continued as Vukovich attempted to take care of the clubhouse. Although a no-nonsense guy himself, Vuk tried hard not to alienate the group of incredibly sensitive players who were in that room. It was a tough balancing act, and almost impossible. How Bowa felt about things was written all over his face. A typical exchange between those two would go something like this. We would be on the airplane, and Bowa would be hot under the collar about something that had happened during the preceding game. He would start mumbling about it, loud enough for Vuk to hear him. Finally Johnny would say, "Larry [putting a lot of emphasis on it, because he rarely called Bo "Larry"], you're a fine little manager, so just keep doing it your way. And since you are my boss, I'll do whatever you say." To which Bowa would reply," I'm *your* boss? Who the %$#&* are you kidding, Vuk? You know I work for you!" It always made me and others around them laugh, and it was a great tension breaker. The irony of Vuk being the cool-headed one in a discussion was as priceless as it was rare.

I think reports of Bowa's temper and alleged browbeating of players were excessive. If anything, as the years went on, Bo really made an effort to keep more things inside. That wasn't really good for him—or anyone else. It may be that he was so wary of his reputation that he tried too hard to go the other way. But the fire and passion remained, and the group of players he'd inherited just didn't respond. Yes, they came close to getting to the postseason, but tension was always percolating right below the surface. A lot of it was the fault of some players who, although talented, were simply soft and unable to stand the heat of playing in Philadelphia, especially for this particular manager. We'd always feared that Bo might have a short shelf-life because in today's climate the players will always win out when a lot of them don't like their manager. The hammer wielded by a guy like Dallas Green in 1980 is a thing of the past. So, as the players kept whining about Bowa's tough demeanor to the front office (they should have seen him in prior seasons), the writing was starting to appear on the wall. Still, Bowa managed to make it to the new ballpark.

In 2004, the Phillies were a team with a lot of injuries. They hung in there and competed, but once again came up short. As the season progressed and the lobbying in the clubhouse continued, the media started being used by those who wanted Bowa gone. Stories surfaced that the decision already had been made, and that Bowa would be let go after the final game of the season. With two weeks remaining, he asked for a meeting with the front office. He was told that he was not about to be fired. But an uneasy atmosphere remained around the club, and the tension was palpable. On Saturday morning before the next-to-last game of the season, the local papers were filled with stories that Bowa would soon be gone. In this instance, it wasn't the media's fault. Somebody who knew something was leaking this stuff. When I went to the ballpark that afternoon and entered Bowa's office to do the pregame show, I wondered what his mood would be like. Not surprisingly, he was visibly agitated. I had seen this many times before, but this time it was different. It was a combination of resignation and righteous indignation that he would be subjected to this stuff after almost 25 years in a Phillies uniform.

Bo asked me what I thought was going on. Since I wasn't privy to that kind of inside information and didn't want to know anyway, I told him the truth. My feeling is, if you don't know, you never need to lie. And I honestly didn't know if he was going to be fired. But I added that if I were Larry, I'd sure as hell pick up the phone and find out. We did the show quickly, without a lot of our normal, off-the-air conversation. I left his office and went upstairs to prepare for the game. I learned later that he'd had a stormy session with the media about the stories in the press. Then he picked up the phone, called Ed Wade, and said they needed to talk. Ed came down and revealed that he was going to make a change, but asked Bowa to manage the final two games. That wasn't going to happen. He took off the uniform with the number 10 for the last time and left the ballpark. (For those final two games, coach Gary Varsho would be acting manager.)

I heard the news about five o'clock as it started to spread like wildfire around the press box. I just wanted to be alone with my thoughts. We had come full circle from two young guys starting out in the major leagues to the almost-inevitable day when a manager gets fired. But this was different. Larry Bowa was the manager being let go, and it didn't sit right with me, even though it was tough to fault Ed Wade. There was enough blame to go around—from those weak, whining players who'd campaigned for his dismissal, to the front-office people who couldn't keep their mouths shut and gleefully leaked the news of his imminent departure. And, of course, there was Bowa himself. He would always have trouble adapting to players with more natural talent who didn't think and work and live the game the way he did. The times definitely had changed. The

Phillies were in their new ballpark, getting a lot better. The fans were back at the games, starting to really like the team. But one of the most popular players ever to wear Phillies pinstripes had just been fired, and it was time to turn the page. Only this time, for some of us, it was a lot harder to move on.

NOBODY KNEW BETTER than Ed Wade that he had a big job on his hands. Having just fired one of the most dominant figures in Phillies history, he had to find a new man to lead his ballclub. Wade was convinced that the Phillies were close to taking the final step to the postseason, but he didn't think they were going to get there with Bowa. So the managerial search began and ended with a guy who had been around the past few years. The Phillies had been down this road before when a change in the dugout brought with it a sweeping change in personalities. Fiery Lee Elia for laid-back John Felske. Emotional and intense Larry Bowa after Terry Francona. I don't know that Ed set out to bring in a man who would be the anti-Bowa in personality, but that's what happened.

Charles Fuqua Manuel really is the poster boy of the baseball lifer. He had become a part of the organization in 2003, when Wade hired him as a special assistant. Charlie was an experienced baseball man with no ties to the Phillies. Sometimes a GM needs somebody who has no personal stake in the players being discussed. It's human nature for someone to try to protect a player he may have signed and brought through the organization. But a fresh set of eyes can be invaluable in the unscientific world of analyzing talent. That was what Manuel brought to the table. Wade could send Charlie to watch a minor-league team for a few days and get an honest report on what the organization had down there—or, more importantly, didn't have. Manuel was a likeable man who had lived the minor-league life. He knew how to relate to those whose careers were dedicated to showing young men what it takes to get to the majors, and to the players themselves.

Wade interviewed a number of qualified people for the job and finally settled on Manuel. Yet from the first day, Charlie was under siege for reasons totally out of his control. He had been a successful minor- and major-league coach and a manager in the Cleveland Indians organization. One of his protégés was a mule-strong Illinois farm boy named Jim Thome. Thome became a star player with the Indians and now just happened to be with the Phillies. The free-agent signing of Thome had been the best thing to happen to Philadelphia baseball since Pete Rose. The town was excited just thinking about what the big slugger could do in a Phillies uniform. So when Manuel was hired to work for Wade, there was speculation that it had been a part of the Thome signing. Some even felt that Thome wouldn't have come to Philadelphia without Manuel getting a job, or that Manuel was around as Thome's personal hitting guru and confidant. All of this was nonsense, but it didn't stop the drumbeat of those predisposed to equating the hiring of Manuel as manager to his connection with Thome.

Then there was Jim Leyland. Leyland had walked away from his contract with the Rockies, citing "burnout." He wanted to spend more time with his family and get away from the grind for a while. So the man who had successfully led the Pirates to postseason play and the Florida Marlins to a world championship kept his name in circulation through a scouting job for the Cardinals. Now he was getting the itch to manage again, and Wade decided to bring him to Philadelphia for an interview. Leyland quickly became a talk-show favorite, and for good reason. He had a proven track record and sounded a lot like Bowa. Leyland felt the clubhouse needed an infusion of new blood. There were too many dead-bodied guys (a nicer term than he used to define certain players), and they had to go. Tough talk always resonates with the passionate Philadelphia baseball fans, many of whom decided he was the man for the job. Ed Wade wasn't one of them, and that's all that mattered.

So genial Charlie Manuel came on board as the Phillies' new manager. Before he knew it, he had a double whammy to face. He hadn't managed a game with his new team when Leyland signed on to manage the Detroit Tigers. All they did was go out and advance to the World Series in Leyland's first season. The second-guessers were having a field day. Couple this with Manuel's seemingly rural

Virginia background and slow, deliberate mannerisms, and he was behind the eight-ball from day one.

One of the first things you learn about Charlie is that he doesn't lack confidence in his baseball ability. He especially prides himself on handling players and the clubhouse, and on his people skills. He felt *that* was priority one with the dysfunctional team he'd inherited. My first conversation with him occurred during spring training of 2003. The Phillies had paid a visit to Cleveland in 2002 during interleague play, when Charlie was the Indians' manager. Larry Andersen made a point the first day, at what was then called Jacobs Field, to take me behind home plate to meet longtime Indians trainer (and Pennsylvania native) Jim Warfield, nicknamed "Waffle." Larry had played with the Indians and knew that Warfield was a fanatical fan of Penn State and Joe Paterno. So "L.A." felt we had to meet. I spent about 20 minutes talking PSU football with Jim, who seemed to enjoy this opportunity to discuss the subject with another rabid fan. Later that summer, Warfield was in the clubhouse and was struck on the head by a falling equipment trunk. Initially, he appeared to be OK, but later he suffered a brain hemorrhage and died. So when I walked up to Manuel for the first time, I thought I'd bring up the fact that I'd met Warfield the previous year. I'd heard that he and Charlie were very close. Manuel smiled at the memory of his friend and went right into stories about Warfield and his love of Penn State. It was at that moment that I remember thinking, "This guy is real. He doesn't know me from the man in the moon, and we're standing here talking like old friends." And this was not an easy subject for Manuel, because he still was affected by the loss of someone he'd grown close to.

That truly is the essence of Charlie Manuel. He is a real person, comfortable in his own skin and totally in love with baseball. He is one of the greatest storytellers I've ever encountered in a business full of them. If you want to talk baseball, he's your man. His memory is amazing. He can remember names, places, and game situations in detail. I love to sit and listen to him tell stories about Ted Williams and his old manager, the legendary Billy Martin. And Manuel likes nothing more than a good belly laugh.

But somehow the Manuel we were getting to know and admire wasn't the same guy being portrayed to the fans. This wasn't being done by the people who covered the team on a regular basis, who also found him to be friendly and accommodating, respectful of what they needed as journalists. No, it was a handful of jerks who were spending their air time making fun of Manuel's inability to articulate his point of view in front of a camera or into a microphone. When he gets into an interview situation, Charlie can become defensive, careful to measure his words. As a result, he can come off as rambling and less than coherent. But if one can get past his halting delivery, the explanation he gives for what happened during a game is honest and fair. Still, it's a far cry from what people see from him when the lights are off and the cameras are put away. He's had to deal with this misconception from day one—that he is a country bumpkin who has no clue.

Charlie does a pregame radio show every day. He knows it's part of the job and that the fans want to hear what he has to say. He doesn't particularly like to sit with a microphone in his face and have to answer questions, but I think we have developed a good give-and-take over the past few years. The show can be entertaining at times, but not always on purpose. If we have to address a touchy situation, I will go over it with him before we start and see what he is thinking and how much he wants to say. I've done that with every manager. We will not duck the issue, but there is no need to belabor it. I try to protect the manager, and if I think something happens during the show that should be edited or redone, we do it, though that's been rare.

I bring this up because there was an incident early in Charlie's career here that made me aware of how certain people were gunning for him. They were just looking for a reason for him to fail. Charlie was an American League guy. In the AL, double-switches are not a big part of the game because of the designated hitter. But in the NL, with the pitcher normally in the nine-hole, managers do have to double-switch, and it is a big part of many games. Early in his first year in Philadelphia, there were a couple of occasions that possibly called for a double-switch. Like almost everything in baseball, there were pros and cons, but somehow it became a popular belief that he didn't know anything about the double-switch. The reasoning was that Manuel is an American League guy and just couldn't comprehend it. It not only became a big deal in Philadelphia, it gained a life of its own in the national media. There are so many talk shows now that are focused on sports, and one question was on every host's list: "How come Charlie Manuel doesn't know anything about the double-switch?" This would come from guys who hadn't even seen a Phillies game, and were getting their information from who knows where.

One day we were doing a show from his cramped visiting manager's office at Wrigley Field. During the show, Charlie said something about a double-switch and then added, "but you know I don't know anything about double-switching anyway." He was smiling as he said it, and I knew he was having a little fun with his critics, trying to make light of it. Although I remember thinking that his response had the potential for trouble, I knew that he was kidding, and imagined that it would be taken that way after the show was aired. How naive I was. We found out quickly enough that a radio station had picked up on the audio and was playing it over and over. They were mocking Manuel and saying it proved their point that he knew nothing about the double-switch. They couldn't really have believed it. But if he added to their negative mantra, it also served as a wake-up call for Charlie. He had to be careful with his words, because there were people out there just waiting for him to slip up and make him look foolish. I believe this hurt him early in his Philadelphia experience and made him even more cautious when there were cameras and microphones around.

I've really gotten to know Charlie well because of the pregame show and the hours and hours we've spent in his office, talking about baseball and life. He has many interests and loves to share them, and he's not always the mild-mannered "Uncle Charlie" that he's sometimes thought to be. He just believes in doing things behind closed doors, not out in the open for show. More than once I've been asked to leave his office while a coach rounds up a player who needs a little one-on-one with the manager. When the door reopens and we are allowed back inside, he will pick up where we left off, rarely discussing what just happened. But rest assured, the situation had been taken care of. The few public instances, notably with Jimmy Rollins last season, were quickly settled with no hard feelings.

One of the best things about what happened to the Phillies in 2008 was the fans' reaction to Manuel. It can take some time in our city, but if you hang in there and don't show weakness, you have a chance to win over our demanding fans. Slowly but surely, they started to understand what the players, many media members, and the front office already knew. Charlie was the perfect man for this team. The players loved him and would do anything for him. Since he always had their back, that provided another reason to win for him. And as for the attacks, even-tempered Charlie would simply reply, "I've seen a lot worse in my life." Surviving cancer and other serious health problems are only a part of it.

When the Phillies beat Washington in the next-to-last game of the season for the NL East title, the celebration in the clubhouse and on the field was spontaneous and raucous. Hopefully, there would be even better days ahead. In that late-afternoon chill, the players, their families, and all the rest of us enjoyed the Phillies' dramatic win and the chance to move on and play Milwaukee in the division series. Players were using the public-address system to thank the fans for their support. Cheers rained down upon their heroes from the many who had stayed long after the game. Then it started. Low at first, but rising in a steady crescendo until it could be heard all over South Philadelphia, fans were chanting, "Char-lie! . . . Charlie! . . . Char-lie!" Could it be they were calling for this man who had been vilified so recently? Suddenly, he came up the dugout steps with that hobbling gait caused by the wear and tear of so many years in the game and the physical ailments he'd overcome. The crowd continued the chant, and Manuel doffed his cap and waved, a huge grin splitting his face.

This scene would be repeated a few more times as the magic postseason of 2008 culminated in that cold night in October when Manuel once again was serenaded with delirious chants. As he held the World Series trophy aloft, he said, "Hey, Philadelphia, this championship is for you." And, of course, he was right—the title was finally for the fans. But Ed Wade also had been right. He knew his man. And as he rode down Broad Street on that beautiful October afternoon, resplendent in his pinstripe suit, looking more like a lawyer than a baseball lifer, Charlie Manuel had won another battle. Holding the World Series trophy on high, he now was adored by the toughest fans in sports.

CHAPTER 8

Our Barnum of the Vet

THERE'S SOMETHING SPECIAL about the opening day of a baseball season. Of course, it coincides with the anticipation of warm weather. There is the sense of a new beginning as the ground thaws and the trees sprout their leaves. The grass is green and the flowers smell sweeter. Baseball and spring arrive together. There is nothing like the sound of the crack of the bat when you haven't heard it in months. Or the unmistakable pop when a baseball hits a glove. I'm sure in other sports they also look forward to the beginning of each season as a moment when time stands still and memory meets anticipation. But for me, there's nothing else like the start of a new baseball season.

Opening Day at Citizens Bank Park, whatever the hour, is something to see. Normally, there will be a choir singing the National Anthem. A huge American flag is unfurled in the outfield. And the players have recently started the tradition of making their way to the home team's first-base dugout from center field, flanked by rows of fans. It's quite an impressive sight. However, it will never match my memories of those openers at Veterans Stadium when the delivery of the season's first pitch wouldn't come, as it does now, from a special guest. Back then all eyes would be trained skyward, or at some remote point of the old oval. Every year was a new adventure. The fun would start on Opening Day and continue throughout the year. It was all presided over by our own supreme ringmaster, a man with boundless imagination who could have been a lineal descendant of P.T. Barnum.

Bill Giles came to Philadelphia in 1969, sharing everyone's anticipation of the opening of a spacious, spectacular new multipurpose
stadium at Broad Street and Pattison Avenue. Bill's father, Warren,
had been president of the National League from 1951 to 1969. Pre-
viously, the elder Giles had been president and general manager of
the Cincinnati Reds for five years, so Bill grew up around the game.
His home base was that field of dreams, Crosley Field, and the team
he rooted for, the Reds. Bill had started his own career working with
teams in the Red's minor-league system before moving to the ex-
pansion Houston Colt .45's, later to become the Astros. While gain-
ing valuable administrative experience, Giles looked forward to
their move into an exciting new facility called the Astrodome. It was
already being touted as the "Eighth Wonder of the World."

To young Bill Giles it presented dazzling challenges and opportunities. It was here that he earned his reputation for merging baseball
with showmanship, like a latter-day Barnum. What a setting to work
with! Giles' most spectacular achievement was an "exploding"
scoreboard. The renown he gained in Houston helped him land a
position with the Phillies as vice-president, business operations. And
Philadelphia baseball, enhanced by a new stadium of its own, was
about to experience a tsunami of innovation.

Giles loved Opening Day, subscribing to the theory that its significance really was unique to our sport. His new title encompassed a
good deal more, but at heart Giles was a PR man and publicist, his
goal to direct as much attention as possible to the Phillies. On Opening Day 1971, Giles had the season's first ball dropped from a helicopter to catcher Mike Ryan. It was fun to watch, if not as much of a
headline-grabber as some of Giles' subsequent stunts that would forever mark the Vet as probably the most entertaining venue in sports.

Many of them, especially throughout the 1970s, had their birth in
Giles' tiny first-floor office. That's where he would convene his
weekly Tuesday-morning staff meetings. We had a very small front
office in those days, so the meetings consisted of only about 10 people. We used to jockey for seats. I always tried to get the corner of a
very comfortable couch where I could position myself behind someone who had turned his chair at a perfect angle. That way I could

hide behind him and sleep. During almost every meeting, Bill would toss a rolled-up piece of paper at me and tell me to wake up and contribute something. To this day, I hate meetings—in my opinion, there is so much wasted time. But Larry Shenk and I were part of the group, and had to try to act interested. More than anything else, we wanted to limit requests for the use of players' time. And since we were the ones who had to put the often-unrealistic plans of others into action, we did our best to tone them down. Although we viewed ourselves as the voice of reason, to some around Giles, in the wondrous words of Spiro Agnew, we seemed more like the "nattering nabobs of negativism." But we did share a front-row seat at the circus. Speaking of politics, I still remind Bill that after our election day meeting in 1972, he suddenly blurted out, "And make sure you all vote for Nixon because this country will be in real trouble if McGovern wins."

Giles was looking for a more spectacular way to deliver the first ball in 1972. His goal was to sell out the 56,371-seat Vet (later expanded to 63,000 for baseball) for the opener, and he was convinced that he had come up with a winner. "Kiteman," later to be known as "Kiteman I" because of his parade of successors, was to be the headliner. Bill had read an article about this guy who jumped off cliffs with a kite on his back. He had him come up to Philadelphia, where he agreed to do his act at the opener. Kiteman told Giles he'd need an 80-foot ramp to be built in the outfield. He would ski down it, go airborne, and land at the mound with the ball. So Bill decided to build the ramp, at a cost of $5,000. The first time he brought up the idea at a staff meeting, Shenk and I just looked at each other. One of us, probably Larry, summoned up the courage to suggest to Bill that the start of the season might be delayed by an unfortunate accident, let alone a fatality. Giles calmly replied that since this guy had assured him he could do it, that settled it. The plan was put into motion.

Unfortunately, it turned out that a labor problem between the owners and the players' association forced the season to start a little late. Meanwhile, Giles received a call from his Kiteman that he had to go to Mexico to teach the president of that country how to water-ski. (I'm not making this up.) He was booked and couldn't get out of it. Did that bother Giles? No way. As he later described it in his entertaining book, *Pouring Six Beers at a Time, and Other Stories from a Lifetime in Baseball,* "We were stuck. We had advertised heavily: 'Come see Kiteman!'" So Bill, quick-thinking as always, managed to come up with a substitute, a guy named Richard Johnson from Cypress Gardens, Florida, who said he would give it a try.

As luck would have it, Opening Night was cool and very windy. And when the wind swirled around the Vet, it was tough enough with balls hit in the air. What would it do to the trajectory of our Kiteman? I was in the scoreboard control room, and Giles was in the back of the room with a walkie-talkie. He was communicating with Paul Callahan from our sales department, who was supposed to cue Johnson to start his descent. Don Baker gave the intro on the PA, and organist Paul Richardson played some tension-building music to help make the moment. But Kiteman didn't move. Baker and Richardson tried it again, and still nothing. Even Bill Giles was verging on panic. The crowd was getting restless, and the inevitable boos had begun. Bill yelled into his walkie-talkie to Callahan, "What's the matter? Doesn't he hear the intro?" To which Callahan replied something like, "Yeah, he hears it, but he looks like he's scared to death." Denny Lehman and I just sat there shaking our heads. Hadn't Larry Shenk warned him? Ever the optimistic showman, Bill kept pleading for someone to just push this guy, or something.

Suddenly, our substitute Kiteman regained his courage and started down that long ramp on the journey that was supposed to take him to the mound. Unfortunately, about halfway down a gust of wind blew him sideways, and he crashed into the 600-level seats instead. I feared that the poor guy must be badly hurt, if not dead. It was that violent an impact. But the crowd just started to boo again. Then, like a phoenix rising from the ashes, Richard Johnson suddenly got up, took the baseball—which had been taped to his kite—and attempted to throw it all the way to the mound. Naturally, it went sideways into one of the bullpens, and the fans had something new to boo about. But at least we hadn't killed anyone, and we could finally start to play ball. There is a really funny clip in the Phillies' 1972 highlight film of Frank Rizzo watching Kiteman nearly splatter himself. The mayor's look of anticipation had been replaced by one between "What just happened in my stadium?" and "How do I get away from this disaster?" Which summed up the way a lot of us felt during the endless minute or so that it took for Johnson to somehow deliver the season's first ball.

One way or another, even if unscripted, Giles had a way of entertaining a crowd. And he was nothing if not tenacious. There would be Kiteman II, III, IV, and V. Kiteman II had a wider ramp, launched successfully, and looked like he was going to make it this time. However, his flight landed in shallow center field, and he ran the rest of the way with the first ball. Despite such initiative, he also got booed. The efforts of his three successors were better performed, but a lot less fun.

WHEN A TEAM receives a copy of its home schedule for the season, there are certain dates when it would be preferable to be on the road. It's just tough to draw crowds on those dates, and there's little you can do about it. Back in the days of the spacious Vet, Easter Sunday was such a day, when many fans would simply prefer to stay home. The promotions department always wanted the club to be on the road—or at least have Easter fall in March, before the start of the baseball season. In 1973, Easter Sunday was in April, the Phillies were scheduled to be at home, and that was that. We needed a crowd-pleasing promotion.

During one of our winter staff meetings in Bill Giles' office, a lot of ideas had been kicked around. I don't remember very many of them since I was probably half-asleep, but one got my attention. Someone had suggested that a softball game between members of the media and a group of Playboy Bunnies might be a good draw. Imagine, live Playboy Bunnies cavorting on the Vet AstroTurf on Easter Sunday. Thankfully, someone in the meeting, probably David Montgomery, nixed such a likely PR disaster. The man had decision-making potential even at that point in his career. After all, we were promoting Phillies baseball as a family venue, especially at Eastertime.

Finally, a more traditional idea was concocted. How about some kind of big Easter-egg hunt involving lots of kids? Now that sounded a lot more logical. Of course, Bill Giles didn't think it was original enough to put people in the seats. And since he had become so fond of aerial shows, he came up with another classic—the "World's Highest Jumping Easter Bunny." The Phils would convince some poor sap to put on a rabbit suit and get into a hot-air balloon. That balloon would then "jump" out of the Vet and land somewhere in the Delaware Valley. That's how we would promote the stunt. Bill would come up with some valuable prize for the first person to find and approach this hopefully still-breathing "bunny." It sounded like great fun, at least to some members at the meeting. Once again, Larry Shenk and I rolled our eyes, but already dubbed the "negative twins," as usual we were ignored.

The promotions department, led by a wonderful man named Frank Sullivan, who had come over from Connie Mack Stadium, now had to find someone to fill the suit. His first idea was to get a local DJ and have his radio station promote it. However, a well-publicized accident had recently occurred with a hot-air balloon in a radio-station promotion down south, and that discouraged any local personality from volunteering to be our bunny. So Giles did one of things he was best at. He took a look around the front office and came up with a volunteer—the aforementioned Paul Callahan from our sales department. Now I don't want to disparage lefties, although some left-handed pitchers do tend to be a little off-center, but Paul was a lefty and fit the part. This guy we all called "Calhoun" was living at the time in a storage area on the fourth floor of the Vet. It was not temperature-controlled, and when it got hot, the place was smoking. When it was cold, Calhoun needed extra blankets. So he seemed a natural candidate to be Bill's bunny. Nobody asked Bill just how he convinced Callahan to do it. Bill Giles was not the kind of man to threaten anyone with "Do this, or it's your job." Anyway, one thing Callahan failed to do was to sign some release papers handed him by the front office. He never even read them. Well, how much could a guy who lived in a storage room have to leave in his will, anyway?

The big day arrived, and once again those tricky winds were swirling around the Vet. They hadn't even practiced with a real hot-air balloon. Instead, the staff had released regular-size balloons to test the wind currents. We were told that some had gone out of the stadium according to plan, but others had been impaled on the roof lights. No matter, Paul Callahan put on the bunny suit, his balloon was inflated near second base, and the show was on.

As everyone knows, Dan Baker still does a great job as our PA announcer. Having witnessed all kinds of wacky events, he could make the most mundane sound like a world championship fight. So he started working the crowd: "Ladies and gentlemen, you are about to witness one of the greatest shows ever seen on the East Coast, or anywhere else in the world." I'm not certain this is exactly what he said, but you get the point. He was doing his best to sell this crazy stunt. Dan continued: "Right before your eyes, the World's Highest Jumping Easter Bunny is going to jump right out of this stadium and land somewhere in the Delaware Valley. And some lucky fan is going to be rewarded with a great prize." Denny Lehman and I were in the scoreboard room as usual, just looking at each other, with that uneasy feeling that always accompanied one of Bill's stunts. We and Larry Shenk never got used to them. Dan went on: "Now we need all of you to send him off. So when I give you the cue, please start counting down from five, and the bunny will take off." Now it was getting really windy. And at the Vet, the wind would come in from the open areas in the lower levels of the stadium as well as from up high. So the count began. "Five . . . four . . . three . . . two . . . one," bellowed Baker. The balloon started to rise, and then the unforeseen occurred. The winds were coming in so strong from the lower levels that they literally were creating a wind ceiling. The balloon couldn't get any higher than 15 feet. It suddenly stopped as if it had hit a roof, and then began to descend. Lehman and I couldn't stop laughing. Fortunately, Bill Giles wasn't in the room with us. Ever the pro, Dan Baker worked up his energy level again and restarted the countdown. Same result. And then he tried it a third time.

After the first attempt the crowd was amused. The second attempt brought a few murmurs of discontent. Since this was a family-oriented crowd on an Easter Sunday, they weren't the type of fans who were given to booing. However, after the third attempt failed, the World's Highest Jumping Easter Bunny was hearing sounds normally reserved at the Vet for a multiple-strikeout victim. As the balloon's basket started to tip over, Callahan had the sense to jump out. It must have been getting pretty hot from all that propane gas. And then our bunny suddenly bolted from the area, running out of the stadium like a real rabbit. Fortunately, our backup promotion had also been put into effect—that mundane Easter egg hunt on the field. Kids roaming all over the place stopped searching to stare at that disappearing bunny and each other, wondering what else was going on. They must have some vivid memories to tell their own kids, and grandkids, about what it was like at the old Vet on that memorable Easter Sunday.

Another Giles spectacular had failed but nobody had gotten hurt, and it was another story for the ages. As for leaping Paul Callahan, he went on to greater heights, eventually becoming a successful businessman. He married a great lady, Janice Meehan, whose father, Bill Meehan, was head of the Republican Party in Philadelphia. The last time I saw him, we talked about that unforgettable Easter in 1973 and his days of calling the Vet his home. Life may have gotten a lot better for our old Calhoun, but could it be more exciting?

WHEN YOU LOOK around professional sports these days, mascots are as commonplace as three-hour games. But back in the '70s, this wasn't the case. They were pretty much confined to the colleges. However, in San Diego, there was a great act known as "The Chicken." He was never actually the mascot of the San Diego Padres, as many believe, but instead the product of a local radio station, and a welcome visitor at their games. The guy inside the costume was a comedic genius named Ted Giannoulis, a really creative crowd-pleaser. The Chicken would interact with the players, both home and visiting teams, and they responded to him as much as the fans did. He'd stride around the field and have some hilariously animated arguments with umpires. Giannoulis was so distinctive that he could even get away with being a bit off-color at times. We couldn't wait to go to San Diego to see what this guy had in store for the Phillies. Eventually, of course, The Chicken went on the road, becoming a national attraction.

For some time, no other team seemed all that interested in coming up with their own creation. I think it was a combination of the conservative nature of the sport and the idea that no one could top The Chicken's original act anyway. But, of course, this didn't faze our man Bill Giles. He was always on the cutting edge of entertainment. Because Bill himself gets such a kick out of life, the more that fans of all ages enjoy their visit to the ballpark, the better he likes it. But Bill had something very different in mind than The Chicken— just as creative but maybe more lovable. So naturally he turned to the people on *Sesame Street*.

Bill put out feelers to Bonnie Erickson and Wade Harrison, designers of the "Big Bird" character. Ungainly yet appealing, he was kind of the symbol of that remarkable TV show, intended for preschoolers yet universally popular. On their second attempt, Erickson and Harrison came back with a design and a costume that Bill really liked, and the Phillies had the makings of their own mascot. Naturally, there were a few problems. Giles now possessed a pile of green feathers punctuated by big feet, an enormous head, and a large snout. And don't forget, the club was run by Ruly Carpenter, a truly traditional baseball man. Generally, he tried to look the other way when Giles got that glint in his eye, about to unveil another of his big "ideas." But Carpenter was also cost-conscious. So now Bill had to explain why he'd already bought into a concept he couldn't guarantee would work. The price tag was $2,900, but the creators retained the copyright. For only $5,000, the Phillies could own it outright. Being a realist, Ruly agreed to the lower figure. Giles wasn't about to press his luck by pushing for the alternative. Of course, it would eventually cost a lot more to buy the copyright. The Phanatic went on to become one of the most popular mascots of all time, probably at the top today—not only the symbol of the Phillies, but very nearly of Philadelphia itself.

Naturally, the Phillie Phanatic didn't become an entertainment phenomenon because of the costume alone. Giles had to find someone to make it come to life. David Raymond was a young guy working in the mailroom. The irony was that he had gotten his job because of Ruly Carpenter. Raymond had been a punter and place-kicker on the Delaware Blue Hens football team coached by his father, the legendary Tubby Raymond. And the Carpenter family was a huge supporter of the University of Delaware and its football program. Dave was, and is, a fun guy. At the time, he was also young, athletic, and very energetic. The idea was for the Phanatic never to talk, to be a mime and express everything with his body. It was a great concept, but who could pull it off? Giles glanced at Dave Raymond and saw just what he was looking for. The rest, as they say, is history. Dave had the right instincts. He turned out to be a natural, filling that ungainly costume with personality. The moment he stepped onto the field his act simply worked, as distinctive as The Chicken's but more endearing, almost innocent—even when he sat on people's laps and squirted them with water. All in good fun. Not only kids loved him, *everyone* loved him, including visiting players, whose interaction with our mascot provided so much pleasure to the fans.

That is, almost everyone except Tommy Lasorda. The Phanatic, of course, loves props, and one of his favorites used to be a nearly life-size doll, complete with padding, wearing the authentic uniform of the Dodgers manager. When L.A. was in town, Raymond would continually run over it with that unique little all-terrain vehicle he'd adroitly ride around the Vet. During one game, Lasorda decided he'd had enough. The venerated Dodgers uniform was being desecrated by this . . . furry creature. Lasorda rushed out of the dugout, grabbed the doll, and whacked the Phanatic with it. This was no act. The players on both teams loved it, none more than Steve Sax of the Dodgers, who'd given Raymond the Lasorda uniform in the first place. If you think about it, the Phanatic has to walk (or wobble) a fine line. There he is, going throughout the stands, riling up the crowd to support their team, leading cheers, standing on top of the dugout putting the whammy on opposing batters, using and wearing all kinds of props to make fun of the visitors as well as himself. He's very much part of the game-day experience, but he has to do it in a way that doesn't intrude directly *into* the game—or really offend anybody. It takes skill and judgment to know just where to draw the comedic line.

It also takes sustained strength. The Phanatic's costume is heavy, somewhere around 40 pounds, and even heavier in the hot summer months when sweat adds to the weight. Dave occasionally would pass out and have to be revived by the ground crew behind home plate. At first, they—like the spectators—thought it was part of the act, until they realized he really needed help. Dave learned to strap ice packs to his body to keep from overheating. But, trooper that he was, the show would always go on. As the Phanatic became popular beyond even Giles' expectations, Raymond started taking it on the road, entertaining crowds throughout Philadelphia and around the country until retiring, in 1993, to start his own company. Today, Dave Raymond helps other aspiring Bill Gileses come up with their own mascots to make sports more fun for fans. But I wonder if any will ever match the originality of the Phillie Phanatic. And for Dave, it all started in the mailroom.

The Phillies are very fortunate that the Phanatic still is a top-shelf attraction, even without Raymond. He had so many commitments to fill that Tom Burgoyne gained experience as his backup Phanatic, duplicating Dave's distinctive moves and persona before he retired. Beyond filling in for special appearances at the Vet, he'd play "Mom Phanatic" or the Phanatic's girlfriend, expanding the act. Tom stepped right into the costume, and the act hasn't skipped a beat. As someone who still thinks that a lot of mascots are a waste of time, I'm fascinated by what our guy does in every game. His act is always fresh and fun, seemingly spontaneous, and I love to sit there like everyone else and enjoy it. Even Ruly Carpenter grew to like the Phanatic. And, although he no longer owns the team, he still smiles when he thinks about how Bill Giles couldn't quite work up the will to come to him and ask for the extra money just to buy a pile of feathers.

· · ·

I'LL ALWAYS BELIEVE that the greatest promotion in the history of the Vet was the one that caused the most terror and angst. As we've discussed throughout this chapter, our own "P.T. Barnum" loved aerial acts. Giles couldn't get enough of them. At the time, the greatest high-wire act was a family calling themselves "The Flying Wallendas." They were world-renowned and were led by the patriarch of the family, Karl Wallenda. Prior to 1972, Bill decided to extend an invitation to Wallenda to walk across the Vet on his cable from foul pole to foul pole. This daring feat was to be staged between games of a Sunday doubleheader. Normally, Larry Shenk and I, the negative twins, were the only ones who had doubts about an act. This time we were joined by others. But no consideration of the potential consequences could deter Bill's desire to have this death-defying show staged right in South Philadelphia.

I had made up my mind that I wasn't going to watch it. Call it chicken or overreacting or just plain panic, but that was my personal decision. What would we do, or say, if something went wrong? And there were plenty of things that day that could have conspired to make it go very wrong. If this 67-year-old man fell to the rock-hard AstroTurf, he had no chance to survive. And, while it may sound insensitive, we *did* have another game to play that day.

Our PR office was on the fourth floor of the Vet. About 50 feet from where Larry Shenk and I worked was the promotions office of Frank Sullivan. Frank had a couch that was perfect for a nap, or for just relaxing when entertaining visitors. The easiest way to make a final pregame visit to the men's room was to walk out of our office and past the door leading to Sullivan's office. In those days, I was still working in the scoreboard room. It was nearing the start of game one, so I had gathered up my stuff and was making that quick trip down the hall. I imagine there were a lot of such trips that day. As I walked past Sullivan's office, I heard a sputtering sound, like a lawnmower about to run out of gas. I can still remember the sense of amazement at what I saw in front of me. There on the couch, head back against the cushion, sat The Great Wallenda, sound asleep. What I'd heard was his snoring. I just stood there and stared. I was scared out of my skin about what we were going to do between games, and here was the star of the show in dreamland, like he didn't have a care in the world. I tried to tell myself it must be OK to relax, that everything was going to be fine, but I didn't believe it for a minute.

I only know what happened because of watching the video and talking to others who witnessed it. One of the things that could go wrong was the condition of the wire. We had just played a game, so there was no way it could be raised across the field until it ended. Then the race was on to stretch the five-eighths-inch cable from the right-field to the left-field foul pole. And since it had to be done in a hurry, there could be quite a bit of slack, even though the supporting wires held by men on the ground were pulled as tight as possible to keep Wallenda's cable taut. Now I don't know too many people who could recite the dos and don'ts of high-wire walking. But I don't think anyone would consider it a good idea to walk on a wire that wasn't tight. You sure don't want the thing swaying. But that's what happened.

Wallenda started his walk to the cheers of the crowd of over 33,000. About 15 feet into the journey, he suddenly sat down and started waving to the men below to pull on their guy wires to make them tighter and his cable more stable. These weren't professionals but people from our regular ground crew and the Vet's ushers. Once satisfied that his wire was taut enough, Wallenda slowly resumed his walk. Right over second base, *he stood on his head!* Then, right side up, he started walking again as Paul Richardson played "You'll Never Walk Alone" on the stadium organ. As I sat in the office with the TV off, I could hear the crowd start to cheer and the organ growing louder and louder. Wallenda had made it to the left-field foul pole. We had dodged another bullet with no one killed in front of all those witnesses. Eventually, even my heartbeat returned to nearly normal.

I'm told that Wallenda had a couple of beers before the walk, which may have accounted for his nap. When he met with the media afterward, he switched to a stronger form of adult beverage. I don't know if the reports of his heavy drinking were accurate or simply part of the lore, but Giles in his book recounts that he saw this fearless aerialist consume 10 ounces of scotch in about 30 minutes. For his part, Wallenda declared that his high-wire act that day had been the scariest of his career.

At least it was over and we'd never have to go through that again. Right? This turned out to be more naiveté on my part. Emboldened by such success, Bill Giles brought The Great Wallenda back on Memorial Day, 1976 as part of the year-long Bicentennial celebration. Then 71, he took a 20-minute walk that included the unfurling of an American flag. On both ends of his balancing pole he had 13-star U.S. flags. Quite a spectacle, but I didn't watch that one either.

Less than two years later, Karl Wallenda was attempting to walk between the towers of a hotel in San Juan, Puerto Rico. A gust of wind knocked him off his wire, and this incredible showman fell to his death. It seemed almost inevitable that it would happen some day. However skilled, his was such a high-risk occupation. I couldn't help thinking how it might have happened at the Vet. But my most vivid memory of Karl Wallenda will always be of him sleeping like a baby before walking from one foul pole to the other. Thanks to Giles, he put on the two best shows ever seen at our ballpark. Even those who couldn't watch them would agree.

FORTUNATELY, MOST OF Bill's promotions were less hazardous. He remains a master showman who enjoys entertainment in any form. One of my favorite photos of Bill is of him gleefully holding up the "world's largest hot dog" to honor "Charlie Frank," a popular Vet vendor (with Jay Johnstone on the other side). As a sound executive, he understood that once he could induce young fans to talk their parents into bringing them to the ballpark, we had that family hooked for life. No one in baseball has tried harder to come up with original promotions since the legendary Bill Veeck (whose autobiography was aptly subtitled *Rhymes with Wreck*). They might not always work, but Bill was never deterred.

There was, for example, the Hot Pants Patrol Duck Race. An usherette was lined up behind each duck and was supposed to shoo them toward the finish line. Unfortunately, a major storm was in the area that night, and a crash of thunder sent them scurrying throughout the Vet. The ducks, not the girls. It took a while to round them up. Then there was the time Giles somehow talked Harry and Whitey into a miniature bicycle race. That was a sight to behold as they tried to pedal these little bikes with their knees up in their faces. Later he induced our two main broadcasters to participate in an ostrich race. All they had to do was get into a cart behind each bird and then see which one won. What Bill didn't take into consideration was that such high-strung birds could get agitated by the crowd noise and start attacking the amateur jockeys riding behind them instead of racing each other. It turns out that ostriches also have a mean streak, or at least these two birds did. Well, Harry and Richie decided they wanted no part of this, and they jumped out of their seats and took off faster than Calhoun. Then the ostriches decided to spread out and greet some fans in the stands, who also departed as quickly as possible. Once again it was left to our long-suffering ground crew to take charge and help the handlers recapture their swift-footed birds and take them back to whatever was their natural habitat.

That ground crew had a lot to do during the golden age of Bill's promotions. Giles not only loved aerial acts, he was also partial to circus animals of all sizes. After all, with the combination of Astro-Turf and dirt cutouts at the Vet, any "accidents" could be readily cleaned up, right? Although normally sensitive to everyone's needs, Giles was oblivious to the potential scale of that problem for our ground crew. But those poor guys spent many a night cleaning up piles of manure after the appearance of those immense elephants and most everything else in the animal kingdom.

Every opening day or night meant a memorable act. Who could forget "Cannon Man"? Hugo Zucchini shot himself out of a cannon near second base into a net behind home plate. It was loud and spectacular, but thankfully, he walked away. And what about "The Great Monique," who rode down a wire on her bicycle from the right-field foul pole to the first-base dugout, and actually made it? Then, at another season opener, there was "Benny the Bomb." His skill was to place himself into a decorative coffin, which would then blow up. Yet, miraculously, Benny would appear out of the mist and also walk away. Well, the explosion that night was the loudest I've ever heard. Once the smoke cleared, here came Benny, staggering toward the middle of the infield like an over-served patron leaving a bar at two a.m. To this day, I don't know if he was wobbling on account of the explosion or whether it was a part of the act. The main thing is that he, too, had survived. Bill Giles had done it again, and we could begin another season without an accident.

Nor was Bill immune to discreet sex appeal. Beyond the attractive Hot Pants usherettes, he hired personable ball girls to be stationed down the lines. Everyone remembers the lovely blonde, Mary Sue Styles, a South Jersey girl from Collingswood—as nice as she was pretty. She became a local celebrity in part because Whitey liked to talk about her on TV whenever a ball went to left field, and the camera naturally would focus on her. It tested Mary Sue's pleasant composure that for a short time there was a picnic area down the third-base line. It came equipped with its own beer keg, and was sometimes rented by guys from local colleges. Let's see—beer, college boys, and Mary Sue. It had the potential to get a little crazy, but at least they were contained.

The same can't be said for the San Diego Chicken on the night he made a guest appearance at the Vet. He had a tendency to get a little out of control in that suit, and figured he could get away with just about anything. That night, The Chicken came out between innings and started wandering down the line toward Mary Sue. Suddenly, he ran after her, grabbed her, and started rolling around the warning track with her. Unfortunately, that stunt resulted in a chipped tooth for Mary Sue, but however she felt, she didn't make a fuss about it. I don't think The Chicken ever returned. As for our most popular ball girl, whom everyone called "Susie," she wound up marrying an FBI agent and moved to the D.C. area and then Atlanta, where she still makes her home. I've seen her several times over the years at Braves games, and she's still a great person with a wonderful smile. The Phillies made sure she got that tooth repaired.

. . .

IN REMEMBERING HOW different the Vet was, I keep thinking about its AstroTurf. Most players and fans would be hard-pressed to come up with a positive feature. But one thing is that it did prevent a lot of rainouts. A good many games were played that could never have been started or completed on grass and dirt. I recall some entertaining scenes during rain delays when the Zamboni machine, which we think of more in terms of ice hockey today, would come out to suck up the excess water on the turf. Drainage was not a strong point in the early days of artificial surfaces, so huge puddles would form. The Zamboni drivers were city employees, and rumor had it that one or two were inclined to hoist a few before and during rain delays. Then one of them would don his raincoat, mount the Zamboni, and go out to vacuum up the water and make the field at least passably playable again. After filling up the huge tank, he'd have the Zamboni's hose empty it over the outfield fence into some drains. This worked most of the time, but occasionally the driver would press the wrong button and the water would come out another hose and go right back into the field of play. Paul Richardson would make his organ music sound like laughter, and Denny Lehman would come up with a funny quip for the scoreboard. The crowd loved it. Whether it was simply operator error or the result of a Bud overload, some have probably wondered if Bill Giles was behind that, too.

CHAPTER 9

Sharing the Booth

I TALKED IN CHAPTER I ABOUT what my childhood was like, how I first became interested in broadcasting and baseball, and that whim of Whitey's that actually launched my career in the booth with the Phillies. In the many years since, I've worked with a remarkably diverse group of personalities and professionals. Like almost anyone fortunate enough to have a job doing what they really want, a lot of things had to go right to make it all possible—involving a lot of people. What I've called my "perfect storm" was most of all a matter of being in the right place at the right time.

As a kid growing up in rural Newtown Square, I always had some kind of summer job. My dad was a hard worker, but never made a lot of money. Besides, I wanted to have a little pocket change. I turned 15 in August 1960. Still a year away from driving, I would pedal my bike over Route 252 to the Llangollen Hills Swim Club. There I held down the prestigious post of locker-room attendant. I would clean the toilets and showers, store the members' valuables, and collect and burn trash. Yes, open incineration was not yet a crime. That was the summer I met a girl named Susan Harvey, and we started to date, or whatever two 15-year-olds did in those days. She told me her family lived on St. David's Road near Aronimink Golf Club and her father worked for WCAU Radio in Philadelphia. I remember going home and telling my mom and dad that I'd met this nice girl and she'd invited me home for dinner. When I told them her name and that her father worked for a radio station, I didn't think it was a big deal until I saw the looks on their faces. "Is her father Ed Harvey?" asked my mom. "I don't know," I replied, "I haven't met him." And that would be my first brush with celebrity and a kick-start to a taste of the broadcasting business that already had intrigued me.

In the late '50s, radio was pervasive. We were still in the age of morning variety shows that featured singers, skits, and comedy—all the things we now associate with late-night TV. And the king of local radio was Ed Harvey at WCAU 1210. Meeting his daughter was the start of a great friendship with this man who would be a huge influence on my life. My dad died suddenly of a heart attack when I was a sophomore at Penn State, and Ed had already advised me to switch my major to communications. He would see to it that I got a job at his station, at that time one of the strongest in the country. You could hear the WCAU signal hundreds of miles away.

I had no idea how this was going to happen, but Ed had a plan. I was late into my junior year at PSU when Ed called one afternoon. "What's your class schedule for tomorrow?" he asked. I told him it was pretty light. He said, "Get in your car and be at the station by three p.m. And be sure to bring your glove and spikes." Back then, I was just a few years removed from playing a lot of baseball, and could still move around a little. And the WCAU softball team was a passion for the station's general manager, Jack Downey. Now Jack was very competitive. He always wanted to win the league that was composed of radio and TV stations, along with local advertising people. Harvey said to me, "Downey doesn't like our team this year. He thinks we're too old and slow, and should get some younger players." So, he continued, "I want you to work out before our game tomorrow night. He'll see you, and you'll wind up with a job." I did as directed. It was pretty easy for a 20-year-old to get noticed, working out with a lot of 40-something guys. Ed said to leave the rest up to him. I got to see my surprised mom that night in Newtown Square, and the next morning I drove back up to Happy Valley, wondering what would happen next.

Within days, Ed was on the phone again, telling me I had a summer job. I'd already done some play-by-play basketball as well as baseball on the Penn State radio station. A month later, I was sit-

ting in the WCAU newsroom that was used by both the radio and
TV side. One by one, people like John Facenda, Herb Clarke, and
Tom Brookshier would come by and introduce themselves. The
radio side also had legendary personalities like Bob Menefee, Jack
McKinney, and Harvey. I would have the summer of my life before
returning to college.

But that was just a warmup for the following summer. My job
had been extended for another year, and now Downey had an idea.
Aerial traffic reporting had become a staple of morning and afternoon drive-time radio. Philadelphia's airwaves were filled with the
sounds of John Carlton and the ARCO Go Patrol. Carlton would fly
in a helicopter and broadcast his reports. Not to be outdone,
Downey decided to purchase a single-engine Cessna 180 Skylane
and commission his service, Traffic Alert. I can still see the green-
and-white plane with the identification on the tail, N2088X. That
tail number became very important to me because I later became a
traffic reporter. Downey and Mike Grant, then the news director,
didn't want to take a chance on one of their big-name personalities
getting killed in a plane crash. So they put me up there. Our pilot
was a guy named Dave whose other job was as a milkman. When he
would fly the plane in the mornings and afternoons, he was a little
sleepy since he had been up delivering milk since two o'clock. Because I loved airplanes, he taught me how to take off and land. One
of the more important things to know was how to contact the control tower at Philadelphia International Airport just in case something happened to him. Dave occasionally would nod off, and I'd
have to nudge him awake. But thankfully, we never had to make an
emergency landing with me at the controls.

This airplane would feature again in my budding career. Harvey
called me one day in May and said Downey had decided the team
had a good chance to win the league in 1967, and he wanted that
young kid shortstop from the newsroom to play more games. When
Harvey told him that it was a nearly four-hour drive from University
Park to Bala Cynwyd, Downey replied that they'd send the Traffic
Alert airplane to Penn State to pick me up. I'd play the game and fly
back the next day. He was that into softball. I actually did this a

couple of times, something my college buddies found hard to believe. A plane is going to fly me to Philadelphia and back just to play softball? So, one warm afternoon, three of them followed me out to the airport to see for themselves. That same airport now has a long runway that can handle jet planes loaded with Big Ten athletes. Back then, all it had was a passenger waiting room, some offices, and the control tower. After about a 15-minute delay, I was starting to get a little anxious. Then a small dot appeared near Mt. Nittany. It got bigger and bigger and sure enough was on final approach for landing. As the plane taxied toward us, it was easy to see the lettering: WCAU Radio 1210 TRAFFIC ALERT. Dave the milkman cut the engine; I picked up my equipment bag and waved to my wide-eyed, open-mouthed buddies, and ran to my personal charter. Off we went on the beautiful, one-hour trip to Philadelphia. And back to our off-campus house went my friends, still not quite believing what they had just witnessed.

The next step was to get a taxi, head to the station at City Line and Monument Avenue, and dress for the game. One June afternoon, when I arrived and headed for the newsroom to check in, a guy came running up to me, shouting, "Hey, my wife just had a baby. Would you take my car and go out and get some cigars?" The date was June 7, 1967 (6/7/67), an easy date to remember in later years. The little girl's name was Luanne. Her very proud father became my first broadcasting partner. No one would teach me more about the business. And if Whitey finally got me behind a mike, it was Andy Musser who got me into the building.

ANDY MUSSER AND I got to know each other during my first summer at WCAU. Even though my job was to write news stories, I naturally gravitated to the sports guys. Andy could see that I had a real passion for baseball. One of my lasting memories of that first summer was getting into Musser's car and heading for Connie Mack Stadium and a Phillies game. Riding in that car on many nights was Philadelphia baseball legend Jimmy Dykes. Jimmy had been a player, coach, and manager and was an amazing storyteller. He had been hired to co-host a sports-talk segment with Musser that aired in the afternoon. With his cigar ablaze, Dykes would talk about his A's teammates—men like Jimmy Foxx, Mickey Cochrane, Lefty Grove, and Al Simmons. He had actually played against Ruth and Gehrig, his A's beating that legendary Yankee team for the American League pennant in 1929. Then the A's went on to win the World Series, besting the Cubs in five. Here I was listening to this man's mesmerizing accounts of competing against and knowing the greatest players of all time. Beyond his admiration for these icons of his generation, there was one name that he respected the most. His manager had been Connie Mack. Here was this man in his 70s who had hit .327 for the great 1929 A's. Yet, when he discussed his former manager, it was always "Mr. Mack." How I loved sitting in the back seat of Andy's car, listening to Jimmy Dykes.

I moved from WCAU Radio to WBBM Radio in Chicago, then to New York and CBS Radio. Musser was making a name for himself in Philadelphia as the voice of the Eagles and 76ers. I came back to town in 1971 after a CBS layoff (unfortunately, the nature of the business), and was working for General Electric at their missile and space facility in Valley Forge. Writing news releases with little enthusiasm, I kept sending out résumés. Of course, I sent them to all the sports teams in town—Phillies, Eagles, Sixers, and Flyers—although baseball was always my preference. And one of my prized references was Andy Musser.

After I'd spent another tedious day at GE, Musser called one night. "I've got some good news for you," he said. "Larry Shenk just called me. He needs an assistant now that they are in the new ballpark, and he pulled out your résumé. He wanted to know if you were the kid I used to bring to Connie Mack Stadium with Jimmy Dykes. I not only told him you were, but that I believed you were his man." The Baron later told me how much Andy's recommendation meant. Shenk said that only a disastrous interview would have denied me the job. So—still not believing my luck—I started my career with the Phillies. But broadcasting being the transitory business it is, Andy moved on to jobs in New York and San Diego before eventually returning to Philadelphia.

By Saam had announced his retirement in 1975, after his long and distinguished career as the primary voice of the team. In 1990, he would be inducted into the Baseball Hall of Fame, winning the Ford C. Frick Award. So the search was on for a successor, and it was time for me to return the favor. I couldn't have been happier when I was asked to call Andy Musser in San Diego and see if he would be interested in applying for the job. He had done very little baseball, but it was certainly attractive to him. And I think he wanted to come back east. Although one of many to send tapes to the Phillies, Musser was hired. He worked on radio alone that year and did some TV with Harry and Whitey. It wasn't easy for him at the start because he lacked a baseball background, and he had to fit in as third man to the team's great lead broadcast team.

Then came my own big break through Whitey on that clinching afternoon in Montreal when I made my unscheduled TV debut. Now I was going to be on radio in 1977, and my partner would be my old friend from the decade before. He and I still laugh about the first game we did together. The Phillies and Pirates were scheduled for a two-game exhibition series in San Juan, Puerto Rico. We were going to broadcast the games on radio, and the experienced Musser warned me that there would likely be problems. And there were plenty. What I remember most is that our location was right out in the middle of the press box. No broadcast booth for us. They had constructed a flimsy partition to separate our location from a Spanish-speaking broadcast right next to us. I was really nervous that night, and the accommodations weren't exactly conducive to a nice, relaxing debut. But we made it work. The game the guys next to us were doing in Spanish sounded a lot more exciting than the one Andy and I were broadcasting. They made it sound like the seventh game of the World Series, and did their voices carry! So you could hear a lot of Spanish in Philadelphia that night. But I had survived an entire game on radio and couldn't wait for the next one.

I'll always be thankful that I had Andy Musser as my first partner. He was definitely the professional in the booth, and I the new guy. But he encouraged me from the start, saying that I had a feel for the game and to just be myself. We worked well together for a long time, eventually doing games on PRISM and SportsChannel. Andy was the same guy every night, prepared and focused. Sitting there before games and during innings, he'd calmly listen to one of my emotional rants about something or other that might be bugging me. He always knew the right way to calm me down and get us focused on the game. He would call the play, and I'd analyze it. The thing he did better than any partner I've ever had was to set me up to sound good. I'll always believe that the most important thing sportscasters do when calling a game is to improve each other. If we mesh, then the broadcast is more entertaining and fun for the listener or viewer. Andy would ask me questions that he felt would bring out pertinent information. As a result, I started to get more and more confidence that maybe I *could* do this well and be relaxed at the same time.

Andy's last year in the booth was 2001. Unlike some guys in our business, he had a lot of other interests. He knew he wanted to do something else with his life while still young enough to enjoy it. He had tired of the endless road trips, hotel rooms, rain delays, and long games. Whatever you do, once it becomes a job, it's probably time to go and give someone else a shot. I remember when another broadcaster, getting ready to retire, was asked what he wouldn't miss. His answer was the loud knock on a door plainly displaying a "Do Not Disturb" sign, accompanied by the shrill sound of "Housekeeping!" Anyone who travels a lot can identify with that.

Andy had become a beer enthusiast over the years—more in terms of business than consumption. He had struck up a friendship with Fritz Maytag, the CEO of the Anchor Brewing Company of San Francisco. They had talked about Andy eventually working for Anchor as its eastern representative, or "brewery rep." One day it all came together. Musser left broadcasting and never looked back. He is now a proud grandfather, thanks to Luanne and son Alan, with a lot more time to spend with his family. He and his Korean-born wife, Eun-Joo, whom he met overseas at an Army radio station, still live in the area. Andy is out there teaching Anchor Steam distributors about the products so they can sell them more effectively, and he's thoroughly enjoying life. I'll always admire the way he walked away from the booth on his own terms. And I'll always be grateful to him for telling Larry Shenk that I was the guy he should hire.

Although this chapter on my colleagues over the years isn't entirely chronological, it makes sense to start with Andy, the partner I spent the most time with and learned the most from. I've been lucky to work with a lot of other talented broadcasters, including ex-players, during the 33 years I've been on the air. Here are some thoughts on each of them.

I GUESS IT'S pretty clear by now that when I was a young, rabid baseball fan, I loved listening to games on the radio. I know television is the primary source of information now, but baseball on the radio was my way of following the Phillies. And it's still a magical means of getting your baseball fix. The radio guys who are able to master the difficult play-by-play skills of a major-league baseball game, and put that image in your mind, still amaze me. Bill Campbell has been nicknamed the "Dean of Philadelphia Sportscasters," and it's well deserved. He was one of the voices of my summers. Bill had a great flair for calling a game, putting you right in the ballpark. He lived in Broomall, Pennsylvania, on Stoney Brook Drive, across the street from my Marple-Newtown High School buddy, Ed Pappas. We used to play touch football in Ed's back yard. Part of the fun was imitating Bill doing football play-by-play. We'd also mix in some Phillies action. Our hope was that one day he would be outside, hear us, and come over and call some plays for our little game. Of course, it never happened, but that didn't stop us.

I got to know Bill—or "Soupy," as a lot of his friends call him— when I started with the Phillies. He'd had a tough experience with the team when Bill Giles let him go and brought Harry Kalas to town. So Campbell was pleased when the Phillies gave him a chance to call the games on PRISM in 1979. I was lucky enough to be his partner, and it was great. Many nights, I caught myself sitting there just listening to him, imagining that I was back riding around Newtown Square with the car radio on. Then it would dawn on me that I was sitting next to one of my childhood idols, and he was asking me a question. I think we both enjoyed that year, one that for me was a learning experience from one of the great pros of the game. It's always a kick to receive a phone call from Bill Campbell or to see him in the press box and talk about the game that he still loves. And every year on September 7th, I make a point to wish him a happy birthday on the air. That date just happens also be the birthday of Bill Giles and my father. These three men have had such an impact on my life.

NICKNAMED THE "SECRETARY of Defense" during his playing days, Garry Maddox took a shot at broadcasting in 1987. Recently retired, he was looking for a way to stay around the game, and he was offered a role on the PRISM telecasts. Now just because a guy played the game doesn't mean he's going to be able to put on a headset and impart his knowledge. But Garry was a natural from the first time he sat down. Many times he was offered a larger role, but on each occasion he would turn it down and say he only wanted to work the middle three innings. So he would come into the booth at the start of the game, normally bringing in a sandwich. He would sit next to me, enjoy his food, and closely watch the game. Then Garry would come on the air in the fourth with some great insights on what he had observed. A bright man who now has two successful businesses in the Philadelphia area, Maddox wanted to learn all he could about television. He would never stop asking questions, always trying to improve. He made me laugh one night when he inquired, "Man, how come you keep asking me all those questions that you already know the answers to?" Although I appreciated that he thought I knew the answers, I explained that he was the guy who had been down there on the field, and people wanted to hear what he had to say.

Garry remained part of the various cable TV teams assembled through 1996. He liked his role and was comfortable with what he did. He used to say how much he enjoyed driving home after the sixth inning, listening to the game on the radio. And he loved to needle us about how, after he got there and turned on the TV, sometimes watching us go into extra innings, he could turn it off whenever he got tired, never having to worry about a late night with a long game or a rain delay. Garry Maddox would have been a success at whatever he chose to do. With his talents, had he wanted to, I think he could have been a great network TV analyst. But his family and his business interests were more important.

It doesn't seem all that long ago that the sports section of your daily newspaper was *the* place to go for information. Newspapers were the mainstay of media. There were some solid guys covering the Phillies in my early years. The Philadelphia *Bulletin* was a big part of a reader's afternoon and evening. Promoted by the slogan "Nearly everybody reads *The Bulletin*," it had some renowned sportswriters. One of the best in the business was columnist Jim Barniak. Nicknamed "Barns," Jim was a good reporter with a sly sense of humor. He was one of the first in our area to make the move from print to electronic media, and PRISM was the place where he found a home. Jim was a good listener. He was quiet, almost studious, but didn't miss a thing. I think that's what made him such a perceptive interviewer. His features on PRISM produced many classics, like the one he did with one of his childhood idols, Johnny Unitas. The program was called *Sports Scrapbook* and won Jim numerous local Emmys. One program that was *not* nominated for an award was the one he did with me in the late '80s. I was dragged, kicking and screaming, into co-hosting a PRISM cruise with Jim. And my reluctance had nothing to do with the co-host. I've never liked boats because of a tendency to get seasick, but I went on this one, fortunately returned intact, and Jim produced a show about the cruise, making me a big part of it.

One year he attended our Dream Week baseball camp, where fans pay for a week in Clearwater, learning and living with ex-big-leaguers. At least, that's the way it was advertised. Bobby Wine and I were managing a team. When it came time to draft our players, Wine decided to select some media guys like Barniak and radio personalities Don Cannon and Tony Bruno. When I asked "Wino" why, he said simply, "I want to get on TV and radio." The team was brutal. It was so bad that one day Bobby picked the names of his starting lineup out of a hat. The pitcher was a little left-hander named

Ben Lerner, who was a public defender at the time. Ben now is a judge in Philadelphia, and he beat a Mets Dream Week team that had to be even worse. Barniak played in the games while his crew filmed them. He always believed that the hilarious award-winning feature on that team was one of the best things he'd done. It was certainly the most fun.

In 1990, PRISM and SportsChannel, both doing a package of Phillies games, decided to have separate broadcast teams. Barniak was teamed with Garry Maddox and Mike Schmidt. I worked on SportsChannel with Andy Musser. In 1991, Barniak and I handled the PRISM telecasts. It could get a little confusing for the viewers with all the different combinations, but Jim and I looked forward to 1992, when we were slated to do the games again. Then one night during the off-season, he was rushed to Chestnut Hill Hospital with internal bleeding. An aneurysm had ruptured in his abdomen, and he was admitted in critical condition. I visited his room a few times, hoping to get a chance to talk again with this good man, but Jim never regained consciousness. He died much too young, but he left a tremendous body of work as his legacy. I know he really enjoyed his second career as a broadcaster.

MENTIONED EARLIER IN this book was a man I definitely didn't like when he was a player. And it wasn't because he was a nasty guy or anything like that. In fact, everyone who had anything to do with Kent Tekulve said he was one of the nicest people in the game. But it seemed like he was always beating the Phillies during that great rivalry with the Pirates in the '70s. Sometimes it seemed like "Teke" would pitch *every* game. And to make it even worse, he'd pitch three innings out of the bullpen. This guy had a rubber arm and the heart of a lion. After he came over to the Phils in 1985, and pitched for the team until 1988, we found out the rest of the league was right about him. He *was* one of the best guys ever, and remains so today.

Teke recalls how he'd look forward to pitching in Philadelphia when he was with the Pirates. "Sure it was mean and hostile," he said, "but there was nothing better than coming into a game, getting the Phillies out, and shutting up those fans. I loved that more than anything." Nevertheless, after Tekulve came to the Phillies, he was one of the most popular guys in the clubhouse. He was a "geek" before that term became popular, always fiddling with gadgets. One afternoon he found a way to hook up VCRs at the players' lockers. They loved it. But this was soon considered too much of a distraction, and the players had to disconnect. Teke also loved to make milkshakes for Phillies employees. He would go around taking orders from his favorite people and return with an afternoon delicacy. Unfortunately, that practice also was discontinued because he was running up a pretty big bill for dairy products, and the expenses weren't coming out of his check.

Sam Schroeder, the vice-president and general manager of PRISM and SportsChannel, could sense the way that the business was changing, especially television. John Madden probably started the trend that made the analyst the main part of television sports, initially in football. Baseball was starting to follow suit with strong personalities like Tim McCarver and Joe Morgan. Schroeder wanted the analysts on his channels to stand out, and he started to experiment with different guys. I was lucky enough to be the play-by-play announcer with a lot of them, one being our milkshake man, Kent Tekulve. Teke came aboard in 1991, and would be a part of the telecasts through 1997. He worked both channels and was knowledgeable and funny, with a self-deprecating sense of humor. Like me, Teke realized that he was another guy with a face for radio. When he and Andy Musser worked SportsChannel games one year, they were quite a sight opening each telecast. Both tall and extremely thin, even with the 10 pounds that TV can put on a broadcaster, they comprised a pretty gaunt picture. One night, when they came on wearing their identical blue blazers, it was suggested that the telecasts be named "Undertaker TV." They resembled nothing more than two guys greeting mourners at a wake. Both got a kick out of that characterization. I only wish I could remember who said it so that I could give him credit.

We spent a lot of time together during the course of a long season. Andy Musser often observed that a guy either does or doesn't "wear well." Teke was a colleague who wore well on and off the air. He's now back with the Pirates, a valuable part of their organization, and he retains his popularity. I guess Teke will always be a Bucco at heart, but he certainly changed the opinions of a lot of us who never thought we'd grow to like this formerly tireless on-the-field opponent.

SOMETHING ELSE I mentioned a lot earlier was my radio job as keeper of the out-of-town scoreboard. This could be rather tedious when coupled with cueing up the replays and trying to watch the game to provide some analysis. So I was always looking for a way to get out of these duties. On Sunday afternoons, Todd Kalas would accompany his famous father to the Vet and sit in the radio booth. He was probably around 12 when I decided I would offer him the cherished opportunity to keep the scores. I knew he was smart and responsible and that he would do a good job. He turned out to be a tremendous help to us on those Sundays.

Todd went to the University of Maryland following graduation from Conestoga High School, then finished at Syracuse University. Joining our telecasting team from 1994 to 1996, he was a good addition. I served as his analyst one season. Although Todd has always had to work in the prodigious shadow of Harry, he's established a distinctive style of his own. After leaving Philadelphia, Todd started working for the Tampa Bay Devil Rays, now the Tampa Bay Rays, and he is still a big part of their telecasts, doing pre- and postgame shows. He also fills in on both TV and radio with play-by-play. It was a little strange during the World Series to hear him as a voice of the opposition. That he got to work an inning with Harry during game one meant a lot to both of them. I've always felt that Todd could be a number-one guy with a major-league team, and I hope it happens for him, a class act even when he was a kid.

I DON'T HAVE to tell you that the 1993 team was loaded with characters. They may have been a one-year wonder on the field, but many of them remain a big part of Phillies history. That team went wire to wire and relished their reputation as, well, a bunch of dirt-balls. The '93 Phillies would fall a little short to the Blue Jays in the World Series, but the fans loved them. However, the fact is that they were not so great for the media, or even for their broadcasters. They could be a surly, intimidating bunch—very different from the fun guys envisioned by the fans. John Kruk was one of the most popular. He had a sloppy, everyman appearance that people could identify with. A lot of guys would wake up in the morning, look in the mirror, and see something of "The Kruker" in themselves. After all, not many of them could say they looked like Darren Daulton. Kruk was funny and irreverent, but for whatever reasons, not a happy guy. However, no one has changed more than Johnny since his playing days, an assessment with which he agrees. He still has the endearing irreverence, but he is a different man now. He has a wife and two children. Kruk has also become a tremendous studio commentator for ESPN. But back in his playing days, some of us didn't like to be around him, and he was fine with that.

I mentioned how Sam Schroeder wanted analysts who were a little on the edge. When he told me that Kruk was coming to Comcast to work with me in 2003, I wasn't very happy. Sure, I thought he would be good at the job, but I didn't exactly have a warm relationship with him when he was a player, so I wondered what the chemistry would be like. Those trepidations vanished in a hurry. We worked a few games in spring training, and it was easy. You could see that Johnny wanted to be in the booth. And since he was at a happy place in his life, the edge was gone and the fun guy was back. He had an immediate feel for the mechanics of a telecast, and it never got in the way of Kruk being himself.

If you've seen Kruk recently, I don't have to explain how he can make you laugh one minute and then say something really perceptive that could only come from a former ballplayer. What amazed me was not only his knowledge of all facets of the game, but how he could explain things quickly. He never liked hearing criticism as a player, but now he wasn't afraid to do it on the air so long as it was respectful. Sometimes ex-players come up to the booth and forget how tough it was to play the game. I don't think that ever was the case with Kruk. Larry Bowa was our manager that year, which played right into John's act. Bowa had been his manager in San Diego and John liked him, but he enjoyed needling Bo and gently making him seem like a nutcase.

I thought Johnny would be a part of our team for a long time. I was looking forward to another year. However, in January 2004, we were asked to make an appearance for the Phillies at a radio sponsors' luncheon in Lancaster. I got there early and was sitting in my car when my cell phone rang. It was Kruk. "What time are we supposed to be there?" he asked. I told him I was going to go in about 15 minutes. I asked if he was lost and needed any help. "No," he said, "look out your window. I'm right beside you." And there he was, sporting a big grin and enjoying the "gotcha" moment. Johnny then came over to my car, and we sat and talked. I wondered if he'd enjoyed doing the games and was looking forward to 2004. He heaved a big sigh and said, "Wheels, I had a great time this year. But ESPN called my agent, and they are offering me a job for big money. I don't see how I can turn it down." He didn't, and that season would be his only one on the Phillies' broadcast team. But John Kruk has gone on to do bigger things for a national audience. He remains a Phillie at heart and may be the most beloved of that band of characters who brought so much joy to Philadelphia in 1993. Who would have believed that of all those guys it would be John Kruk and the "Wild Thing," Mitch Williams, who would make it big on TV?

Speaking of popular Phillies, one of the fan favorites was outfielder Jay Johnstone. Nicknamed "J.J.," he had a reputation as a troublesome flake when Paul Owens brought him to Philadelphia. The Pope was not averse to acquiring guys who'd had some problems on other clubs. Owens would do his homework and then reach his own conclusions about potential trouble. Most of all, could he help his ball club? Johnstone was a skilled offensive player, and Paul decided he was worth a shot. Jay didn't disappoint, giving the Phillies some solid years from 1974 through 1978. His playing time started to diminish after the Phils traded for Bake McBride, but he performed well off the bench before eventually being traded.

Jay went on to play for a number of other teams before retiring and starting a second career as an author of several books and an organizer of charity events. He was always a people person, however eccentric, and at ease in any crowd. Not surprisingly, Sam Schroeder approached him prior to the 1992 season about a TV job. Jay accepted and was announced as a member of the PRISM team for that season. Since I was going to be the play-by-play man working with him, Schroeder asked for my opinion of Johnstone. In turn, I asked him what he expected of his new hire. Johnstone had a reputation of being fond of practical jokes. But he had another side to him, one that was not as obvious. I told Sam that J.J. was a good guy, but not the crazy clown he felt he was getting. If Schroeder thought Johnstone would provide a lot of humor and lighten up the telecasts, I didn't see it that way.

Jay tried very hard to do a solid job, and I think he succeeded. He was at the ballpark early and was always prepared. I think he liked the job, but he was never the wacky prankster some felt they were going to get, including Sam Schroeder. Jay came back to the booth for the wild ride of 1993, when he and I had a week to remember. We were on the air for the famous twi-night doubleheader with the San Diego Padres—the one that started at 5:05 on a Friday night and ended at 4:37 on Saturday morning. It was just the two of us, and J.J.'s energy level never waned. He was upbeat until Mitch Williams lined that pinch hit in the 10th inning of the second game to give the Phillies a split. Five days later, when Mitch blew a save in the ninth against the Dodgers and we played 20 innings, it was still "Jay and Chris" for the whole game. The temperatures and humidity were unbearable. I think he did his finest work in those games, but he left following that season. Jay makes his home in the Los Angeles area today, not far from Dodger Stadium, and is involved in a lot of business ventures. We run into each other once in a while, and can still laugh about that amazing week. We did three games that seemed like three weeks—a memory we'll always share.

· · ·

IF I WERE TO describe all the ingredients of a man who knows every facet of broadcasting, it would be Scott Graham. He had been a pre- and postgame host on our flagship station, 1210, for a number of years before joining the radio team in 1999. Scott put together the best production pieces I've ever heard. He had a tremendous talent for conducting interviews. Then he would incorporate sound and music, and it was great stuff. Scott has one of those classic radio voices that are perfect for almost any kind of work. He did both radio and TV with us before leaving after the 2006 season. Scott remains a talented football and basketball announcer who is heard throughout the Philadelphia area. He also does voice-over work for NFL Films, has his own production company, and is the morning voice on Sirius/XM with Buck Martinez. He and I used to play some golf together, and the game drove him nuts. But, like anything he tried, Scott worked hard and improved. More important, he stands as one of the most competent and professional broadcasters I've ever known.

LET ME MENTION someone else who was a big part of those PRISM telecasts, but didn't get a lot of credit. Larry Rosen, a native Philadelphian, was a man with instinctive talent for interviewing and production. He was the ultimate behind-the-scenes guy, but he also did a great job on the air and was the heart and soul of our telecasts. His love for baseball showed in his production pieces. Larry realized a lifelong dream in 1996 when he got a chance to do some play-by-play on the PRISM games. After he left Philadelphia, he became part of the NFL's Baltimore Ravens organization. I've missed his wisdom and advice since he departed. Larry had a real feel for what makes a good telecast.

ALTHOUGH THERE'S ALREADY a lot in this book about each of them, this chapter wouldn't be complete without some additional mention of Richie Ashburn and Tim McCarver. And so here's a story that involves them both.

Tim was treading lightly in his new broadcasting career, while working some innings with the highly regarded team of Harry and Whitey on Channel 17. He just wanted to fit in, and he'd been warned about Whitey's penchant for saying almost anything on the air. But Tim had a healthy sense of curiosity, and also loved a good story. He ventured to tell one during a telecast more in terms of education than amusement. It seems that pitcher Larry Christensen, a native of Marysville, Washington, had recently returned to that area following the spectacular eruption of Mount St. Helens. L.C. had brought back some ash from the volcano and was showing it to anyone interested. One of them was a fascinated Timmy. During the telecast, he expressed surprise at how smooth the ash was, saying he'd expected it to be coarse. Meanwhile, Ashburn just sat there, occasionally saying something about the game, then taking a long drag on his trademark pipe. How many times had I witnessed that— and wondered what he might eventually come out with? Finally, Whitey turned to McCarver and said, "Timmy, that's a fascinating story you've just shared with our viewing audience. But to be honest with you, I always thought that if you'd seen one piece of ash, you've seen them all."

McCarver later told me how many thoughts ran through his head at that point. One was the premature conclusion of his own broadcasting career. Another was simple incredulity—how could *anyone* get away with saying that on the air? Well, maybe only a Richie Ashburn could, and he did. Anyway, the telecast went on, Whitey chuckling quietly and Timmy vowing to be more careful with even innocent-sounding subject matter in the future. It's part of Ashburn lore now, tying together two of my favorite people, and another reminder of the times we shared in the booth.

THERE HAVE BEEN a lot of changes in broadcasting the games since I first came on the air in 1976. For the last two seasons, we have had a six-man team. The duties are split between radio and TV. However, starting in 2007, the Phillies have tried to put together separate teams for the two mediums, as opposed to a lot of crossing over. Larry Andersen and Scott Franzke do the bulk of the radio. It's been Harry Kalas, Tom McCarthy, Gary Matthews, and I on TV. So I have saved the final part of this chapter to talk about the guys with whom I've shared the booth most recently.

Although Gary Matthews only wore a Phillies uniform from 1981 to 1983, "Sarge" is a guy loved by the fans. He personified the hard-nosed, Phillies-fan type of player who gave up his body in the outfield and on the bases. At the plate, he was an aggressive hitter who never saw a fastball he didn't like. And he always tried to hit one early in the count. His game plan was simple: Swing hard, and hit the baseball harder. Gary had the tough, top-sergeant demeanor that got him his nickname from Pete Rose. But under that gruff exterior was a gracious man who loved life and people. Quick to smile and share a laugh, he's fun to watch and even more fun to be around. As a player, Matthews was the perfect teammate, and he was a joy for those of us in the media.

When he broke into the major leagues with the Giants in 1972, Matthews was one-third of one of the best outfields ever assembled. The other two guys were Garry Maddox and Bobby Bonds. I thought they would be together for a long time. But Sarge was traded to the Braves in 1977, and Maddox to the Phillies in 1975. Gary was National League Rookie of the Year in '72, and hit .281 with 234 home runs during a career that ended with Seattle after the 1987 season. He almost single-handedly beat the Dodgers in the 1983 NLCS with a great performance that earned him series MVP. Gary joined our broadcast team last year, and having been a hitting coach for the Blue Jays, Brewers, and Cubs, he contributes his own observations on the complexities of hitting a baseball. Sarge admits that he enjoys watching the hitting a lot more upstairs with us than down on the field. The life of a coach is not very rewarding. For the most part, the player gets credit when things go right; when the player or the whole team slumps, it's the hitting coach's fault.

Matthews also is a great ambassador for the ballclub. He is completely at ease in any social situation, and the Phillies use him a lot to chat up sponsors. He also mingles effortlessly with fans, wearing one of his trademark hats, and genuinely enjoys it. Sarge is an avid golfer who keeps trying to get better. He brings the same intensity to the golf course that he did to home plate. I swear the man leaves the ground on certain shots, just the way he did when he played.

Sarge has a lot of potential as a broadcaster. His evident respect for what it takes to be a player doesn't prevent him from giving his honest opinions without mincing words. The fans have welcomed him to his new career, and I just like being around the guy.

IN 2006, SCOTT GRAHAM was given a larger role on the broadcast team and was named TV play-by-play man for the middle three innings. The club now needed someone to handle pre- and postgame duties, plus the middle three innings of radio play-by-play. There are a lot of good young announcers working in the minor leagues. Just like players in the minors, their goal is to get a big-league job. And with the advent of so many ex-players now occupying broadcast booths, their opportunities are few and far between. Besides, people who are lucky enough to do this for a living have a tendency to hang around as long as possible. Even with all of the traveling, it's a great life, so why retire? When the word went out that the Phillies were hiring, the audition tapes predictably poured in. The club set up a committee to listen to them and come up with the right choice. This was not a favorite period of time for anyone in the booth. You always wonder what the next guy will be like. It's so important that broadcast teams establish good working relationships. Guys don't have to be best friends off the air. But on the air, everything has to work smoothly and with as little tension as possible. It is, after all, as much a team as the one on the field.

The choice was Scott Franzke, then a 34-year-old graduate of Southern Methodist University. A native of Dallas, Scott had experience calling games for the Kane County Cougars, a Single-A affiliate of the Florida Marlins. He also had two stints with the Texas Rangers as a pre- and postgame announcer. And he had play-by-play experience. On paper, Scott had all the right stuff. But what kind of person were we getting? We had been very lucky over the years in that everyone coming on board was somebody we already knew. But now we were in uncharted waters.

Franzke turned out to be not only a talented broadcaster, but also a great guy who fit in right away. He possesses a wicked but dry sense of humor and a genuine love of the game. You could tell right away that he was going to come into the booth unobtrusively and not try to take over. Scott developed an immediate bond with Larry Andersen, and they are the ideal radio team. They just have that elusive chemistry. Franzke has learned to bring out the wit and wisdom of the playful L.A., and Larry has come into his own as a really good broadcaster. Scott has one of the smallest egos of anyone I've ever met in this business. He never hesitates to ask questions and learn from people who have been around a lot longer than he has. However, I don't think he needs a whole lot of help. We hope to have him broadcasting Phillies games for a long time to come.

I'VE ALWAYS ADMIRED people with the ability to cover different sports. Baseball may be the toughest to broadcast because of all the downtime involved. To some enthusiasts, its pace has a kind of poetry to it. But to broadcasters, all that time provides opportunities to say stupid things they will regret later. In other sports, the play-by-play announcer and analyst have to move with the action more quickly. I'm sure each presents its own set of challenges, but it never ceases to amaze me how anyone can excel in the demanding requirements of broadcasting several different sports. It's almost like being a three-sport collegiate athlete—increasingly rare in these more specialized days.

Tom McCarthy is the epitome of the professional who can do it all. He's a Central New Jersey native who had an extensive minor-league background with the Trenton Thunder, the former Double-A affiliate of the Boston Red Sox. Starting his minor-league baseball career in 1993, Tom's earliest job included selling hot dogs and counting the money. However, he soon graduated to broadcasting games for the Thunder before going on to host a talk-radio program on ESPN. He was another guy who started with the Phillies as a pre- and postgame radio host in 2000, before working his way into some radio play-by-play in 2004. Following the 2004 season, Tom received an offer he couldn't refuse. He had grown up a Mets fan because of the proximity of his hometown to Shea Stadium, so we can cut him a little slack on this. The Mets came calling with a great offer to join Howie Rose as their radio play-by-play team on WFAN. The lure of the New York market was hard to resist. Tom did the Mets games for two seasons, and we would see him a lot. But I always had the feeling that he still loved the Philadelphia market. Besides, it was much easier to commute from his home near Trenton than to deal with the problems of driving to Queens.

The Phillies had been thinking about starting to groom a young announcer for the inevitable day when Harry Kalas would conclude his career. So Tom jumped at their five-year offer to be a TV voice. And I think Phillies telecasts were actually better after his return. Tom is one of those guys who never seem to have a bad day. With his energetic delivery, you can hear him two or three booths away. Tom also regularly broadcasts college football and basketball, with no less enthusiasm. When he enters a room, with his big presence and booming voice, things just seem to pick up. I think it is clear that the Phillies were right. He was the perfect man at the perfect time to go into doing TV play-by-play.

Big things were coming to Philadelphia sports television in 1998. After years of planning and development, Comcast SportsNet had started operations in late 1997. Their first year of televising Phillies baseball was on the horizon. However, a tragic event had put the future makeup of the broadcast team in question at a time when this new network needed anything but problems. Richie Ashburn had died of a heart attack in his hotel room in New York City in early September 1997. He certainly would have been a big part of the new network. But now the Phillies and CSN had to come up with someone else. And how could anyone step into the booth and try to fill Whitey's shoes?

Larry Andersen had two stints with the Phillies during his 25-year professional baseball career. It took him a while to get to the big leagues, but Larry made the most of it after breaking in with the Indians in 1975. He had a 17-year major-league career, also pitching for Seattle, Houston, Boston, and San Diego. He was with the Phillies from 1983 to 1986, and again from 1993 to 1994, pitching in two World Series. He then spent three seasons as a minor-league pitching coach for the Phillies, at Reading (1995-96) and Scranton (1997). He almost took a broadcasting job in 1997 when the Astros offered him a TV spot after Larry Dierker left the booth to manage Houston. With his informal, relaxed personality and offbeat wit, Larry was a guy you just had to like.

I've mentioned Sam Schroeder a lot in this chapter. Having asked me about Jay Johnstone, he once again sought my opinion on the guy now known as L.A. We used to call him "Andy" when he played with the Phillies, and many of us still do. Sam wanted to know if L.A.'s zany off-the-field demeanor would be a part of his on-the-air personality. As with Johnstone, I told Sam that I thought Larry would be a good choice, but not to expect someone whose antics as a player would be all that evident in the booth. He wouldn't be giving colleagues a hotfoot. Larry is one of the most naturally funny men I've ever met. But behind a kind of innocent approach to life is a keen mind. He doesn't want people to think he's some kind of goofy character who just had the ability to play baseball. So Sam brought Andy on board, and he has been a big part of our team for 12 years.

L.A. has found his niche on the radio with Scott Franzke. He really enjoys radio and doesn't care to return to TV. As he likes to point out, "There is no dress code on radio." It suits his laid-back personality and brings out his natural humor. I miss our days of working together on TV because he became really good at it. But focusing on radio has worked out well for both Larry and the listeners. The fans love him because he is real. And we still get to enjoy his company, and that distinctive off-the-wall wit, just as before.

In 1968, I was called to complete my six-month active-duty stint in the U.S. Army Reserves. I spent basic training at Fort Polk, Louisiana. Then it was off to Fort Sam Houston in San Antonio.

There my MOS (Military Occupational Specialty) was medical corpsman. Yes, I know it's a frightening thought, but I was actually trained to be a medic. I really missed listening to Phillies games, so I did the next best thing. Often I would spend a hot, humid evening sitting outside my barracks, listening to a Houston Astros game. They had two lead announcers. Gene Elston was a future Ford Frick Award winner. The other guy, Loel Passe, had a "good old boy" shtick that I guess worked well in Texas, but he didn't seem to know a whole lot about baseball. He was more into coming up with such strange country phrases as "Now you chuckin', Larry." I learned that meant that Larry Dierker was pitching pretty well. I guess it was in either the fifth or sixth inning of every game that another voice would take over. And this guy was good. He knew the game, sounded great, and was the perfect radio play-by-play man. I couldn't help noticing that he never had any byplay with either Elston or Passe. Many times, his inning would fly by, and that was it. I found myself wanting to hear more of him. And this became my introduction to a man I would get to know very well just three years later—Harry Kalas.

Bill Giles caused a real firestorm when he brought Harry to Philadelphia in 1971 to replace Bill Campbell. Giles had worked with Harry during their Houston days and felt he was ready to become a number-one guy on a broadcast team. Everyone loved Bill Campbell, so this was anything but an easy decision. Giles has made a lot of controversial moves that turned out well, and I think he would put this hire right near the top. It didn't take long for Harry to establish his own rapport with the fans.

"Harry the K" developed a great working relationship with Richie Ashburn, and they became a unique team. Harry covered the nuts and bolts of the broadcast, while Whitey provided the humor. I first worked with Harry, reporting the middle three innings, in 1977. Andy Musser would head over to TV to work with Whitey, and Harry would come to radio. It may sound confusing, but it was fun, as Harry did the play-by-play and Todd Kalas kept the scores on Sundays. Harry taught me a lot about every aspect of finding your niche as a professional broadcaster. He had an amazing ability to rise to the occasion when something exciting happens in a game, and an uncanny knack of getting the play right. His home-run calls became legendary, and his distinctive voice added authority to other productions, such as NFL Films and national commercials. In personal appearances, he became the face as well as the voice of the team, and really of Philadelphia itself.

The best advice Harry gave me was simply to be myself and not worry about criticism. He said that if you never express any opinions on the air, you'll never develop any type of personality. People relate to distinctive personalities, not carbon copies of others they hear or see. There is no better illustration than Harry and Whitey. Harry and I spent a lot of time together off the air and had many discussions about every aspect of broadcasting. His philosophy about sharing the booth with a partner was sensibly simple. He gave the analyst room to say anything he wanted to, in his own way. Just don't expect a lot of back-and-forth, because Harry didn't stress conversation. He understood the unique rhythms of baseball, its pauses as well as its action, as well as anyone I've ever known.

In 2002, Harry was inducted into the broadcasters' wing of the Baseball Hall of Fame at Cooperstown. I think winning the coveted Ford Frick Award was the highlight of his career, one that spanned nearly four decades in Philadelphia. In recent years, when the subject of retirement came up, Harry inevitably replied that he would know when the time was right, but that for now he was enjoying everything about his job, and felt he was still doing it well. Certainly there were few complaints from the fans. It reminded me of Joe Paterno at Penn State. He had surely earned the right to keep going as long as he liked. Of course, it turned out that Harry Kalas would be denied that decision. Yet the shock of April 13, 2009 was tempered by the knowledge that, to the end, Harry was doing what he loved. His will always be the voice of the Phillies.

CHAPTER 10

Two Parades

THE TRIUMPH OF EVERY major professional franchise in Philadelphia has been followed by a parade down Broad Street, ideally suited for a procession of sports heroes—and tons of fans to salute them. When the Phillies, after years of coming close, brought home their championship trophy in 1980, the town erupted into a memorably massive celebration. Who can ever forget Tug McGraw holding aloft that *Daily News* with the "WE WIN!" headline? And all the prior highlights of 1980, from the most dramatic playoff series in baseball history to the six-game World Series victory over the Royals? The whole town went crazy. Could we imagine it would take 28 years to experience it again?

"Everyone loves a parade." And so, over time, the fans' fixation on when, if ever, the Phillies or any other team in town would do it again became focused on "When will we have another *parade*?" This chapter, encompassing my own memories of the Phillies' title years of 1980 and 2008, culminates in what it was like to take those two memorable rides down South Broad Street as part of a championship organization—a story of two parades.

Earlier chapters have had a lot to say about 1980. That was the year the Phillies, a veteran team loaded with homegrown players, exorcised the demons of past failures, battled their manager, and kept the fans on edge throughout a grueling season. Eventually, the heartaches of 1976, 1977, and 1978 were swept away on that October night when the South Philadelphia sky lit up with fireworks and

Tug McGraw stood on the mound, waiting for Mike Schmidt to embrace him first, an act the two had choreographed earlier.

Tug and Mike lived in suburban Delaware County—Mike in Media near the Springton Reservoir and Tug in Wallingford. They would drive to the ballpark together many times, two of the most diverse personalities on a team of distinctive personalities. The Phillies had won a thrilling game five in Kansas City on October 19th. They had trailed 3-2 in the ninth, and were facing ace closer Dan Quisenberry. RBI hits by Del Unser and Manny Trillo and a heart-stopping save by McGraw had sent the Phillies home with a chance to end it with a win in game six.

As they had done throughout the year, Schmidt and McGraw planned to ride to the Vet for what could be a momentous evening. During the course of the ride, with Schmidt at the wheel, they came up with a plan. Steve Carlton was the Phillies' starting pitcher, and that made everyone think that something special could be on tap. Always the analyst, Schmidt said to McGraw, "Tug, I have a good feeling about tonight. We have Lefty on the mound, and what could be a better way to end this thing? Plus, you know you are going to be out there at the end." Schmidt continued, "Now, I've been watching other guys celebrate winning a World Series, and there always seems to be one picture that gets the most attention. And I want to be in it when we win. So remember, after the final out, look for me." This may have sounded pretty good, but what were the odds it would happen?

Who can forget that ninth inning of game six? McGraw was practically out of bullets. He had been remarkably effective throughout the season and postseason to get the Phillies to this point. But, as he would later point out, by now he barely had feelings in his fingers, that's how much his arm tingled, as if his hand was asleep. But he faced a struggling hitter in Willie Wilson at the plate. Wilson had struck out 11 times in the World Series. Could McGraw make it 12?

When Wilson swung and missed at a two-two pitch for the final out—there are many indelible memories of that. But the one that would be shown over and over in photos and video involved Schmidt and McGraw in the scenario they had envisioned during their afternoon drive. The still photo shows Schmidt leaping into McGraw's waiting arms. But how did they get there? Watch the video of the final out. Wilson waves and misses, McGraw leaps off the mound with his hands held skyward as catcher Bob Boone walks calmly toward the mound. Then it seems to dawn on McGraw. Oh, yeah, Schmitty had said, "Wait for me." Sure enough, McGraw turns to his right just at the moment Schmidt comes flying through the air into his waiting arms. It seemed so spontaneous. Yet these two great players had dreamed that moment, and the biggest memory of their baseball lives had come true. It was 11:29 p.m. on October 21, 1980.

One of the questions we often get asked is, "Where were you when Tug struck out Willie Wilson?" My story is not as exciting as it should have been. In fact, it was one of the low points of my baseball career. And it occurred on a night when everything should have been perfect.

In 1980, the World Series was not broadcast by the local announcers, so we watched the game like everyone else, and it was more than a little frustrating. I was only a few years into my broadcasting career, but still had a dual role as Larry Shenk's assistant. As the ninth inning started, Larry informed me of my postgame duties should the Phillies win. Television had started its steady climb toward domination of live sporting events, but the print media still occupied a major position. Shenk, an ex-newspaperman, wanted to make sure the writers got their due. He said to me, "If we win, Mike is the MVP. You have to grab him as soon as he comes into the clubhouse and get him to the media room right away." Shenk continued, "I know it will be tough, but get him out of the clubhouse as fast as possible."

So downstairs I went. As I walked into the clubhouse, I saw a platform set up in the middle of the room, and there on a table sat the gleaming World Series trophy. It was then that the magnitude of what could happen dawned on me. We were three outs away from the first championship in Phillies history. I remember NBC's Len Berman positioned on the platform. We exchanged hellos and a little small talk. Then I had to decide where to watch the top of the ninth. Tug had been making things pretty exciting lately, so there was no reason to think it would be a one-two-three ninth. Of course, he didn't have to make it as exciting as it turned out to be.

I didn't want to be around a lot of people, so I walked into the back room where the bats and washing machines were kept. The room was the domain of a sweet man named Pete Cera. He had been a trainer and equipment man with the Phillies for over 30 years, and he wore a perpetual smile. A native of Hazelton, Pennsylvania, "Petey" was sitting on his favorite stool, watching the ninth on a little black-and-white TV that had terrible reception. I asked him if we could watch it together and he nodded OK. When I saw that even the affable, chatty Cera was as uptight as I was, it was apparent that we had a chance to share a pretty unique moment. Petey stayed on his stool while I paced his room like an expectant father. The half-inning seemed to go on forever. Then Pete Rose made his great catch on the ball hit by Frank White that had bounced off Boone's glove. Who can't still picture that scene? Two outs, bases still loaded, and it was 4-1 Phils. One out to go. I kept pacing as Pete Cera sat motionless. Swing and a miss. Wilson struck out and the Vet went nuts! Inside that little room in the back of the clubhouse, 35-year-old Chris Wheeler and 60-year-old Pete Cera grabbed each other in a bear hug, and the laughter and tears still resonate.

Then it dawned on me—I had to get Schmitty to the interview room. After the celebration on the field, the players started pouring through the double doors at the end of the long tunnel leading from the dugout. The champagne started to flow, and it was pandemonium. I kept looking for Schmidt, and suddenly he appeared in the tunnel. As he came through the door, I rushed toward him and he saw me. We exchanged hugs, and I remember him saying in his typically understated way, "Hey, Wheels, how about this?" I told him what Larry wanted him to do, and that fast we were out the door and down the hall to meet the media.

Mike did a great job, answering every question about winning the World Series and how it felt to be MVP. Meanwhile back in the clubhouse, the postgame TV interviews were in full swing. Check out that postgame video and you'll see Ruly Carpenter, Paul Owens, and Dallas Green drenched in beer and champagne, accepting the trophy from Commissioner Bowie Kuhn. Then came the parade of players, led by the exhausted McGraw tearfully hugging Owens. It was a scene to treasure. But keep looking, and the one guy you will not see on TV who *should* have been there was the MVP of the World Series. Thanks to my outstanding effort, Mike Schmidt never made it to live TV to accept his award. I know that seems impossible when you consider the pomp and ceremony involving the presentation of the award today. But that's what happened, and it's one of the lowlights for both Larry Shenk and me.

Mike eventually received his trophy from the commissioner, but to add to our misery, he later commiserated about how he had wanted to say something to his sick grandmother back in Dayton. It was the perfect mess-up, a good idea gone bad. Schmitty teased Larry and me about that night for a number of years. During the off-season, Larry made a point of informing the league's other PR directors about what we had done in order to make sure it wouldn't happen again. To his credit, The Baron took the blame and made a positive out of the negative. I still apologize to Mike occasionally, and he's still good-natured about it. But I don't think I'll ever completely get over what we denied him that night, despite our good intentions.

One significant change did come out of that postseason. The Philadelphia fans were irate that the Phillies broadcasters were not a part of the postseason coverage. Major League Baseball was inundated with complaints, and the following season it was decided that at least local radio broadcasts of the World Series would be permitted. It was just another example of the passion of our great fans. They actually changed MLB policy, and that's never easy.

I did return to the clubhouse in time to get drenched, and it never felt better. Then I headed up to the Stadium Club, where a huge front-office party was under way. It was a boisterous celebration, and I know a few people reeked of beer and champagne after hugging me, but nobody seemed to care.

Few can forget that as the ninth inning started, police dogs entered the field from behind home plate and made their way, with their handlers, to the first- and third-base dugouts, and that there were also mounted police. The city wasn't sure how much crowd control would be needed if the Phillies won that night, so they were taking no chances. We had been instructed to park our cars inside JFK Stadium in case things got out of hand around the Vet. So, after spending some time at the postgame party, I went back to our office, packed up, and headed across the Spectrum parking lot to find my car. Police ringed the huge stadium and smiled as we passed them to go inside. I drove to my town house in Roxborough, thinking about what had just happened, yet knowing the fun was far from over.

There would be no rest for the new world champions. The parade had been scheduled for the next day, and that day had already arrived. I walked into my house around two a.m. and turned on the VCR to watch Tony Kubek and Joe Garagiola describe that ninth inning. It was the first time I'd been able to sit back and relish the moment.

Now it was about three a.m., and we had been instructed to meet at the Philadelphia Museum of Art at 8:30. To say it was a short night is an understatement. It was a bleary-eyed bunch of players, broadcasters, and front-office personnel who staggered into that waiting room to receive instructions about what was to transpire. We were told that buses were waiting to transport us to the floats. There was a lot of yawning and coffee-guzzling and not much enthusiasm, despite the victory. The floats, which were mounted on huge open flatbed trucks, were numbered, and we were given our assigned vehicles. Then it was off to the buses and who knew what.

The floats were parked in a long line on JFK Boulevard. Everyone piled on, and they started moving. I remember being so drained at that point that I wanted to be anywhere but on that float. There were a few people scattered around in the street, but no big deal. We went east on JFK and turned right, or south, onto 22nd Street. It was then that we started to notice a few more fans. As the floats headed toward Market Street, the sun started to shine brighter, and there was some noise up ahead. As we reached Market Street, we all received the wake- up call of a lifetime. Thousands of people lined the street, waving and screaming at their new heroes. The tall buildings were filled with office workers, and confetti rained down from some of them. I was riding with David Montgomery and Denny Lehman. We looked at each other a little wide-eyed, sensing we were a part of something very special. Then it was east to Broad Street and the sight of thousands of fans as far as the eye could see. I will never forget the looks on their faces as they watched the floats go by. Some were laughing, others crying. The *Daily News* had printed a special edition, its front page headlined "WE WIN!" It was proudly held aloft by many adoring fans, as it would be later by McGraw.

The ride seemed to go pretty fast, and I thought that was about the end of the party. We'd heard that the parade was going to end in massive JFK Stadium, where over 100,000 fans had watched many an Army-Navy game. The prevailing thought was that some fans probably would be there, but that we had seen the bulk of the celebration. As the floats approached the stadium, I remember thinking there seemed to be a lot of people in that place. But they probably were all in one location, and there would be an expanse of empty seats. Yet, as the floats entered this historic venue that had hosted everything from heavyweight fights and great political speeches to sold-out concerts, the roar was deafening. The place was packed with 100,000 fans who had waited hours to welcome the ballclub, and they weren't going to be denied. Harry Kalas was handed the mike, and he started introducing the team to roars of approval. Mike Schmidt told the delirious fans to "savor this world championship because you all deserve it." Finally, it was left to the little leprechaun, Tug McGraw, to finish the public celebration. Tug thanked the fans and praised them for all they had done to make this day come true. Then the former Met took his now-famous shot at the Big Apple by telling the New York fans what they could do with this championship. The crowd went crazy. Tug was high-fived by his teammates. We took one more look at this possibly once-in-a-lifetime scene, and the floats headed out of the stadium to the waiting buses. They transported us back to the Art Museum and our cars. With almost everyone, the rush of adrenaline had replaced our early-morning weariness, but there was still no time to rest.

Bill Giles had put together a huge party for Phillies personnel scheduled for that night at seven p.m. at the newly opened Wyndham Franklin Plaza Hotel. Two people had skipped the earlier parade for their own personal reasons: Whitey Ashburn and pitcher

Ron Reed. And believe me, by then I wanted nothing more than to go home and get some sleep. That would have turned out to be a huge mistake, because nobody could organize a party like Giles. It was like Kiteman, Wallenda, and all his spectacular promotions compressed into one room. The night was filled with laughter and a shared sense of accomplishment. The sights and sounds of the parade still vividly in our minds, we got to celebrate with the people who had been through the tough years of the early '70s and the seasons of thwarted glory that followed.

One memory stands out for me that night amid all the balloons, food, and music. Since the Phillies were world champions for the first time in their long history, we were wondering about World Series rings. We knew that all front-office employees were going to receive them, as well as the players themselves, but we wondered when and how. So who better to ask than the man who had won more than a few? I went up to Pete Rose and inquired, "When do you guys get your rings?" I sure didn't want to make it sound like I was interested in mine. After all, what had I done to deserve a ring? Rose, with his very expressive face, just looked at me like I'd asked him the dumbest question imaginable and said, "Opening Day. How come you don't know that?" Thinking the answer should be obvious, I thanked him and walked away, eager to share my newfound information.

I imagine we all slept very well that night after such a whirlwind of events. I knew in my heart that I had just experienced the greatest 24 hours of my life. How could anything ever come close to matching what had just occurred? And 28 years later, I would have to revise that mindset. Our city was about to experience another day that would create memories for new generations of Philadelphia sports fans. And I would be lucky enough to be a part of it again!

THE CHAMPIONSHIP WON by the Phillies in 1980 was the first in their long history. Although optimism that another might be in the immediate future was dimmed by events, how long would it take to contend again? We've already mentioned the problems our still-talented team incurred in 1981 with a lengthy players' strike, followed by the disjointed postseason playoff that the Phillies lost to Montreal. In 1983, the "Wheeze Kids" made it to the World Series. A decade later, that exciting wire-to-wire run by the 1993 team also produced a trip to the fall classic. However, the Baltimore Orioles and Toronto Blue Jays would win the respective rings. Our organization seemed stuck on that one shining moment. Already in my mid-thirties when the 1980 team made their triumphant ride down Broad Street, I began to join many other Philadelphians in wondering if we'd ever see another parade like it.

Beginning in 2001, the Phillies turned the corner and became a more competitive team. With the exception of a season under .500 in 2002 (80-81), they consistently had seasons with victories in the high eighties. This led to three straight second-place finishes from 2004 to 2006. In 2007, the Phils won the NL East with a strong finish and the collapse of the Mets. However, they were quickly wiped out in three straight games by the red-hot Colorado Rockies. So the talk during the off-season was that the 2008 team once again should contend. And if they were able to get into postseason play, perhaps they had learned something from their early exit the year before.

One of the keys to success was to get off to a better start. In recent years, the Phils had some terrible Aprils. As a result, they found themselves behind the eight-ball, trying to get to the .500 mark as late as June. However, the season didn't start well. The Washington Nationals scored some late-inning runs on a cold, dreary March afternoon to win the opener 11-6. Two days later, the Phillies went down again, 1-0, despite a great job by Cole Hamels. And things were looking similarly grim in the third game of the season before the Phillies rallied late to tie the game. They won it in the 10th on a walk-off, bases-loaded walk to Jayson Werth. The win enabled them to avoid a 0-3 start at home, and they went on to have a 15-13 record for April. Their opening series opponents, the Nationals, would be back for the final three games of the season. How could we know what drama that weekend would produce?

The season bore out the baseball maxim that it's always a marathon and never a sprint. Even though the team stayed relatively healthy, there were disability-list stints by both Jimmy Rollins and

Shane Victorino early in the year. Brett Myers had his problems, made a trip to the minor leagues, and came back a different pitcher. He went 7-2 in his final 13 starts, with a 1.80 ERA. Chase Utley got off to a blistering start that seemed to have him destined to win the third straight MVP for the team, following Rollins and Howard. A hip injury requiring postseason surgery would soon hamper his efforts.

From May 23rd on, the Phils occupied either first or second place, their largest lead of four games coming on June 13th. As the crucial month of September began, they were 75-62 and trailed the first-place Mets by one game. The Mets had cooperated the year before by blowing a far more substantial lead, one of the largest collapses in baseball history, reminiscent of the Phillies' own nightmare in 1964. It seemed we'd always be chasing the Mets.

There are moments in such a long season when even optimists conclude that things are hopeless. Baseball is a sport so steeped in failure that anyone who hits safely one-third of the time is deemed a success. It's easy to forget that a team that wins 100 games still loses 62. You can go a week without a win and look terrible, but any player, striving for consistency, shares with fans the inevitable peaks and valleys. For me, the roller coaster reached the bottom on the hot, humid afternoon of Wednesday, September 10th. The Phillies played a lethargic game more suited to July or August. It lasted just two hours and 45 minutes, but seemed to go on forever. The Florida Marlins dominated the contest and won 7-3. The Mets' victory that night increased their lead to three and a half games, and four in the all-important loss column, even more important late in the season. During the more than two-hour ride home in the late-afternoon rush-hour traffic, it seemed to me that the season was over. The Mets weren't going to go belly-up two years in a row, and the Phillies placidly had just lost two of three to the Marlins. Where was their sense of urgency? The division title looked to be pretty much gone. Of course, the wild card possibility remained, but the Phillies trailed the Milwaukee Brewers by four full games.

Now it just so happened that next on tap for the team was a four-game home series with the Brewers. Four-game series are not all that common. And with the Brewers in the Central Division, the odds

were slim that their one visit to Citizens Bank Park would come near
the middle of September. But that's how it had been scheduled. The
opportunity was right there. How would the Phillies react, after
looking so feeble against the Marlins? As it turned out, like a different team. The Brewers series started with a 6-3 Thursday-night
Phillies win behind Jamie Moyer. Then torrential rains wiped out the
Friday-night game. A day/night split doubleheader would now be
scheduled for Sunday. On Saturday afternoon, Cole Hamels won the
second game, 7-3, setting up a long day and night of Sunday baseball. The team had won two straight, but needed an improbable
sweep. However, a couple of controversial bullpen moves by Brewers manager Ned Yost blew up on him, and the Phillies went on to
win the day game with a late-inning rally. Three straight.

So it would come down to a four-hour wait for the most important game of the season. Win this one, complete the sweep, and the
Phillies would be tied for the wild card. Lose it and the Brewers
would leave town two up and still in control, with only 12 games remaining on the schedule. As noted, Brett Myers had stepped up big-
time since his trip down to Triple-A Lehigh Valley to regain his
confidence and his stuff. He dominated the Brewers, winning 6-1,
and suddenly, just like that, the air was back in the balloon.

Whatever the emotional condition of the fans (and at least one
broadcaster), if the 2008 team had a constant, I think it was a state
of perpetual calm. When everything seemed to be crashing down
around them, they remained remarkably steady. A lot of that came
from the atmosphere provided by Charlie Manuel. Behind the
scenes, Charlie would get upset at the seemingly lackadaisical style
of some of his players. But Manuel knew that if he and his coaches
showed signs of panic, his team would reflect it. On the way to Atlanta late that Sunday night, there wasn't a whole lot of celebrating.
The players were cheerful but hardly buoyant. They were a bunch of
guys, playing day to day but never doubting they were going to win
in the end. That a lot of people like me didn't share their quiet confidence didn't matter.

They went on to sweep the Braves in three games, winning all
nine played in Atlanta. Then it was off to Florida for a weekend with

the smoking-hot Marlins. Buried by the Fish on Friday night, the Phils then won two tough games, finishing the road trip 5-1. Meanwhile, the Mets were struggling with a leaky bullpen. Returning home for the final six games of the season in first place with a game-and-a-half lead, the Phils promptly lost two of three to the Braves. Fortunately, there was a day off on Thursday. Next up were the Washington Nationals, the team they had opposed on Opening Day way back on March 31st. Winning Friday night, the Phils were set to play a Saturday-afternoon game with a two-game lead over the Mets, and only two games left in the season. That made the math pretty simple. Win the game and go on to postseason play for the second straight year. Lose, and the Mets still have life.

There are a lot of shared memories from 2008, but the top of the ninth inning in game 161 of the season was the one that launched a month-long party. The Phillies led 4-3, but the Nats had the bases loaded with one out. The sellout crowd, in a frenzy at the start of the inning, now was squirming with every pitch. Brad Lidge had been perfect all season, but had run out of wiggle room. Up stepped tough Ryan Zimmerman. Suddenly, the ball was headed up the middle for what looked like a 5-4 Washington lead, a blown save for Lidge—his first of the year—and possibly a crushing loss. Out of nowhere, Jimmy Rollins darted to his left and went to one knee, gloving the hard-hit ground-ball. He flipped it to Chase Utley, over to Ryan Howard. Double play. Game over. Pandemonium at the ballpark. The Phillies were Eastern Division champions.

Forget the serenity. Now this group, which had hung together through so much during the long season, was celebrating with a massive dog-pile near the spot where Rollins had possibly saved their season. The scene on the field and in the clubhouse was anything but subdued. Yes, it had been that way a year earlier. Some speculated the Phillies had spent so much emotion that day that they were ill-prepared for the playoff games that followed. But I had a different feeling *this* time about *this* team. To a man, they talked about what they had learned from the sweep by the Rockies. The Milwaukee Brewers were coming back to town for the division series. Despite their performance in Philadelphia two weeks earlier, they had put together a great run of their own and had won the wild card. A best-of-five for the right to play for the National League championship was set to get under way. Would the home team move on this time?

THERE WAS A lot of anticipation when the National League Division Series opened up at Citizens Bank Park on October 9th. The fans were fired up after the dramatic clinching of the NL East on Saturday. To a lot of people, the Brewers were merely a speed bump on the way to bigger things. But the Phillies knew the Brewers were a team that presented a number of problems. They'd had to win almost every game the last two weeks just to get to the playoffs, and several of the wins had come through dramatic walk-off home runs, giving this young team a sense of renewed confidence. They lived and died by the long ball, and they were hitting a lot of them. Plus, they had a big-time pitcher in C.C. Sabathia. Acquired from Cleveland at the July 31st trading deadline, Sabathia had been brilliant for his new team. The Phillies had managed to avoid him in their four-game sweep, but he was ready to go in game two of the playoffs. Before then, our young ace, Cole Hamels, showed an early sign of the dominant pitcher he would be throughout the postseason. He went eight shutout innings, and the Phillies won their first postseason game in 15 years, 3-1.

The crowd, a factor from the start, really came into play in game two. Sabathia took the mound against Brett Myers. C.C. had been pitching on three days' rest for a couple of weeks, still getting the job done. However, he needed some quick innings to keep his pitch count low. The pivotal inning for the Phillies was the second. For the second straight game, they did all their scoring in one frame. Needing only one more out to end the inning, Sabathia ran into trouble with, of all people, Brett Myers at the plate. Myers, never noted for his bat, battled him relentlessly, fouling off pitch after pitch. The crowd was eating it up, waving their rally towels in a sea of white. I don't know whether baseball fans in other towns would have reacted so vocally to foul balls, but the Philly fans understood how badly Sabathia needed quick outs. When Brett finally earned a walk, Sabathia, obviously rattled, walked Jimmy Rollins to load the bases. Up next, Shane Victorino lined a grand slam into the seats in left. I think this finished the Brewers, and not only for this game. The Phillies won, then went to Milwaukee and lost game three. But Jimmy Rollins' lead-off homer in game four took some of the enthusiasm out of the raucous Miller Park crowd. Pat Burrell hit two homers that day, and Joe Blanton pitched well. The Phils won the game 6-2, and with it the series, three games to one.

There is nothing like winning a playoff series at home, but it's also pretty neat on the road. It's amazing to hear a crowd that has been at a fever pitch all day grow eerily quiet. And that's what the final out did in the ninth inning of that fourth and deciding game. There was a celebration on the field and in the clubhouse. However, it was very subdued compared to the win that had ended the regular season. It had been an exciting series, another significant step, but this team was on a mission. The Los Angeles Dodgers and Manny Ramirez were coming to town, and the smart money was convinced that the Phillies had reached the end of the line.

The Dodgers had swept the Chicago Cubs in three games, adding yet another chapter to the perpetual misery of Cubs fans. Trying to make it to a World Series for the first time since 1945, I think the Cubs had the best team in the National League. But the Dodgers came into Wrigley Field and smacked them around for two wins. Then they took the series back to Dodger Stadium and got it over quickly, sweeping the series. Many "experts" felt that the Dodgers simply had too much starting pitching for the Phillies. On paper, they may have had a point. But the Phils were a team riding a wave of emotion, especially when buoyed by the excitement generated by their home crowd.

In game one, after Ramirez had given L.A. a quick lead with a first-inning double that missed being a home run by inches, Derek Lowe was just sailing along. The Phillies were trailing 2-0 in the sixth when Victorino reached base on an error by shortstop Rafael Furcal. Then, just like that, Utley smashed a two-run shot to tie it. One out later, Burrell's solo bomb gave the Phillies a 3-2 lead, and our bullpen, solid throughout the postseason, made it hold up. In game two, played during the daytime, Brett Myers didn't pitch quite so well, but came up with three hits and knocked in three runs. There was no lack of emotion in that game after a Myers pitch went behind Manny Ramirez, but the Phillies won 8-5, and headed for the West Coast.

I've referred a lot to memories involving the Dodgers. On the long flight to L.A., my mind drifted back to 1978 and a similar flight. This time it was a lot different. That year the Dodgers had the Phillies down two games in a five-game series. Now the Phillies were up two in a seven-game series and had all the momentum. Of course, we've seen how little that can matter in this wonderful, maddening, original "game of inches."

The Dodgers fans have been portrayed throughout the years as quiet and laid-back. They'd come late and leave early. And, throughout the years, that assessment seemed accurate to me. But the fans who showed up for game three were more like an East Coast baseball crowd. They were loud from the first pitch. And when their team jumped off to a 5-0 first-inning lead, they really started giving it to the Phillies. The atmosphere on the field and in the ballpark became a little tense when Hiroki Kuroda threw at Victorino in the third inning. Obviously, it was in retaliation for what had happened with Ramirez. Victorino started yapping at the Dodgers, and the benches emptied. But now both teams were energized, and it was clear this would turn into a tough series.

Following their 7-2 win in that game, the Dodgers came out with renewed life in game four the next night. So did their fans. And their team didn't disappoint them. They built up a 5-3 lead going into the eighth inning, and it looked like the series was about to be even at two apiece. I think that was the pivotal moment, launching the sequence of events that propelled the Phillies to their world championship. Victorino had become the Dodger fans' whipping boy, and they were all over his every move. But our "Flyin' Hawaiian" was only motivated by the abuse. With a runner on base, he lined a ball to right that looked like it would hit the top of the Phillies' bullpen fence. You could hear a pin drop as the more than 56,000 fans in that classic ballpark grew quiet. The ball just cleared the wall, and the game was tied. But that was just the warm-up. Carlos Ruiz picked up a base hit, and Charlie sent Matt Stairs up to pinch-hit. What happened next is already part of Phillies lore.

Bright House Field brightens Clearwater.

Citizens Bank Park lights up the night sky.

Rooted on by Phanatic and fans . . .

"The Philadelphia Phillies are 2008 world champions of baseball!"

The parade said it all:

from City Hall . . .

to the ballpark.

Elvis and Pat led
the way.

Charlie, dressed for the occasion,
"This is for the fans."

Series MVP Cole Hamels:
"Let's do this again and
again and again."

Jamie Moyer: "I was a fan
just like you."

Perfect closer in 2008—
Brad Lidge

Brett Myers: "You have won my heart."

"The Flyin' Hawaiian" gets his turn.

Chase Utley: "World [bleeping] Champions!"

. . . and my reaction (back row, head down)

Ryan Howard looks it over.   Jimmy Rollins sums it up.

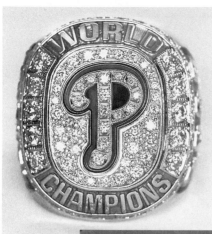

The ring

Harry and I at ALS
charity fashion show

And the beat goes on...
Raul Ibañez in 2009

Foursome at Pebble
Beach: with Charlie
Manuel, Frank Coppen-
barger, and Tom
McCarthy

At the White House

"Phillies Navidad!" With
Renée and Nittany

When Pat Gillick acquired Stairs, the feeling was that maybe he could win a game or two with his bat. Stairs, a Canadian who at age 40 resembled a coach more than a player, was a guy known as a professional hitter. Give him a fastball in the zone, and he could crush it. On the mound for the Dodgers was right-hander Jonathon Broxton, who must weigh about 280 and looks like an NFL lineman who just happens to have a 97-m.p.h. fastball. What a good matchup for the Phillies: a fastball hitter versus a hard thrower. Stairs got ahead in the count, and Broxton fired a belt-high fastball. Stairs swung, and I swear the contact between bat and ball was one of the loudest I've ever heard. It was a home run off the bat, deep into the spacious right-field pavilion, up into an area where few balls land. If the crowd had grown quiet when Victorino hit his homer, now they were almost funereal. As Stairs rounded the bases, an instant Philadelphia sports hero, the only audible sounds in the ballpark came from celebrating Phillies fans. And you could also hear Stairs' teammates clapping their hands, waiting for him in the first-base dugout where he received a memorable welcome.

Then the bullpen, our strength all season, did their job once again. Six outs later, the Phillies had a lead of three games to one over the demoralized Dodgers, and were only one game from the World Series. The Phils were ready to wind it up. Unfortunately, there was a scheduled TV off-day, so the teams had to wait an extra day to get back to business. Could L.A. shake it off? It reminded me of nothing more than what the Dodgers had done to the Phillies on Black Friday in 1977, snatching victory from a seemingly certain defeat. You never want to get too far ahead of yourself in this business, but after a win like that, weren't the Phillies destined to play for a shot at a ring?

On October 15th, Cole Hamels once again did a great job. He had to work out of a few jams. But, in the late-afternoon twilight, the Dodgers uncharacteristically threw the ball all over the place, doing their part to secure a Phils victory. Then, with two outs in the ninth, Brad Lidge continued his perfect season and popped up Nomar Garciaparra to end the game and the series. Who would represent the American League in the World Series was still undetermined. Maybe because the clinching win took place on the road or because there was more work to be done, our celebration was spirited but not off the charts. A large number of Phillies fans remained after the game to cheer the players as they came onto the field to celebrate with their own families and front-office personnel. I talked earlier about Charlie and the team enjoying everything that happened, but always staying focused. And I couldn't help but smile, thinking back to the disappointments of 1978.

I've made quite a few "red-eye" flights from California back to the East Coast—not generally very enjoyable—but the flight that night and early morning was very satisfying. I'd been around a lot of good teams, but this one had the aura of something special. Every time they faced adversity, they reached down deep and conquered it. Of course, it's not all skill and will; so much of baseball is also bounces and breaks. But they made a lot of their own luck. The sun began to rise about an hour from touchdown at Philadelphia International Airport. As we landed and our Delta charter taxied to the private area near Island Avenue, I could see a lot of activity. There were police vehicles and dignitaries waiting to meet the flight. Mayor Michael Nutter greeted David Montgomery and Charlie as they got off the plane and we headed to the buses. Then it was off to the ballpark, where quite a few fans had gathered in the early-morning hours, many looking like they hadn't slept, but had partied all night. And who could blame them? We were home with the National League Championship trophy. But one more goal remained. The World Series would be starting in the American League champions' ballpark in a week. That's one advantage of winning the All-Star Game. Would it be the Boston Red Sox or the upstart Tampa Bay Rays—experience or enthusiasm? We still didn't know, and really didn't care. The Phillies had done their part. Now all we could do was wait.

IN 2007, THE Colorado Rockies had roared through the NL postseason, sweeping the Phillies and Arizona Diamondbacks. And while their 7-0 record was impressive, they also had to sit around for a week for the start of the World Series. Now almost the same situation awaited the Phillies, who had vanquished their two opponents, 7-2.

The Red Sox and Tampa Bay Rays were involved in a tremendous series that would go to a seventh game, set for Sunday night, October 19th. Phillies director of travel Frank Coppenbarger had passed out two itineraries. Packing for them involved very different alternatives. The weather forecast for Boston was cold and rainy, with temperatures in the 40s. The Florida forecast was a lot better. The Phillies were scheduled to depart Philadelphia aboard their charter flight around noon on Monday, so we had two piles of clothing ready for the same suitcase. The Rays and Red Sox played a great game seven, finally won by the Rays around midnight. Well, at least we knew we were headed for warm weather, set to start the World Series against a very dangerous team coming in on an emotional high.

As we boarded the buses at the ballpark on Monday before heading for the airport, the atmosphere was festive. The chance to be part of a World Series traveling party doesn't come along often, so why not enjoy every minute of it? No one could envision what lay ahead—10 days of baseball for the ages. The thought of going to St. Petersburg for baseball in October was a reach in itself. At the start of the season, some had predicted the Phillies could win the NL East. But to pick the Rays as champions of the AL East, the division containing the Red Sox and Yankees? Who could imagine that scenario? It would be the second Pinellas County World Series. That part of Florida is a narrow strip of land that encompasses a large population in a very small area. It is the spring-training base of the Blue Jays and Phillies, but also contains the Rays' regular-season hometown. The first World Series between teams training in the county had not gone well, as the Jays beat the Phillies in six in 1993. But there was something comfortable about the organization returning to this part of the country for the sport's showcase. It felt almost like going home, where each of our seasons begins.

After a routine flight, our descent through the broken clouds suddenly brought the plane over a familiar body of water. Below was the Gulf of Mexico, and off to the left, the west coast of Florida. The flight was scheduled to land at St. Pete-Clearwater Airport. The approach brought us over Dunedin, home of the Blue Jays. Off to the right was the island of Sand Key, with its high-rise condominiums where many of us live during spring training. We could see old Jack Russell Stadium, then Bright House Field, as the plane banked right and headed for landing on a spectacular, 75-degree day. It felt like we were back in town for spring training, but this time the stakes were a lot higher.

The teams had an off-day Tuesday before starting the series on Wednesday, October 22nd. Just as Rollins had done in both the Brewers and Dodgers series, Chase Utley got the Phillies off to a fast start with a two-run home run in the first inning. Cole Hamels ran his postseason record to 4-0 with seven strong innings as the Phillies silenced the incessant din from those annoying cowbells with a 3-1 win. However, game two would go to the Rays, 4-2, as the Phillies stranded 11 base runners and went 0-13 with runners in scoring position. But a split on the road in a seven-game series is a plus. The Phillies headed home knowing they would not see this part of Florida again until February, if they could just win the three home games set for Citizens Bank Park.

Having won four straight postseason games, the Phils couldn't wait to open the series in front of our home fans, who by now had been whipped into a frenzy by this team they had grown to love. Our home games were a sight to behold. Football, basketball, and hockey crowds can be intimidating and make life uncomfortable for visiting teams. Football players need to hear the quarterback, and noise can be a problem. Basketball and hockey are played indoors, and the sound can't escape. But baseball is played outdoors (except in St. Pete and a few other places), and the crowds rarely are a factor. Postseason in Philadelphia in 2008 would be the exception. If there was an indoors dome din in St. Petersburg, the Phillies' crowds were absolutely wired throughout the playoffs. The atmosphere at the start of World Series game three was especially electric. Maybe it was the 15-year wait. Or just the anticipation of finally getting the game started after 10 p.m. following a 91-minute rain delay. There were few empty seats even when the game neared two a.m., tied at 4-4, at the bottom of the ninth inning. With the bases loaded and nobody out, the Rays decided to play a five-man infield. Carlos Ruiz sent the crowd home happy with an infield hit to third; the throw home was high, and the Phillies led the series, 2-1.

The Phils broke open a tight game four with a barrage of home runs, including one by winning pitcher Joe Blanton, as they romped 10-2. Unlike the Saturday-night game, Sunday night's was dry and pleasant. The whole city was set to erupt in joy if the home team could just win one more game. And they had Cole Hamels set to face the Rays in the possible clincher on Monday night. The planets were aligned. The anticipation was palpable. And nobody wanted to go back to Florida and play another game in Tropicana Field with those miserable cowbells.

The weather forecast for Monday night, October 27th, wasn't very promising. We have a broadcast workroom at Citizens Bank Park, and there were a lot of people in and out throughout the afternoon. They had been in meetings and knew that Major League Baseball was being told by *three* different weather sources about the chances of playing the game to completion. The consensus seemed to be that it was not going to be a very nice night. Light rain would start falling around 10 p.m., and heavy rain would hit the area around midnight. With the first pitch set for 8:32 p.m., it was decided that the game would start on time and hopefully be played to conclusion. Later there would be reports from others who said they had a forecast that the heavy rain would begin a lot earlier and the game would probably never be completed. Still others said they understood a full-blown nor'easter was about to form, and that it would rain for two days. No matter, we were in for a night that would provide fodder for world-class second-guessing.

The game started in a light rain, but the heavy stuff came a lot earlier than midnight. With the Phillies holding a 2-1 lead and the Rays batting in the sixth, in my opinion (along with many others), the field became unplayable. Yet play continued. The Rays tied the game with two outs, and the umpires called time, knowing the game would not be resumed. Eventually, it was determined that it would be suspended at that point and resumed when Mother Nature decided to cooperate.

But it wasn't that easy. Nobody knew what was going on during this perfect storm of screw-ups. Baseball rules provide that if the home team holds the lead after four and a half innings and the game is called, that game is official. Nobody thought a World Se-ries–clinching game should end that way. What would the Phillies do, run out on the field and roll around in the rain? That scenario was not attractive to anyone, yet no one in authority would make the decision to stop the game and not continue playing in this del-uge. Thus, when the Rays scored to tie it, everything appeared to be made a lot easier for the commissioner. And many Phillies fans blis-tered Bud Selig and the umpires as if they had conspired to give the Rays a chance to tie the game before calling time. None of this was true, of course, but the situation was handled so poorly throughout that such a theory gained credibility.

The bottom line was that everyone was unhappy. Well, maybe not the Rays, because they now had a tie and a better chance to sur-vive an elimination game. The night that had started with so much emotion and anticipation had turned bitter. The cold rain continued to whip the area—indeed, a nor'easter *had* formed—and we were told there would be no baseball until at least Wednesday. We all waited, amid negative vibrations from the fans that somehow vic-tory had been snatched from our team. Having grown up in the area and experienced all of the years of disappointment, I could under-stand the uneasiness. However, the Phillies would bat first when the game resumed in the bottom of the sixth, and they would have the potential of four at-bats to the Rays' three. And we still held a 3-1 lead in the series. But we are what we are in Philadelphia, and po-tential positives can be overshadowed, at least temporarily, by our doomsday mentality.

The game resumed on Wednesday, October 29th, after a 48-hour wait. Now that's some rain delay. When the first pitch was thrown to pinch-hitter Geoff Jenkins, all the negativity and trepidation van-ished. The re-energized crowd had come to will the Phillies to a world championship, and they were poised to explode. Jenkins set the tone by blasting a 3-2 pitch for a double to right center. The crowd erupted, and the emotion inside our beautiful ballpark for the next hour and a half defies description. I've never heard any-thing like it, and the players later stressed how much they fed off that controlled frenzy.

There probably never will be another series of events that come together to create what happened in those three innings. The Phillies had been one of the worst teams in baseball for situational play. Our team struck out a lot and didn't advance runners. But Jimmy Rollins hit a ground ball to the right side, sending Jenkins to third. The Rays opted to play the infield in, and Jayson Werth's blooper scored the go-ahead run.

It was pandemonium again, but not for long. Rocco Baldelli's homer tied it 3-3 in the top of the seventh. So it was fitting that Pat Burrell step up and play a starring role in this drama. The first over-all pick in the 1997 draft, he had had an up-and-down, love-hate relationship with the fans. He was hitless in the World Series when he worked a 3-2 count off left-hander J.P. Howell. As the ball left his bat, it looked like a home run. On a hot summer night, the ball would have been deep into the seats in left center field. But on this cold, windy night, it clanked off the fence atop the wall and bounced back into play. Burrell was slow out of the box. He knew his home park and thought it was gone. As he stopped at second, Eric Bruntlett came trotting out of the dugout to run for Pat. He would later say it crossed his mind that this could be his last game in a Phillies uniform. He soaked up the standing ovation as he headed to the dugout. Now he could only sit and watch.

For the second time in this nerve-wracking game, the Phillies played winning baseball. Shane Victorino got Bruntlett to third, and once again Joe Maddon brought his infield in. Pedro Feliz had no problem grounding a single through the drawn-in infield, and the Phillies had the lead again, 4-3.

After a scoreless eighth, Brad Lidge emerged from the bullpen to start the ninth, and 45,940 fans were on their feet. Lidge had put together a remarkable season. He had saved 47 games in 47 tries. Only one more would bring the Phillies their second title. Could he do it one more time? I remember looking to my right, where Harry was calling the game. Beside him was a cameraman with his camera pointed right at Harry. We were doing radio, but they wanted to tape his call of the final out on TV. Now I admit to being very superstitious—it's a part of the business—so my first reaction was to ask the guy to get the heck out of the booth. It would be a lie to say we weren't thinking the same thing as the fans. Lidge was overdue to blow a save, and what could be a worse time than now? And if he did, it had to be the fault of that camera. Irrational? Of course, but it made sense to me. Naturally, the spunky Rays were not about to go quietly. They had a runner at second base with one out when Ben Zobrist ripped a line-drive to Jayson Werth in right for the second out. We only needed one more. Pinch-hitter Eric Hinske was all that remained between the final out and who knows what.

I was a frayed nerve ending. It's such a long season, starting with pitchers and catchers reporting in February, right through the endless road trips and the inevitable emotional ups and downs of a season that now had extended almost to Halloween. I don't think anyone can be prepared for what happens at the moment *when* it happens. Lidge got Hinske in the hole, 0-2, and buried him with a slider. I remember hearing Harry yell, "Swing and a miss, struck him out! The Philadelphia Phillies are 2008 world champions of baseball!" The rest is a blur.

The crowd let loose all the pent-up energy of a city that had waited 28 years for this moment. The players buried Lidge in a massive pile near the mound. I remember wondering what was happening throughout the Delaware Valley. There had to be generations of fans hugging and crying in reaction to what we were witnessing at the ballpark. Smiles were everywhere as we were given "World Champions" hats and tried to sum up on the air what had just happened. Finally, our part was finished and we could go downstairs. I walked out of the third-base tunnel area and onto the field, and I just stood there and looked at the most amazing sight. The awards ceremony in center field had ended. Cole Hamels had received his MVP without somebody like me dragging him to an interview room. Things were done a little differently than in 1980. David Montgomery and Charlie Manuel had thanked the crowd for their support. And the fans responded with deafening noise that seemed to go on forever. Now things had calmed down a little, but the scene remained awesome. Few fans had left the ballpark. It was as if they had waited for this moment their whole lives and didn't want it to end. I spent a lot of time walking around, embracing players and front-office friends in this unique time of bonding that really is inexplicable.

It was a cold, raw night, and I wanted to make sure the champagne celebration had stopped before entering the clubhouse. It was not a good night to get soaked. As I walked down the dugout steps and up the ones toward the clubhouse, a blur came flying around the corner with a bottle of champagne. Chase Utley was finished with the clubhouse interviews and was headed out to the field to celebrate with his wife, Jen, and the fans. As our eyes met, he threw on the brakes and ran toward me. I said to him something like, "Man, you are a world champion." He laughed and replied, "Yes, *we* are champions," which was typical of Utley. It's never about him; it's always about the team. Then it was on to Charlie's office. This good man, who had been through so much in his life and in this town, sat calmly behind his desk, still wearing the bright red windbreaker he had worn while accepting the championship trophy. He had a big smile as he got up and about crushed me with another of those hugs that are a big part of the aftermath of what had just happened. I then looked off to my right and saw that there was one other man sitting in the room—Dallas Green. Manuel and Big D had some tense moments, culminating in a blow-up in the tunnel near the Phillies' dugout a few years earlier. But after that, they had become good friends, and now here they were, the only two men who had ever managed the Phillies to a world championship. It was one of the more touching memories of a night that will always be a highlight of the great life that I've experienced in baseball.

I left the clubhouse and wanted to head out into the crowd to find Renée and her family. I had seen them waving from the field and knew that they were still part of the crowd that wouldn't go home. On the way out the door near section 124, I ran into veteran umpire Tom Hallion, who was waiting to meet some friends. I've known Tom for a long time, and he smiled and offered his congratulations. We talked for a few minutes about what a great series we had just witnessed, and then it was out to celebrate some more. Later that evening, Renée and I went to a big postgame party in a tent down the third-base line. Like everyone around the ballclub, I felt drained. There was a tremendous feeling of satisfaction for what the players and the organization had accomplished. There were lots of smiles and more hugs, and then I saw *it* for the first time.

There were big-screen TVs all over the place, and they were tuned to some postgame shows. I think Comcast was still on the air. Several people were laughing and pointing at the screen and telling me to watch. I couldn't believe my eyes. There I was, acting like a crazy person. Later described by John Gonzalez in the *Philadelphia Inquirer* as a "full body spasm," I saw what had happened in the booth when Hinske struck out. All I remembered was consciously trying not to make any noise as Harry called that final out. When the Phillies won the World Series in 1980, we were not on the air. So this was Harry's first shot to call the final out of a World Series, and the moment was his. I saw myself alternately flinging my arms into the air and simulating someone attempting to hit a punching bag. I thought I looked like an idiot and would get all kinds of heat about it. What I later learned was that the fans enjoyed what I'd done for the sheer emotion involved. They told me that's what they were doing, too, and it was real. I still have people asking me to do "The Wheeler," and I'm happy to try. But I'm not sure how to do it. There was no choreography. It just happened.

I was just one of millions of fans that October night who shared an experience that brings a community together. You don't have to be a sports fan to get wrapped up in the joy that a championship can bring. Philadelphia is known as a city of neighborhoods, and they all came together after that strikeout by Lidge. Mayor Nutter had announced that there would be a parade on Friday, October 31st. The team and their legion of fans would have some time to catch their breath. And if everyone does love a parade, there was a big one coming to which everyone was invited.

IF THE BEGINNING of the week had proved to be a weather disaster, Friday morning, October 31st, was absolutely beautiful. It was a perfect day for a parade. The forecast was for clear skies and temperatures near 60. This time we had been told to meet at an area east of the Navy Yard. From there, the buses would take everyone up to Front and Spring Garden, where the truck-floats would be waiting.

I couldn't help noticing the difference between 1980 and 2008. Everyone showed up looking rested. The day between the clinching game and the parade had done wonders for us all. Instructions were given about who was to ride on which float, and then it was time to go. On our bus, Doris Gillick sat with me while her husband, the GM, chatted up a member of the front office. She and I talked about their future plans. I asked her if she thought Pat was serious about retiring. She said he was finished with the full-time position and was ready to move on. Later he would be named to that special-assistant role that has become so popular, and today he remains a valuable advisor to Ruben Amaro. During the course of our conversation on the ride up I-95, Doris made it clear that she wasn't the one influencing Pat's decision. She said he had made it on his own and was comfortable with it, having completed what he'd set out to accomplish.

I was to ride on float one with the broadcasters, the ball girls, and a few others. We had gotten to the staging area early, so there was a lot of time to just talk about the great season and what lay ahead. I was one of only about 10 or 15 people on board who had made the last triumphant Phillies ride down Broad Street, so I was getting a few questions. I told Sam, one of the ball girls, that it would be a great experience, adding how it would start out slowly and then pick up in intensity. I felt that the most important thing was to enjoy every minute of it. It would go by awfully fast, and you never knew when this might happen again. The floats were due to hit 18th and Market around noon, and the whole parade was supposed to take about two hours. In 1980, everything had been pretty much on schedule and moved along quickly.

I wondered what this one would be like. We already were seeing a lot of fans dressed in red and white a long way from the parade route. Fans had had time to prepare their excuses for missing work, kids skipping school—whatever it took to be a part of this day. The city was expecting a big crowd and had urged everyone to use SEPTA and ride trains downtown. That seemed like a great idea, but it turned out to be a problem because the volume of people simply overwhelmed the system. It was getting near late morning, and the sun was breaking through the late-fall haze. We were getting anxious and just wanted to get started.

Instructions were given about the vehicles. We were asked not to reach down and shake hands if people got close to the floats. Then the engines roared, and off we went west on Spring Garden. Music blared from the speakers. I probably heard "We Are the Champions" a hundred times that day, and if I heard it even more, that would have been fine. Fans were starting to line Spring Garden as the floats went by. Not big crowds, but a preview of what was to come. We crossed Broad Street, and it was starting to get a little louder. We went north on 18th Street, and the excitement started to build. Then we got to 18th and Market, and it was 1980 all over again. There were thousands of people lining the streets and waving from the office buildings. Our float turned the corner and started down Market Street, where it came to a dead stop. We would sit there for almost half an hour. We later learned that the police were trying to clear Broad Street so the official parade could begin. There were so many fans blocking the street that the huge floats—with police cars, motorcycles, and horses assigned to both sides—just couldn't make it down even this wide boulevard.

So we sat there and soaked it all in. I think it was at that point that I realized something was different from the 1980 parade, and it was pretty simple. This day was going to be louder, crazier, and more fun. And the reason was the fans. Maybe because we'd all had time to prepare, they were there to have a really good time, and we were happy to be in the show, however long it might take. We finally got started and inched down Market Street. Soon something else became apparent that was different from 1980. There was no open space anywhere. People were packed into every available spot, sometimes as far as we could see. And they all seemed to be wearing World Series merchandise. Granted, that stuff wasn't as readily available 28 years ago, and fans had more time to buy it from well-stocked stores that opened early. But it was an incredible sight—Phillies red everywhere.

The ride down Broad Street was magic. One thing I remembered from the first parade was the look of joy on the faces of the fans.

The parade of 2008 was the same—except, if possible, they seemed even happier. And so many people looked up at the floats and yelled, "Thank you! Thank you!" That's when it hit me how much this championship meant to everyone. They really liked this team, and now they could identify with them as winners. I started saying "thank you" back to the crowd. After all, it was these fans who had come out in record numbers and were such a force at the ballpark. They had been the driving motivation behind the success of their team, and we *should* be thanking them. As many of them saw me, they started doing "The Wheeler," which had already become popular on YouTube. I finally got to enjoy whatever it was that I had done after that final out.

All the way down Broad Street, it was the biggest street party in the city's history. Every part of the route was jammed with fans. The floats had to stop numerous times so the police could part this virtual red sea. As a result, we were getting way behind schedule, but who cared? During one stop, I noticed that someone was trying to climb up on our float. We figured no one was going to try that because of the police presence, but here was this big guy making his way on board. And he looked really familiar. It was Pat Burrell. He came running past us to the front of the float where the Porta-Potty was hidden behind a curtain. He emerged with a huge smile and said, "Thanks, guys. We don't have one of those on the Budweiser wagon." Pat, his wife Michelle, and his bulldog Elvis were leading the parade, and our left-fielder knew he wasn't going to make it without a pit stop.

We finally reached Citizens Bank Park, where the surrounding streets were lined with people who had either waited for the floats or followed them to the ballpark. We got off and went inside, while the players were taken over to Lincoln Financial Field, where thousands more waited to greet them. I felt like I'd been at a rock concert. As I walked down the long tunnel by the right-field line, headed for the clubhouse, my ears were ringing from the noise. The whole experience had been unforgettable. The sheer volume of fans and their enthusiasm dwarfed what we had experienced in 1980. As I approached the clubhouse, there were convertibles parked in a long line, ready to parade the team around Citizens Bank Park. We hung out in the dugout before Scott Palmer started introducing the broadcasters and front-office officials, and we took our places on the huge stage set up at second base.

Then the real show started as one by one the players, coaches, and Charlie entered the arena like conquering heroes. And in a way they were. Everyone had done something huge in the postseason, and the fans roared their approval and chanted their names as the cars made their way around the warning track. Each occupant was greeted by David Montgomery and Mayor Nutter. We just sat there and watched, and I remember thinking, "Did this really happen?" The World Series flag was unfurled out in center field, and the crowd kept screaming. One by one, Harry Kalas brought people up to the mike to speak to the crowd. And the message was almost universal. The players thanked the fans for all they had done. And they kept talking about the incredible parade, and how much they wanted to do it again . . . and again.

And then it was over. The guys did one more victory lap around the ballpark, holding up the trophy. The sun was almost gone, and a chill had started to replace the warm sunshine of this magnificent day. There was some more milling around, and food was served in the third-base dugout as the fans started to leave. But much like after the clinching game, nobody really wanted this day to end. We finally started back to the buses that would head over to the Navy Yard. I spent a lot of time just walking around, thanking the police officers who had done such a magnificent job of keeping us in one piece. They were our unsung heroes. There were a lot of things that could have gone wrong, because people were so excited. But they kept thanking us. The bus I boarded was practically empty. I headed back to the seat I occupy on road trips—second from the last on the left side—and I have no idea why. Cell and text service was impossible because so many people had the same idea.

I was starting to doze off when I saw Pat and Michelle Burrell headed to the back of the bus. And sure enough, leading the way was the ubiquitous Elvis. What a day for that canine! He had been the lead dog in the biggest parade in Philadelphia history, riding with his owner, a man who had been through the ups and downs experienced by so many Philadelphia athletes. Pat looked exhausted as he got into the seat behind me and started talking about the day. He was in awe about what he and his teammates had just witnessed. It had forever changed the way they would look at our fans in the future. Chase and Jen Utley Jen got on right behind Burrell. Elvis needed a drink, so Jen produced a big bottle of water and Elvis started drinking. And drinking and drinking. Then he passed out on his side. The day was over and everyone was mentally and emotionally drained.

Once we got back to the Navy Yard and our cars, we all started to scatter and take with us our memories of what for me was a twice-in-a-lifetime day. I couldn't wait to get back to Blue Bell where Renée and our friend, longtime season ticket–holder Eileen Pluck, were waiting at the Blue Bell Country Club for dinner. I got into my car, and the perfect day hit a little snag. I had driven down to the staging area in the early morning with my lights on and, you guessed it, I now had a dead battery. Almost everyone had left except the highway patrol officers on their motorcycles. I sheepishly walked over and told them what had happened, asking if anyone had jumper cables. One officer said to wait and he would drive to their headquarters and get some. I managed to find one person left in the lot—Dave Schofield, one of our photographers, who said he'd wait with me. Out of the darkness came the cop on the motorcycle, and he got my car started. If the players were the fans' heroes that day, that highway patrolman was number one with me, with an assist from Dave.

As a man lucky enough to have been a part of two World Series parades in our great sports town, it's hard to describe the magnitude of both of those October days, 28 years apart. They were so different, yet each as special as the teams and personalities who won the championships that made them possible. Yes, everyone loves a parade.

CHAPTER 11

Clearwater Then and Now

MARCH IS A TRANSITIONAL month, with occasionally milder days bringing tantalizing promise of more to come. After a winter of anticipation and speculation, spring training itself is chronicled these days as intensively as a presidential primary— the prelude to the main event. Cameras follow the players' every move. Not only do local TV stations send reporters to document the preparation for the start of a new season, but the national sports media also descend upon increasingly elaborate training complexes, whether in Florida or Arizona. Reporters move around solo or in packs with open notebooks, documenting the words of anyone will- ing to share his thoughts. Blogs are part of the newspaper business these days, and anything new can be on the Internet in a matter of minutes. Like it or not, we live in the era of instant gratification and constantly updated "breaking news" (or non-news), in our case fo- cused on the Phillies.

But it wasn't always this way. To this young baseball fan in the '50s and '60s, the news about our favorite players came in bits and pieces. We had to wait for the stories of famed writers like Allen Lewis of the *Philadelphia Inquirer* or Ray Kelly of the Philadelphia *Bulletin*. And those stories always began the same way, with capital letters: CLEAR- WATER, FL. To a kid who considered visiting his Aunt Rosie in Warminster an adventure, I was fascinated by this far-off place. I liked geography and knew that Clearwater was on the west coast of Florida, about 1,200 miles from my house. But what was it like to be playing baseball down there when it was so cold up here? Some of my friends talked about going to California or some other distant place. All I wanted to do was to go to Clearwater and see the Phillies.

Having started working with the ballclub in July 1971, I had been with the team for five months when Larry Shenk began talking about spring training. He said he would need my help down there, and I would have to think about making plans to leave town in February and return in late March. That winter went by pretty fast. I had to have my bags packed at the ballpark by the date when our equipment truck would be leaving to go south. The Phillies would rent a car for me, and I would pick it up at the airport in Tampa. I knew that was somewhere near Clearwater.

Larry and I flew to Tampa and waited for our luggage and rental car. He said we would be going west on Route 60 over a large body of water, and to follow him. That drive from Tampa to Clearwater, about 12 miles over the Courtney Campbell Causeway, will always be breathtaking. But that day in February 1972, I thought I was in paradise. I had my windows rolled down and music blaring on the radio. It was 30 degrees when we'd left Philadelphia, but now the weather was more suited for a convertible. I wish I'd been driving one. I kept following The Baron as we finished our ride across the water. Then we got on a road leading through a little town full of palm trees. I'd never seen a palm tree—now there were hundreds. Soon we arrived at our destination: the legendary Jack Tar Hotel (formerly the Fort Harrison) in downtown Clearwater, the spring-training headquarters of the Philadelphia Phillies. I already knew this place because Ray Kelly and Allen Lewis had written about it so many times.

The next day, I saw the Carpenter Training Complex for the first time. Then it was off to the ballpark I'd heard and read so much about—Jack Russell Stadium. Named after a former major-league pitcher, later a local oil dealer, it was situated at the corner of Seminole and Greenwood. Across the street was a beat-up field where spring training had been held until the complex was built in the late '60s. I remember the players had named it Iwo Jima, and I could see why. It was in bad shape after years of neglect, and now served as a parking lot. Even when it was in "good" shape, it had to have been a terrible place to try to field a ground-ball.

A typical day in 1972 would start with the morning workout at the training complex. There I would learn for the first time how little I knew about this game I'd thought I understood so thoroughly. Pitchers and catchers report first to get in shape about a week before the regulars. So every morning they would throw off the six mounds under the watchful eye of pitching coach Ray Ripplemeyer. I couldn't believe the sound the baseball made hitting a catcher's glove. Every guy looked to me like he was throwing 100 miles an hour. Then they would throw breaking pitches, and I just knew that National League hitters had no chance against these guys. They were that good. Of course, that was the year the Phillies won 59 games, finished dead last, and were one of the worst teams in history. Steve Carlton still hadn't been acquired in the trade for Rick Wise, which would come a few days later. At least I would have been right about him.

Following the workout, The Baron and I would return to our office at the hotel. Back then, all the players and team personnel had to live in the same place. Even some of the media stayed there. We would work on news releases and publications, chatting up anyone who might come by our office up on the second-floor mezzanine of the gracious old hotel. The guys who covered the team were almost part of the family. Everyone would gather in The Cheese Room, where John Quinn would hold court as the alcohol flowed and the stories followed. It was an amazing sight to watch the interaction between the old baseball men and the reporters. It's hard to imagine the camaraderie that existed then. We still were years away from today's more adversarial role. To me, it was fascinating and educational.

Once that part of the night was over, it was time for dinner. The Jack Tar had a bar called the Gaslight Buggy. Everyone would change clothes and head down there for more cocktails. We had few choices of locations for dining. Normally, we'd wind up at the famed Heilman's Beachcomber or the Island House, located across Mandalay Avenue from the Beachcomber. A night at the Beachcomber would include a great meal and some spontaneous entertainment provided by people around the Phillies. There was also a piano in the middle of the restaurant. The woman who played it was named Helen. She was my first look at the kind of pianist Billy Joel would later sing about. Helen had a jar for tips and would take requests. Bus Saidt, a sportswriter for the *Trenton Times,* was a fixture at the Beachcomber, and every night he would head for the piano. Clutching his crème de menthe, Bus would perform his repertoire of show tunes and standards. As I recall, "Fly Me to the Moon" was one of his favorites. I heard it so many times that it's still in my head when I return to the Beachcomber. Once Bus started singing, we knew the night was winding down and it was time to head back over the Memorial Causeway to the hotel and bedtime. Then it would start all over the next day. I was having the time of my life.

CLEARWATER IN 1972 was still a sleepy Southern town. It hadn't been that long since reality had intruded into our world of fun and games. We think of Florida as a land of sun, beaches, and golf courses. But at one time it was a state as much ruled by segregation as Mississippi. African-American and Latin players were not allowed to stay at the team's hotel. Men like Bill White, Tony Taylor, and Dick Allen had to find other accommodations in a different part of town. I would hear them tell stories about those days and try to interject some humor. But the scars and bitterness remained. By the time I got to my first spring training, the Jim Crow laws were gone. Still, I had a hard time believing what so recently had been law in a city that seemed nearly perfect to me.

Fans coming to the area now see many of the same landmarks, but the changes are significant. Many of us live on a beautiful island called Sand Key. You cross over the Memorial Causeway from the mainland and enter Clearwater Beach. Then it's about a mile ride south before a bridge over the Clearwater Pass to an area now populated on both sides of Gulf Boulevard by condominiums of varying sizes. There are spectacular water views of the Gulf of Mexico on one side and the Intercoastal Waterway on the other. In 1972, Sand Key was just that—an island of sand dunes with one public park at the north end. North of the training complex, there was little above

Sunset Point Road. Now there are the communities of Countryside and Palm Harbor. Multimillion-dollar homes, shopping centers, and huge golf courses like Innisbrook dominate the area along Route 19. The bulk of the residents and tourists come from the Midwest. That's because I-75 leads to the west coast of Florida from the Midwestern states. I was surprised to hear fans cheering for the Minnesota Twins and Detroit Tigers during exhibition games at Jack Russell Stadium. It was a home game for them.

The playing field at the ballpark, built in the '50s, was shared with a nationally known championship softball team, the Clearwater Bombers. They played softball on a "skin" (non-grass) infield. So when the Phillies showed up for games in March, the city would hastily put down some turf, and it never had time to take root. It was bumpy, and as the sun beat down, it grew rock-hard. Exhibition games were not a big deal. The ticket prices were low, and the games were sparsely attended, unless the Twins or Tigers came to town. The field was not covered at night by a tarp. If it rained and the Phillies had a home game, it was simply postponed. It's hard to believe today, but that's how minimal the revenues from ticket sales were. In bad weather, the players would hit in the batting cages, the pitchers would throw, and life went on.

All this started to change for the Phillies in 1979. The Cincinnati Reds had trained for many years in Tampa and then had moved about 20 miles northeast to Plant City. So when Pete Rose put on a Phillies uniform and came across the bay to play in Pinellas County, exhibition games for the Phillies changed forever. Sellouts became common. We even got a tarp to cover the field at night in case it rained. Postponements now were important. We wanted to play every game, and the fans were coming out in record numbers. I'll never forget the sight of a rope stretched in the outfield from foul pole to foul pole. Standing-room (or sitting-room) tickets were sold for the overflow crowds. We had to inform the umpires of a new ground rule: Balls hit into the fans in front of the high cinder-block walls were ground-rule doubles. It caused a few problems, but everyone wanted to see Pete Rose, and the Phillies were determined to accommodate as many fans as possible, no matter who they were rooting for.

Throughout the years, Jack Russell Stadium saw a series of renovations to increase the size of the ballpark. The Phillies kept signing lease extensions to assure the city fathers that financing improvements would result in expanding revenues for Clearwater. In turn, the Phillies agreed to stay and invest in this accommodating area for years to come. It was a perfect arrangement. As teams started to move around Florida looking for new locations, the Phillies' established winter home continued to get better. Eventually, the Bombers had their own field constructed near the Phillies' training facility, and a permanent, grass-and-dirt field was laid down at Jack Russell.

Things had certainly improved, but the team and the city started envisioning and talking about a new ballpark in the 1990s. Like any ambitious project, there were a myriad of challenges. How much would it cost? Where should it be? How about guarantees to stay? Still, a new facility seemed almost inevitable. Even though Jack Russell remained a charming old venue, the key word was *old*. It was getting to the point that little more could be done to improve the place. And the foundation, built in the '50s, was starting to crumble. Eventually, the state, the city, and the Phillies got together on a plan and a suitable location. Jack Russell Stadium was about to become part of the long history connecting the Phillies and the city of Clearwater. Bright House Field was on the horizon, but none of us could imagine how much it would change the way the ballclub conducted spring training.

For the Phillies organization, it was an unprecedented time of ambitious plans. The Phils were proposing to build *two* new ballparks, both to open in 2004. Since each had been in the works for a number of years, it was actually a coincidence that both would open at around the same time. But that only doubled the headaches for David Montgomery and so many other people involved in both the hometown and Florida projects.

First up was the new spring-training home of the Phillies. From the beginning, the idea was to build a "mini" version of what the team had planned for South Philadelphia. Both venues had to offer fun for the whole family, but Bright House, in particular, should reflect the laid-back lifestyle of Florida—a tiki bar in left field, but also a really good cheesesteak stand. Fans coming to either new ballpark should be able to see the game from many different angles. The ideal design would be a facility where fans could walk around the whole perimeter of the place and never miss a pitch. Of course, some people might come just to have a good time, and never even see a pitch. There would be no shortage of amenities for them. Beyond its Florida ambiance, the Phillies wanted their new Bright House Field to reflect what was to come at home. It has the same dimensions, complete with that angle in left center field designed to produce crazy bounces and occasionally one of the most exciting plays in baseball—a triple.

Like a lot of people, I had mixed emotions about leaving Jack Russell Stadium. It was the classic old minor-league park with so much history, and a place I'd envisioned long before I actually got to see it. But it had gotten to the point where it was starting to become a safety hazard. In fact, at a time when the ballpark proponents were trying to win over the critics, a Clearwater city commissioner named Hoyt Hamilton fell through part of the crumbling structure and landed in the old right-field clubhouse. After suffering a broken ankle in the fall, he didn't need to be persuaded that something had to be done. So we went through the final spring training in 2003 at Jack Russell, savoring the memories and looking forward to what was to come.

Spring training, 2004 was the time to christen Brighthouse Networks Field (its original name). A Pinellas County cable company, they had purchased the naming rights, just like in the big leagues. The name was a mouthful, but at my first sight of the new ballpark, I forgot I'd ever put Jack Russell Stadium on a pedestal. I was asked to emcee the opening-night ceremony. We couldn't have had a worse night. It was really cold—temperatures in the low 50s with a stiff wind out of the northeast. But the festive atmosphere of the evening helped take away some of the chill as, one by one, the dignitaries responsible for putting the deal together came proudly to the podium to appraise their final product.

The earliest indication we received that the Phillies and the city of Clearwater had built the best ballpark in Florida came on the first trip across the bay by the Yankees. They had opened their own facility a few years earlier and named it Legends Field, an appropriate choice for a franchise with the history of the New York Yankees. George Steinbrenner still was front and center in those days. The first game between the two teams was played on a Chamber of Commerce day. It was just perfect—sunny, with a temperature in the 70s—and the place was packed. I know I'm prejudiced, but although very attractive, Legends (now George M. Steinbrenner Field) isn't quite legendary. There is no nicer place to watch a ball game than Bright House Field on such a day. The grass berms in left and right center field were filled with fans lounging on blankets, soaking up the sun. The concession stands were packed. Frenchy's Tiki Bar was 10 deep as the bartenders hastened to serve so many cheerful patrons. All this was taken in by Steinbrenner, who was being entertained in one of the suites along the first-base line. We later heard that he ripped into his people about how the Phillies had put the Yankees to shame with their new playpen. A customary eruption from George can't have been pleasant, but all of us enjoyed hearing that the wealthiest, most famous franchise in the history of our sport envied something that Philadelphians had done. It was a stamp of credibility on the herculean effort to bring what became Bright House Field (the name was shortened two years ago) to fruition.

Attendance has been through the roof since the park opened. Its official capacity of 8,300 often exceeds 10,000. Legions of Phillies fans dressed in red and white make their annual pilgrimage to Florida's west coast to combine vacation and baseball. With few exceptions, they are as one in their assessment of the new ballpark: as family-friendly as it is fan-friendly. Once you've made the migration, you'll want to come back year after year, just as we do. Not surprisingly, on the heels of their world championship, the Phils set a new spring-training attendance mark in 2009. And with some minor improvements each year, the place should keep getting better and better.

CLEARWATER HAS CHANGED so much since my first trip across the Courtney Campbell Causeway in 1971. However, the area's population explosion brings with it all the trials and tribulations that come with success. The highway system is ill-equipped to handle the massive number of people who come here, especially during the months of January, February, and March. The city and state have done their best to keep pace by widening roads and building overpasses on the heavily traveled Route 19, but it's almost impossible to catch up. The whole Tampa/St. Pete/Clearwater area is so aggressively promoted, and Clearwater Beach itself has become one of Florida's prime tourist attractions. Still, more teams have left Florida's "Grapefruit League" during the past few years and headed for the "Cactus League" of Arizona. Unlike many areas of Florida that have been overbuilt, Arizona is a more spacious place where, despite its own development, desert land remains plentiful. It's hard to turn down the great deals offered by cities in that state for ballpark and training complexes. For example, after a long tenure in Vero, Florida, where the famed "Dodgertown" was the crown jewel of training facilities, the Los Angeles Dodgers finally succumbed to the siren song of Arizona and moved to Glendale. It's hard to blame them. After all, they were the Brooklyn Dodgers when Dodgertown opened. Arizona is a lot more convenient than Florida for a team that calls California home. But their move was a great loss to the Grapefruit League, and Florida is now scrambling to convince other teams to return.

The Phillies aren't going anywhere. We now have the best facility in what I view as the finest area of Florida. Every team that comes to Bright House Field raves about it. And if they want to know what it's like to live and train here, we're happy to support the local chamber of commerce in promoting the locale of our second residence. As for home base, Citizens Bank Park in South Philadelphia, I honestly consider it to be the best of all the new, amenity-oriented "retro" ballparks—no matter what some pitchers may think. And that's where I'll be heading after gazing out at the glistening gulf one last time this spring.

CHAPTER 12

Two Weeks in April

OPENING DAY WOULD BE different this year. Spring training, as it always does, unfolded in cycles. First, the pitchers and catchers report. Then, after daily workouts, they get bored and can't wait until the rest of the squad reports. Then the full squad works out, and can't wait for the exhibition season to start. Then they can't wait for the regular season. The cyclical nature of spring training culminates at the end of March when it's time to come home. They can't wait to pack their bags, fly north, and whatever the weather, get those final two exhibition games at Citizens Bank Park out of the way and start the real season, when every game matters.

Except, that is, for people like me who would normally give anything to stay in the Clearwater sun for an extra month or so. I remember even in that strike-delayed season of 1995, when we didn't have Opening Night until April 28th, that was fine with me. I wouldn't have to be dragged up north, kicking and screaming, to face baseball in the chill of a Mid-Atlantic April.

But defending a world championship made everything different in 2009, even to me. We were all really looking forward to getting started, to all the ceremonies, and to receiving our rings. And everything went smoothly, starting with the flight up from Tampa. I arrived home in Blue Bell around 10 p.m. on Thursday, April 2nd. Our annual welcoming reception by the Chamber of Commerce the next day drew a record turnout of their members to the ballpark. In three different locations, from the Hall of Fame level to the Diamond Club, there were to be question-and-answer sessions with the players. Then everyone would come down to the field level for the actual ceremonies.

Afterward, the players would have time to work out, because there would be a game that night, the first of our two final exhibition games against, of all teams, the Tampa Bay Rays, our opponent in the 2008 World Series. And right there, in street clothes, was our old friend and new Ray, Pat Burrell. I walked toward him to say hello. After he'd greeted pitching coach Rich Dubee and bullpen coach Mick Billmeyer, Pat gestured to the Phillies' bench and said to me, "I'll always be part of that bunch over there, the best teammates I ever had." It would be the first of many emotional moments.

We shook hands just before it was time for the program to start. I would be the emcee, but that's not the way it had been planned. Harry Kalas was to have hosted the event. But the prior evening, after our return from Tampa, he'd experienced a health problem, was taken to the hospital for observation, and would remain there overnight. As has been customary for so many years, Dan Baker started things off, introducing David Montgomery, Mark Schweiker (the outgoing president of the Chamber), other notables, and Charlie Manuel, who each said a few words. Then Dan introduced me. I said I viewed it as an honor to substitute for Harry, our "Hall of Fame voice, who we all expect will be back with the club really soon." Then I introduced each player, including those bound for Triple-A and Double-A ball, who although still around largely for the remaining exhibition games, were just happy to be here. I'm no Dan Baker, but I'd been the PA announcer for games in Clearwater since coming aboard in 1971, and it was kind of fun. Originally, I'd been a replacement there, too. I remember Larry Shenk saying to me that the guy who normally did it, a friend of the Carpenter family, had been "over-served" the night before and was temporarily out of action. Could I fill in? Of course, I said yes. I'd never done it, but as I always tell kids who want to get into broadcasting, "Never turn anything down. Whenever you're asked if you've ever done something, either say 'Yes' or 'I'll try it.'" I'd never done any PA work, but I'm still at the mike in Clearwater 38 years later.

The exhibition game that night was to be broadcast only on radio. So I was able to get back home and unpack in a leisurely way, after two months in Clearwater, and enjoy a relaxing evening. The next, and final, exhibition game, on Saturday, April 4th, would start at 1:05 p.m. and be telecast on MyPhl 17. After 34 exhibition games, we just wanted to get it over with. But the fans were excited to see the team on the field. Would Harry be able to make it? Yes, it turned out he would. "I feel pretty good," he said, after being released from the hospital. The tests turned out OK, and he'd been cleared to do whatever he wanted. What he wanted was to broadcast that final exhibition game against the Rays. Harry had minor surgery in January, and many of us were concerned about his health. He had turned 73 on March 19th, and the challenges of constant travel do take their toll. Though 73 is hardly considered ancient these days, it seemed to me that despite his sustained enthusiasm, Harry appeared frail. He still sounded great, but clearly he looked tired. It was suggested that he might want to do only home games this coming season, but he was having none of it. It sounded too much like the first stage of retirement, and he was not about to become a candidate for part-time broadcaster. Ever the professional, Harry the K sounded as good as ever in that final exhibition game.

The next night, Sunday, April 5th, the world-champion Phillies would have the distinction of launching the 2009 major-league baseball season. The game, to be televised nationally on ESPN2, was to start at eight p.m. Our opponent would be our perennial rival, the Atlanta Braves, an attractive matchup. Only *that* game would be played on Sunday. All the other major-league teams were to start their seasons later. When I heard we were the opener, I thought, "Oh, no, it will be a brutally cold April night." Well, I couldn't have been more wrong. It turned out to be a beautiful evening, calm and clear, the temperature hovering above 50 degrees at game time. Pregame ceremonies were spectacular, the special circumstances supplementing what the Phillies normally do so well. Flanked by the customary lines of fans clad in red, this time the players made their way on a more extended route, starting with a parade into Citizens Bank Park, then through the stands and down the steps to the field, high-fiving everyone on the way. There was the customary huge American flag in center field, held by military service personnel, but also our championship flag, raised by Charlie Manuel—a memorable moment with cameras flashing everywhere. Members of the 82nd Airborne parachuted in, although one missed his mark and landed in the parking lot. There's always a little reminder of Bill Giles in the opener. Starting with the coaches, trainers, and support staff, the noise grew louder. By the time the teams were introduced, the decibel level was unbelievable. The Phillies' starting lineup was introduced in reverse order—nine through one—Brett Myers to Jimmy Rollins, a special-occasion innovation. It was all such an effective mix of pomp, ceremony, and spontaneity. A perfect night.

Only Derek Lowe failed to cooperate. The ultimate "worm-killing" sinkerball pitcher, he had it all working. All those ground-ball outs turned Lowe into a dream-killer as well. The Phils just couldn't hit him. Lowe was at his best as Atlanta's starter that night. Myers, on the other hand, struggled in the first two innings. He gave up three home-run balls, and before we knew it, after two, the home team was down 4-0. By the end of this anticlimactic game, which the Phillies lost 4-1, all the persistent questions about the upcoming season had resurfaced. Did we have too many left-handed hitters in our lineup? Two of them, Raul Ibañez and Ryan Howard, had been struck out in the ninth by lefty relief pitcher Mike Gonzalez. What about our starting pitching? Myers had steadied after the second inning, but how consistent would he be throughout the season? And what about Hamels' elbow? The next day we had off, providing more time for premature gloom and doom to set in and simmer. Football must be agonizing to cover—a whole week between games to dwell on all the analysis, second-guessing, negatives, and dissection. But *we* had 161 games to go. Still, it was deflating—such a shame that the high-flying crowd had been silenced by a low-ball pitcher.

Unfortunately, the next game was more of the same. But on Tuesday evening, the weather *was* cold and windy. In the first inning, the Braves jumped out early again. This time the victim was our veteran left-hander, Jamie Moyer. The home-run ball again did the damage, and the final score was 4-0. Against Jair Jurrjens and four relief pitchers, the Phils could manage only six hits, yet left 11 men on base. That had been a perennial problem, even in the championship season of 2008. Well, we'd started the new season 0-2, but the buzz hadn't diminished.

To me and probably a lot of others, the real opener would be the following afternoon, Wednesday, April 8th, slated to start at 3:05, the third and final game of our series with Atlanta. It would be telecast on Comcast SportsNet along with the prior ceremony, starting around two p.m., with the awarding of rings to those in attendance who had played in the championship season, plus the coaches and trainers, their immediate support staff. Everyone else in the organization, including the broadcasters, would receive the rings in June, and we would have our choice of the weighty, full-size version or a smaller replica that is easier to wear. The whole ring process was carried out with exceptional secrecy and a lack of leakage that would do the CIA proud. A committee of seven men and women selected a jeweler and together carefully developed the design. Although some of the players were disappointed that they had no inkling of what their ring would look like, later they realized that it had been a good idea.

I think it's fair to say that, in good times or bad, no organization in sports does a better job of planning and conducting such ceremonies than the Phillies. Imagine what it would be like now that we had finally won. The whole pregame progression began with the laying out of the red carpet for Dan Baker, in black tie as usual, who read off each name. David Montgomery came out to preside, greeting each ring recipient in turn. The afternoon was a bit chilly, but thankfully dry. There was nothing chilly or dry about the reception. A large white van, flanked by motorcycle police, came slowly into the ballpark from right field. After it parked, two ballgirls carefully took out about 40 individual wooden boxes and placed them on two large tables set up next to Baker's microphone. Each presentation box held only a single ring.

First to receive theirs were outgoing general manager Pat Gillick and manager Charlie Manuel. I was surprised to see that Gillick, usually so self-contained, was already crying. And then I realized how much this meant to him. Although he'd guided two prior championship teams at Toronto, this day marked the end of his active career in baseball. He'd stay on, advising his successor, Ruben Amaro Jr., but by his own choice, he'd never be a GM again. I began to reflect on how I'd seen others react to the reality of retirement, both on and off the field.

In *The Boys of Summer*, Roger Kahn wrote, "Unlike most, a ball player must confront two deaths." Just as his contemporaries are hitting their stride in their chosen professions, he is facing the uncertainty of retirement in his. I thought of Tim McCarver, setting out to be a broadcaster at 38. And of the emotion of Mike Schmidt, who'd played every one of his 2,404 games in a Phillies uniform. The day he could no longer make a routine play, in midseason, he had too much pride to continue. I'd stood beside him at that impromptu press conference he held in San Diego to announce his immediate retirement. Perhaps his tears that day endeared him to Philly fans more than any prior accomplishment. And I thought of that other fierce competitor and icon of the 1980s, also too often misunderstood—Steve Carlton. Only Lefty had chosen to continue his career. Harry and I went up to visit him the day after he was released by the Phillies. He was as upbeat and confident as ever, and incredibly gracious, a side not always visible to everyone. And so, I think I could appreciate Pat Gillick's tears. His decision had been determined two years before, and his managerial skills had hardly diminished, but he was still facing the end of an active, productive career in the profession he loved.

One of the most sustained ovations greeted Pat Burrell, who was able to return for the ceremony because his new team was not to play until that evening. He had earlier been greeted by a similar reaction from the fans when he came to bat for Tampa Bay during those two final exhibition games. He just didn't look quite right in their uniform. Behind his dark glasses, it appeared that Pat Gillick was not the only one to shed tears that afternoon.

Each presentation box was about the size of a deluxe cigar box. At first the players, as excited as little kids on Christmas morning, seemed reluctant to open theirs. Jamie Moyer was the first to take out his ring, try it on, and show it to the camera. Then, one by one, other players did the same, their smiles saying it all for PhanaVision. The ring was already up there for everyone to see from the start of the ceremony. It is spectacular, personalized with each player's name and number, an image of the world championship trophy on one side and the Liberty Bell on the other—encompassing 103 diamonds, one for each Phillies victory in 2008, in an immense creation comprising nearly four carats. It's possible to be overwhelmed by such "bling," but it also represents the joy of accomplishment. I got to see it courtesy of Frank Coppenbarger, director of team travel and clubhouse services, and a member of the designing committee that had done its job so well. Earlier he had let on only that it would be "outstanding." In my office, I was able to hold his ring and try it on my finger, appreciating its heft.

Later, when I met Renée and our friends Larry and Eileen Pluck, they too had the thrill of trying on a ring belonging to pitcher Scott Eyre. David Montgomery was hosting a reception in the Phillies' executive dining room for everyone on the team and their families. Scott came by to ask if I'd seen his wife, and to get directions to the party. In the process he showed us his own ring, and Renée, Eileen, and Larry each had a chance to try it on. We took pictures, their faces beaming. Such casual interaction made them Scott Eyre fans for life. It typifies the appealingly generous nature of the players on this Phillies team. It's not difficult to pull for them.

The game that day? It's easier to describe than explain. How could our team take the field to play focused baseball for nine innings after all the emotions of such a ceremony? Perhaps the greatest ovation of all was for Harry Kalas as he walked to the mound to throw out the first ball. He stood there soaking up the adulation of the crowd, and had some fun. Once, then twice, he shook off the sign, imitating a pitcher's reaction to what his catcher called for. Then he one-hopped his throw to the plate, and as the noise got louder, he waved his arms in mock dismay. Finally, he tossed the ball to the crowd before heading to the booth.

Joe Blanton started the game. The Braves hit him with a five-spot in the third, and before we knew it, we were getting smoked, 10-3.

But then it looked like 2008 all over again. In one memorable seventh inning featuring five walks and four timely hits, the Phils scored eight runs. Three successive Braves pitchers simply couldn't find the plate. Later, Bobby Cox, their Hall of Fame manager, said he'd never seen anything like it. Well, didn't Harry always say one of the joys of going to the ballpark each day was the possibility of seeing something you'd never witnessed before? For the first time in the new season, our screaming, intimidating fans had something to cheer about during the game itself. To Charlie Manuel it was like old times, confirming the never-say-die tenacity of his players. Heart-stopping to the end, we eventually won, 12-11.

When, early in the game, our cameras showed a little girl in the stands, carrying a big sign saying "Make My Pfirst Game a Winner," I commented that it would take quite a rally to bring that about. I never dreamed that remark would come true. It would be a stretch to view the third game of any season as pivotal, but despite our miseries on the mound, it was a lot better to take to the road with an initial record of one and two than with three losses. It was off to a three-game series in Denver, followed by three in Washington, and a much-anticipated trip to the White House on Tuesday, April 14th, where Sarge could renew his acquaintance with his old friend from Chicago, the President of the United States. Why Philly to Colorado to D.C.? Well, once or twice each season, the schedule-makers get goofy, and that's just the way it works. It would be tough, flying from Denver and losing two hours in the process, to get to Washington for a game the next afternoon.

On our flights, I usually sit by the window, in the first row facing the bulkhead, just behind first class. Generally, Frank Coppenbarger is in the next row, on the aisle, and we often converse. Harry Kalas normally settled in the back row with the players—the only broadcaster I've known to be accorded this honor. However, on this flight, he sat only three or four rows back on the left side of the plane. "What's he doing there?" I asked Frank. He said that Harry had requested it, that he was a little tired and didn't want to walk all the way back. But it wasn't like him at all. He cherished his acceptance by the players and enjoyed sitting with them.

The pattern continued in the Denver series. Our starting pitchers were lit up, our relief pitching held up, and our hitting enabled us to come from behind. The first game, however, wasn't close, as the Rockies, a good offensive team, put it out of reach. In the second game, which Charlie felt had shown a lot of our "heart," we came from behind to win. It looked like a pattern was developing for the season. But it was the final game in the series that everyone will remember, evoking memories of 2008, and recreating that key playoff game with the Dodgers. The weather in the mile-high city was brutal, cold, windy, and miserable. This time it was Chan Ho Park who had been roughed up. Behind 5-3, Chase Utley tied the score in the eighth with a two-run homer (it had been Shane Victorino in 2008). Then who would step to the plate with a man on base but pinch-hitter Matt Stairs, whose philosophy of hitting is simple: Try to hit the ball as hard and as far as you can. Déjà vu. He rocketed one "outta here," just as he had in that playoff game, where it appeared we'd had no chance. Getting great relief from Madson and Lidge, the Phillies won, 7-5. With those big blows, it was even more exciting than that eight-run inning at home featuring the bases-loaded walks. A lot of us stayed for a while in the visitors' clubhouse to watch the end of an equally exciting Masters. Trying to explain golf to the garrulous Shane Victorino was a challenge. I finally said, "Shane, will you listen to me?" Jimmy Rollins responded dryly, "Wheels, I've been trying to get him to listen to *me* for three years." Then it was off to the bus to catch our flight. We got into D.C. around midnight their time. Our first game with the Nationals, on Monday, April 13th, would be their home opener, and already the third opener we'd participated in. Slated to start at 3:05, it didn't give us much time to rest.

Settled into our hotel in Arlington, Virginia, across the Potomac, we boarded our scheduled 11:30 bus for the 15-minute trip to Nationals Park. On the bus that morning was the normal cast of characters. The broadcast team almost always goes out together along with Frank Coppenbarger. Some players ride with us, but for the most part they go out early and have their own routines. Ryan Madson was the last person to board before the doors closed. I gave

Harry the K my customary "Good morning." I was seated across from Pat Gillick. He was in town to join us for our White House visit the following day. Then he'd planned to fly to different cities so he could personally present their 2008 World Series rings to those no longer with the team. We talked about that, the exciting weekend series in Colorado, and baseball in general.

Pat greeted Harry with a big "Harry Kalas," always kind of dragging the name out, and complimented him on his first-ball toss the preceding Thursday at Citizens Bank Park. Harry sheepishly responded that he was still embarrassed about bouncing the throw. Pat had done a better job on Opening Night. They both laughed, and then Harry looked in my direction to see what I was wearing. That had become an ongoing joke in the last few years. We had started wearing similar shirts, jackets, or pullovers for the TV openings, and sometimes it could get confusing. Either of us could wind up with the wrong color or the wrong outfit. It was a cool day, and I was wearing a leather coat. I told Harry my red pullover, the garb for the day, was in my bag. He told me he also had his, so it looked like we'd match. He laughed and walked to his customary back-row seat. Little did I know those few words were the last we'd exchange.

When I got to the ballpark, I headed for Charlie Manuel's office to record his pregame radio show. Charlie had a lot on his mind that morning and wanted to talk a bit before recording the show. Afterward, I walked out of his office to get some information from bench coach Pete Mackanin in the coaches' room. Now it was time to head for the elevator to the press box.

Wheeling my game-day bag, I was halfway out the door of the clubhouse when I heard Frank Coppenbarger call out my name. "Wheels, come here," he said, "I have to tell you something." Inside the spacious new room, he was seated at a desk, filling out ticket envelopes from the players' comp lists, one of his many jobs. But then his phone rang. It was the Phillies manager of broadcasting, Robert Brooks. Obviously, something serious had happened because Frank said, "No, oh no." With an anguished look on his face, he then glanced up at me with the news. Harry Kalas had collapsed in the booth. "Brooksie says that he is down on the floor and the EMTs are working on him."

What went through my mind I can only try to reconstruct. My first instinct was to get upstairs as fast as possible, yet I was wary of what I'd find. And what could I do, anyway? Then my old PR instincts kicked in, and I went looking for our director of baseball communications, Greg Casterioto. I found him by the indoor batting cage, standing next to Charlie. Later he told me I'd had a strange look on my face. I told them about Harry's collapse, that I didn't yet have any details, but that they'd better be prepared for any eventuality.

Greg and I then walked toward the field-level elevator, saying little. When the doors opened, we heard a commotion. Then we saw a chilling sight—professionals trying to save a life. Several emergency medical technicians were working furiously on a still figure lying on his back on a gurney, his face covered by an oxygen mask. At the same time, they were wheeling him quickly to an ambulance. How often had we seen something like this in the movies or TV? Only this time it was real life. The man they worked on was my friend and colleague of 38 years, Harry Kalas. All this occurred in the space of about 10 seconds.

In shock, I did what came instinctively, taking the elevator up to our TV booth on level seven, the highest press box in baseball. When I got out, I ran into two remaining EMTs. I asked them some questions they didn't want to answer. That is when I heard the "Code Red" on one of their radios. Harry was being rushed to George Washington Hospital. Later, Greg told me he'd heard one of the EMTs say, "I don't think he's going to make it." Greg added that he was glad I hadn't heard that remark.

Finally entering the booth, I saw another scene that will be ingrained in my memory. The floor was filled with the debris of medical paraphernalia. Syringes, cotton balls, rubber tubing, and gauze patches were strewn throughout the empty room, which minutes before had been the focal point of trying to save a man's life. I respectfully circled around it as best I could. I kept thinking not to touch anything. I saw that Harry must have started preparing for the game when he was stricken. His glasses were on the counter beside his media guides and statistics. But there were no lineups on his score sheets, the first thing a baseball broadcaster does when he sits down and goes to work.

There was no way I could unpack my stuff and begin preparing for the game. The ballpark was beginning to fill up. Many of those in attendance were Phillies fans. The Nats' opener would be a sellout. I just sat there, staring at the floor. It was then that I saw a pencil in the middle of all the medical material. Harry always kept score with a pencil. It must have been in his hand when he fell. That was the first time I felt the tears start to well up. Later I learned that a cameraman had found Harry's score sheets and given them to Todd Kalas. The last notation was "Adam." Harry never got to "Dunn." One by one, some of the other guys started to file into the room. Spanish broadcasters Danny Martinez and Bill Kulik, Sarge and L.A., Scott Franzke and Tom McCarthy were doing what I had done—just staring at this awful scene in a room where we normally share so much laughter. Not much time had passed when we received a call that David Montgomery wanted to see us all in the visitors' clubhouse.

We went back downstairs with few words spoken. What was there to say? Inside a side room in the clubhouse, David took charge. I've mentioned him a lot in this book, how we grew up together in this business and how early he demonstrated leadership. On this day, with events moving quickly, he was magnificent. All we knew was that Harry was at the hospital and that things didn't look good. What about the upcoming broadcast? David asked for opinions from each of us. It was decided to bring the players off the field and tell them what had happened before they were questioned by the media. One by one they filed in, filling the eerily quiet clubhouse. David didn't sugar-coat the reality. The players listened intently, and then as they returned to the field, we went into that side room again.

We had just entered when Tom McCarthy looked at his Black-Berry and confirmed our fears, "Guys, I just got a text from Brook-sie, and he didn't make it. He's gone." Each of us had his own reactions to Tom's words, and each took a few minutes to compose. Officials from the Nationals came in and asked David what he wanted to do. He told them the game should be played. It was nearly 1:30. The Phillies were not about to request a postponement, and it is not too much to say that Harry would have wanted the game to go on as scheduled. As we talked quietly among ourselves, David made a couple of quick phone calls, one of them to Harry's oldest son, Todd. Then the players were called back into the clubhouse for a second time, and told the news. It was tough for many of them to believe, and their emotions were not unlike ours. They, too, were close to Harry. To the media gathered outside, David put our heartbreak into four fittingly memorable words. "We've lost our voice," said the president of the Phillies.

I needed some time to gather my own thoughts. I quickly headed back to the press box and was happy to see that it had been cleaned up. I unpacked my bag and started preparing for the game. Our producer, Jeff Halikman, reminded us that we were professionals in this business and, however we all felt, we had to make it through. I'd been through it before, when we'd lost Whitey in 1997. But on that occasion we'd received the news around 5:30 in the morning and had the whole day to consider what we'd say and do. Not this time. The Nationals had a moment of silence before the first pitch, as a large image appeared on their center-field scoreboard: "HARRY KALAS 1936–2009." I kept thinking of times together when our heads had been bowed in honor of others, and of Harry's eloquence before the first game we played following 9/11. He had died on his own terms, in the broadcast booth, his last game a come-from-behind Phillies victory, his last home-run call that Matt Stairs game-winner.

Now we had about four minutes before we would be coming on live. No taped opening, no re-dos. Tom, Gary, and I were just sitting there waiting for a grieving audience to see how we would deal with the shock of this tragedy. We were not quite sure ourselves. Tom had written a few words on an index card, since his role was to start off the telecast, but just before the lights went on, he put it down and spoke from the heart. Explaining how much Harry had meant to so many, he was terrific. Then it was my turn. I said something about losing a good friend, but feeling myself getting emotional, I decided that was enough. Then Gary made his spontaneous remarks, having known Harry both when Sarge was a player and then as his colleague in the booth. Later I managed to recall how that 1993 team of "throwbacks" was Harry's favorite, and to share some smiles remembering Harry through their exploits.

Needless to say, it was tough getting through the game. The guys in the TV truck did an amazing job of finding footage, enabling us to dwell a bit on old times and the fun we'd all had. Fortunately, the game itself was entertaining—full of errors, exceptional plays, home runs, and lots of things to discuss. Afterward, we were told that, under the circumstances, we'd done a good job, providing therapy not only for us, but for so many in our viewing audience who were watching and grieving at the same time. By the next game, the Nationals had placed a vase of flowers in our booth, a touching sign of sharing our sorrow.

When I went back to my room that night, after sharing my thoughts with some members of the Philadelphia media, it was time to see what was on my own BlackBerry. There were 22 voice-mails waiting, and probably 60 text messages and e-mails. I stayed up until two a.m. answering the calls and messages and trying to unwind. After tossing and turning for a few hours, I was wide awake by five and back to communicating again. It was good to be busy. The day involved going on a lot of radio talk shows, but most of all I wanted to get back and thank people who, in the midst of their own sadness about Harry, cared enough to ask how I was coping.

Somehow we all got through the week, but the most emotional part was to come as we returned for a seven-game home stand in Philadelphia. Prior to Friday night's opener against the San Diego Padres, there was a nice, understated ceremony. Harry's three sons—Todd, Brad, and Kane—threw out first balls to representatives of the three eras through which their father had broadcast Phillies games: Mike Schmidt, John Kruk, and Jimmy Rollins. Then Kane, the youngest, sang a beautiful rendition of our National Anthem. The game itself was the most disappointing of the young season. This time it was the Phillies who took an early lead, only to be overtaken by the Padres, and both our starting and relief pitching faltered. The final score, the Padres winning 8-7, only deepened the gloom of a sellout crowd.

Saturday morning, April 18th, was the climax of a city's grief, centered on an extraordinary memorial service at the ballpark itself. Some 9,000 people, a red sea of mourners, filed by the white casket at home plate to pay their final respects to the voice of the Phillies. Many of those who came in the early morning were greeted personally by David Montgomery. Such an honor had been accorded only one other baseball luminary on the day of a game: the immortal Babe Ruth. Over 5,000 fans remained to hear tributes from nine speakers, punctuated by music and video on PhanaVision. Through the crowd one could see Phillies from many decades, among them Robin Roberts, Dick Allen, and Darren Daulton. Bill Giles, who had brought Kalas to Philadelphia, wore white shoes in remembrance of his friend. Introduced by Dan Baker, Tom McCarthy did a great job emceeing the program. From Governor Rendell and Mayor Nutter to Steve Sabol of NFL Films to David Montgomery and Jamie Moyer, each extolled a different aspect of Kalas' career, which had spanned the broadcasting of over 6,000 games. Moyer told of first listening to Kalas as a nine-year-old in Souderton, and then being thrilled that his own name would be spoken by that unforgettable voice.

Perhaps the most eloquent remarks were by Mike Schmidt, called "Michael Jack" most memorably by Kalas. The most poignant were delivered by 20-year-old Kane Kalas, who said in summation, "Most of all, he loved you fans." Then, to the playing of "A Bridge Over Troubled Water," as Harry had requested, his casket was carefully passed down two long lines of players and team personnel to a hearse, and ultimate burial at West Laurel Hill Cemetery.

There will be reminders of Harry throughout the season and beyond. All the Phillies players and coaches are wearing a circular "HK" patch on their uniforms. Our TV booth, that day shrouded in black, has been dedicated to him, as our radio booth is to Whitey. A simulation of Harry's signature was embedded along both the first- and third-base lines, with "H of F 2002." His rendition of "High Hopes" began to be played after games. His recording of "That ball is outta here" will be heard whenever there is a Phillies home run at Citizens Bank Park this season. There are two signs in the outfield with the giant letters "HK" and a microphone in between.

The Phillies lost that night's game, 8-5, Brad Lidge finally blowing a save, but they came back in dramatic walk-off homer fashion the next day as Raul Ibañez went deep. Monday night's game with San Diego was rained out. On Tuesday, April 21st, against Milwaukee, they finally won in traditional fashion, not coming back from behind, but leading wire to wire, 11-4: remarkable 46-year-old Jamie Moyer's second victory of the season. After 12 games within little more than two weeks, encompassing both the glow of last year's triumph and the tragedy that came so soon this season, they are at .500, six and six, four games behind the Florida Marlins in the National League East.

What to make of it? The Phils' starting pitching, with the highest ERA in the league, remains the key question mark. In 12 games, Phillies pitchers have given up 27 home runs. Their hitting, on the other hand, has been encouraging, if inconsistent. Most regulars, except the catalyst, Jimmy Rollins, who is bound to come around, are exceeding their offensive output—especially Utley, Werth, Feliz, and our new left-fielder, Raul Ibañez, who has already been embraced by Philly fans. There are chants of "Raaauul" whenever he comes to the plate. Defense is also much improved, nowhere more than at first base, where a slimmed-down Ryan Howard is excelling in every phase of the game. Where will the team be when you read this? Hopefully, vying for another championship—but, whatever happens, the journey should be as exciting as the destination.

Many years ago, Bart Giamatti, a very wise man who was also Commissioner of Baseball, was asked if he was still an idealist. "I hope so," he replied, and then reflected on the significance of the sport he loved. "Baseball is about coming home and how hard it is to get there and how driven is our need and how good home really is."

I've viewed a lot of life through the booth. If you need to have a lot of little boy in you to play baseball, I think that's also true of broadcasting baseball. I'm constantly reminded, even through this time of tears, of how much fun I've had with these big kids I've been around in this game. Just the other day, Tom McCarthy recalled how Vuk would hide my glasses and then play "hot and cold" before I'd get them back. If Whitey had his pipe, Harry would occasionally puff on a huge cigar, I think as much to annoy me as for any pleasure it gave him. People would send me little fans to help circulate such air as remained in our booth. And then there's the Phanatic, who recently celebrated another birthday, but never seems to get older. He still loves to visit us and toss boxfuls of popcorn all around the booth. It takes days to clean it all up.

I've had a lot of fun taking this trip down Memory Lane, and I hope you've enjoyed taking the journey with me. Baseball and the Phillies were a big part of my life before I was lucky enough to get that call from Larry Shenk to become part of the organization. They may have lost some money over the years because, had I landed somewhere else, I still would've bought as many tickets as I could afford.

Luck has certainly played a large role in my broadcasting career, as it does in anyone's life. True, I had the advantage of a Penn State degree in communications and some prior experience, and I was confident that I could do the job. But there are thousands of people who feel the same way and just never get the opportunity. Whitey gave me my break on that cold, rainy afternoon in Montreal, but I still had to make the most of it.

My philosophy has always been simple—to work hard and prepare for every game. I wasn't born with one of those "magic" broadcast voices. I like to think of my approach as more conversational, just as I view this book as my conversation with you. I do have a pretty good memory that helps with storytelling. That, combined with my passion for this sport, has enabled me to have a sustained career doing what I love. Because I never played professionally, it may have taken some fans longer to accept someone more like themselves who could analyze the game without having worn a major-league uniform.

Fortunately, I've had the supportive advice of many respected professionals in the business, people like "The Dean," Bill Campbell, and the late Flyers broadcaster Gene Hart, who told me early on to just keep doing it my own way. And Harry Kalas, who *was* blessed with one of those distinctive voices, and encouraged me in our conversations after games to develop my own style and never worry about criticism. "It's part of the business," he'd say, and you need a thick skin to survive. He was good enough to add, "Many times you see things I don't." You don't have to have been a manager, coach, or player to develop an ability to analyze what you see on the field. Almost every day, I learn something new about this fascinating game and try to share it with our passionate, loyal, outspoken fans. More than ever, I'm hearing from viewers who, like me, enjoy what I guess might be called "inside baseball." It's a privilege to continue to be even a small part of their lives.

In thanking the Phillies organization for this great opportunity, I'm bound to reflect on those no longer with us who have featured so prominently in this book and throughout my life:

> My parents
> Ed Harvey and Susan Harvey Rhodes
> Joanne Rosati Wheeler
> Jack Downey
> Paul Owens
> Tug McGraw
> Hugh Alexander
> Eric Gregg
> Rich Ashburn
> John Vukovich
> Harry Kalas
> Danny Ozark

We can't look into the future without remembering the past. I've been thinking a lot lately about John Vukovich. How he would have loved the 2008 season. One of the best men I've ever known, when he died in 2007, a part of me went with him. On the final day of that season, I was riding to the ballpark and my mind was all over the place. If the Phillies could win that afternoon and the Mets lose, the team would wipe out what had seemed an insurmountable New York lead and win the division for the first time since 1993. The butterflies were fluttering as I approached 30th Street Station on my ride down the Schuylkill Expressway. As I do every Sunday morning, I was listening to the *Elvis and Friends* show with "Rockin'" Ron

Cade on WOGL 98. The music of the king of rock and roll always re-laxes me, taking me back to those early years growing up in New-town Square, listening to baseball on the radio and not having a care in the world.

Elvis could sing a ballad like no one else. That morning I heard one of my favorites, about dreaming and the positive power in try-ing to make our dreams come true. Tears filled my eyes as I listened to its final verse and I thought about Johnny. I said out loud, "Come on, Vuk, let's make this happen today, and it will be for you." And it did, that late fall afternoon. The Mets lost, the Phillies won the East, and the town went nuts.

I think the sentiment in that song sums up my life. When we are children, we have dreams. Many of them remain just that—dreams. In my case, my four decades with the Phillies have been a dream come true.

In some respects, I haven't had a "real job" for 38 years. I've made many enduring friendships that have lasted a lifetime. Some of these good people are gone, but their influence and memories remain.

I'm a lucky man with a lot of people to thank.

And the one constant remains the game of baseball. Like life, it has its imperfections, but it draws people together like nothing I've ever experienced.

Thanks for the ride. And no matter how bad life may seem, two words can part the clouds like no other: "PLAY BALL!"